First World War
and Army of Occupation
War Diary
France, Belgium and Germany

32 DIVISION
96 Infantry Brigade
Lancashire Fusiliers
15th and 16th Battalion
13 September 1914 - 31 October 1919

WO95/2397/2

The Naval & Military Press Ltd
www.nmarchive.com
Published in association with The National Archives

Published by

The Naval & Military Press Ltd

Unit 10 Ridgewood Industrial Park,

Uckfield, East Sussex,

TN22 5QE England

Tel: +44 (0) 1825 749494

www.naval-military-press.com

www.nmarchive.com

This diary has been reprinted in facsimile from the original. Any imperfections are inevitably reproduced and the quality may fall short of modern type and cartographic standards.

© Crown Copyright
Images reproduced by permission of The National Archives, London, England, 2015.

Contents

Document type	Place/Title	Date From	Date To
Heading	WO95/2397 (2)		
Heading	2nb Bn Manchester Regt 1918 Feb 1919 Mar From 14 Bde 32 Div		
War Diary	Emile Camp	01/02/1918	01/02/1918
War Diary	Het Sas	02/02/1918	04/02/1918
War Diary	Emile Camp	05/02/1918	07/02/1918
War Diary	Houthulst Forest	08/02/1918	11/02/1918
War Diary	Abri Wood	12/02/1918	15/02/1918
War Diary	Corps Line	16/02/1918	19/02/1918
War Diary	Houthulst Forest	20/02/1918	23/02/1918
War Diary	Abri Wood	24/02/1918	27/02/1918
War Diary	Corps Line	28/02/1918	28/02/1918
Miscellaneous	Operation Order No. 21	26/02/1918	26/02/1918
Heading	2nd Division. The Manchester Regiment March 1918		
War Diary		01/03/1915	31/03/1915
Heading	2nd Battn The Manchester Regiment April 1918		
War Diary		01/04/1918	30/04/1918
War Diary		01/05/1918	30/06/1918
Operation(al) Order(s)	Maid Operation Order No. 1 By Lieut. Colonel G.M. Robertson D.S.O. Commanding 2nd Battalion The Manchester Regiment.	18/06/1918	18/06/1918
Miscellaneous	Nov 15 War Diary		
Miscellaneous	2nd Battalion The Manchester Regiment.	18/06/1918	18/06/1918
War Diary	Boyelles	01/07/1918	01/07/1918
War Diary	Blaireville	02/07/1918	06/07/1918
War Diary	La Bazeque	07/07/1918	19/07/1918
War Diary	Proven	20/07/1918	07/08/1918
War Diary	Briquemesnil	08/08/1918	08/08/1918
War Diary	Boves	09/08/1918	11/08/1918
War Diary	Le Quesnel	12/08/1918	12/08/1918
War Diary	Ignacourt	13/08/1918	13/08/1918
War Diary	Fouencamps	14/08/1918	17/08/1918
War Diary	Harbonnieres	18/08/1918	31/08/1918
War Diary	Berny	01/09/1918	06/09/1918
War Diary	Ennemain	07/09/1918	07/09/1918
War Diary	Monchy Lagache	08/09/1918	10/09/1918
War Diary	Villeveque	11/09/1918	11/09/1918
War Diary	Marteville	12/09/1918	13/09/1918
War Diary	Villeveque	14/09/1918	14/09/1918
War Diary	La Neuville	15/09/1918	24/09/1918
War Diary	Tertry	25/09/1918	28/09/1918
War Diary	Vendelles	29/09/1918	29/09/1918
War Diary	East Of Bellinglise	30/09/1918	30/09/1918
War Diary	Berny	01/09/1918	06/09/1918
War Diary	Ennemain	07/09/1918	07/09/1918
War Diary	Monchy Lagache	08/09/1918	10/09/1918
War Diary	Villeveque	11/09/1918	11/09/1918
War Diary	Marteville	12/09/1918	13/09/1918
War Diary	Villeveque	14/09/1918	14/09/1918
War Diary	La Neuville	15/09/1918	24/09/1918

War Diary	Tertry	25/09/1918	28/09/1918
War Diary	Vendelles	29/09/1918	29/09/1918
War Diary	E Of Bellinglise	30/09/1918	30/09/1918
Heading	War Diary Of 2nd Manchester Regt From Oct 1st To 31st 1918 Vol 51		
War Diary	Magny-La-Fosse	01/10/1918	03/10/1918
War Diary	Lehaucourt	04/10/1918	04/10/1918
War Diary	Vendelles	05/10/1918	05/10/1918
War Diary	Hancourt	06/10/1918	18/10/1918
War Diary	Leahcourt	19/10/1918	20/10/1918
War Diary	Bohain	21/10/1918	22/10/1918
War Diary	Busigny	23/10/1918	29/10/1918
Miscellaneous	St Souplet	30/10/1918	30/10/1918
War Diary	Ors	31/10/1918	31/10/1918
War Diary	Pommereuil	01/11/1918	05/11/1918
War Diary	Sambreton	06/11/1918	11/11/1918
War Diary	Prisches	12/11/1918	13/11/1918
War Diary	Avesnes	14/11/1918	14/11/1918
War Diary	Felleries	15/11/1918	19/11/1918
War Diary	Liessies	20/11/1918	20/11/1918
War Diary	Rance	21/11/1918	24/11/1918
War Diary	Froidchapelle	25/11/1918	30/11/1918
Miscellaneous	2nd Battalion To Manchester Regiment.	06/11/1918	06/11/1918
War Diary	Froidchapelle	01/12/1918	12/12/1918
War Diary	Phillipville	13/12/1918	13/12/1918
War Diary	Stave	14/12/1918	14/12/1918
War Diary	Assesse	15/12/1918	31/12/1918
Heading	2nd Bn Manchester Regt Jan-Mar 1919		
War Diary	Assesse	01/01/1919	04/02/1919
War Diary	Field	05/02/1919	05/02/1919
War Diary	Namur	06/02/1919	06/02/1919
War Diary	Field	07/02/1919	07/02/1919
War Diary	Bonn	08/02/1919	28/02/1919
War Diary	Bonn, Germany	01/03/1919	31/03/1919
Heading	WO95/2397(3)		
Heading	15th Bn Lancs Fus. Sept 1915-1919 Oct		
Heading	15th Battalion Lancashire Fusiliers January 1916		
Heading	32th Div Sept 14-Dec 15 15th Lancs Fus Vol I		
War Diary	Salford	13/09/1914	13/09/1914
War Diary	Conway	28/12/1914	28/12/1914
War Diary	Catterick	21/06/1915	21/06/1915
War Diary	Codford	13/08/1915	13/08/1915
War Diary	Boulougne	22/11/1915	23/11/1915
War Diary	Longpre	24/11/1915	24/11/1915
War Diary	Maison Roland	25/11/1915	27/11/1915
War Diary	Boulon	28/11/1915	28/11/1915
War Diary	Poulainville	29/11/1915	30/11/1915
War Diary	Albert	01/12/1915	15/12/1915
War Diary	Becourt	15/12/1915	20/12/1915
War Diary	Albert	21/12/1915	24/12/1915
War Diary	La Boiselles	24/12/1915	29/12/1915
War Diary	Albert	29/12/1915	29/12/1915
War Diary	Henencourt	30/12/1915	31/12/1915
Heading	15th Lancs Fus Vol 2 Jan		
War Diary	Henencourt	01/01/1916	02/01/1916
War Diary	Anthuille	03/01/1916	10/01/1916

War Diary	Henencourt	11/01/1916	21/01/1916
War Diary	Martinsart	22/01/1916	26/01/1916
War Diary	Hennencourt	24/01/1916	31/01/1916
Heading	15th Battalion Lancashire Fusiliers February 1916		
War Diary	Hennencourt	01/02/1916	06/02/1916
War Diary	Authuille	07/02/1916	12/02/1916
War Diary	Millencourt	13/02/1916	17/02/1916
War Diary	Aveluy	17/02/1916	19/02/1916
War Diary	Hennencourt	01/02/1916	06/02/1916
War Diary	Authuille	07/02/1916	12/02/1916
War Diary	Millencourt	13/02/1916	17/02/1916
War Diary	Aveluy	17/02/1916	24/02/1916
War Diary	Albert	24/02/1916	29/02/1916
Heading	15th Battalion Lancashire Fusiliers March 1916		
Heading	15 Lan Fus 32 Vol 4		
War Diary	Albert	01/03/1916	02/03/1916
War Diary	Aveluy	02/03/1916	06/03/1916
War Diary	Authuille	06/03/1916	16/03/1916
War Diary	Bouzincourt	16/03/1916	20/03/1916
War Diary	Authuille	20/03/1916	31/03/1916
Heading	15th Battalion Lancashire Fusiliers April 1916		
War Diary	Authuille	01/04/1916	03/04/1916
War Diary	Bouzincourt	04/04/1916	04/04/1916
War Diary	Mervaux	05/04/1916	23/04/1916
War Diary	Warluy	24/04/1916	24/04/1916
War Diary	Aveluy	24/04/1916	28/04/1916
War Diary	Authuille	29/04/1916	30/04/1916
Heading	15th Battalion Lancashire Fusiliers May 1916		
War Diary	Authuille	01/05/1916	02/05/1916
War Diary	Authuille	03/05/1916	06/05/1916
War Diary	Bouzincourt	06/05/1916	13/05/1916
War Diary	Senlis	14/05/1916	17/05/1916
War Diary	Contay	18/05/1916	29/05/1916
War Diary	Bouzincourt	30/05/1916	30/05/1916
War Diary	Authuille	31/05/1916	31/05/1916
Miscellaneous	Raid carried out by 15th Lanc. Fusiliers on the night of 5th/6th May 1916		
Miscellaneous	Notes.		
Diagram etc	Scheme for Raid		
Miscellaneous	Detail of groups.		
Heading	1/15th Battalion Lancashire Fusiliers June 1916		
War Diary	Authuille	01/06/1916	04/06/1916
War Diary	Aveluy	05/06/1916	07/06/1916
War Diary	Authuille	08/06/1916	13/06/1916
War Diary	Warloy	14/06/1916	27/06/1916
War Diary	Bouzincourt	27/06/1916	30/06/1916
Heading	War Diary 15th Battn. The Lancashire Fusiliers. July 1916		
Miscellaneous			
Heading	War Diary 15th Lancashire Fusiliers 1st July 1916-31st July 1916		
War Diary	Thiepval Sub Sector	01/07/1916	01/07/1916
War Diary	The Bluff on River Ancre	02/07/1916	02/07/1916
War Diary	Martinsart Wood	03/07/1916	03/07/1916
War Diary	Warloy	04/07/1916	05/07/1916
War Diary	Lealvillers	06/07/1916	07/07/1916

War Diary	Hedauville	08/07/1916	08/07/1916
War Diary	Senlis	09/07/1916	09/07/1916
War Diary	Reserve Trenches SE Bouzincourt	10/07/1916	11/07/1916
War Diary	Ovillers	12/07/1916	15/07/1916
War Diary	Senlis	16/07/1916	17/07/1916
War Diary	Halloy	18/07/1916	18/07/1916
War Diary	Bouque Maison	19/07/1916	19/07/1916
War Diary	Croisette	20/07/1916	20/07/1916
War Diary	Boyaval	21/07/1916	21/07/1916
War Diary	Westreham	22/07/1916	26/07/1916
War Diary	Marles-Les-Mines	27/07/1916	29/07/1916
War Diary	Haillicourt	30/07/1916	31/07/1916
Miscellaneous	Maps		
Map	Appendix K.		
Map			
Heading	15th Battalion Lancashire Fusiliers August 1916		
Heading	War Diary 15th Lancashire Fusrs From 1st August 1916 To 31st August 1916 Vol 9		
War Diary	Haillicourt	01/08/1916	05/08/1916
War Diary	Beuvry	06/08/1916	21/08/1916
War Diary	Trenches	22/08/1916	25/08/1916
War Diary	Annequin North	26/08/1916	29/08/1916
War Diary	Trenches	29/08/1916	31/08/1916
Heading	15th Battalion Lancashire Fusiliers September 1916		
Heading	War Diary Of 15th (Service) Battalion The Lancashire Fusiliers. From 1st September 1916 To 30th September 1916 (Volume 10)		
War Diary	Trenches	01/09/1916	10/09/1916
War Diary	Annequin	11/09/1916	20/09/1916
War Diary	Annezin	20/09/1916	26/09/1916
War Diary	Trenches	27/09/1916	30/09/1916
Heading	Diary Of 15 Lancashire Fusiliers Sept 1916		
Heading	15th Battalion Lancashire Fusiliers October 1916		
Heading	War Diary Of 15th (S) Battn Lancashire Fusiliers From October 1st 1916 To October 31st 1916 Vol II		
War Diary	Support Trenches	01/10/1916	01/10/1916
War Diary	Cuinchy	02/10/1916	03/10/1916
War Diary	Trenches	04/10/1916	08/10/1916
War Diary	Le Quesnoy	09/10/1916	10/10/1916
War Diary	Bethune	10/10/1916	14/10/1916
War Diary	Ourton	15/10/1916	15/10/1916
War Diary	Magnicourt-En-Court	16/10/1916	16/10/1916
War Diary	Mazieres	17/10/1916	17/10/1916
War Diary	Orville	18/10/1916	21/10/1916
War Diary	Vadencourt Wood	22/10/1916	23/10/1916
War Diary	Brick Fields	24/10/1916	26/10/1916
War Diary	Warloy	27/10/1916	31/10/1916
Heading	15th Battalion Lancashire Fusiliers November 1916		
Heading	War Diary 15th Lancashire Fusiliers From November 1st To 30th. 1916 Vol 12		
War Diary	Herissart	01/11/1916	14/11/1916
War Diary	Thiepval Area	14/11/1916	17/11/1916
War Diary	Beaumont Hamel	18/11/1916	30/11/1916
Heading	15th Battalion Lancashire Fusiliers December 1916		
Heading	War Diary Of 15th (S) Battn Lancashire Fusiliers. From 1-12-16 To 31-12-16		

War Diary	Montrelet	01/12/1916	31/12/1916
Heading	War Diary Of 15th (S) Battn Lancashire Fusiliers 1-1-17 To 31-1-17 Vol 14		
War Diary	Montrelet	01/01/1917	06/01/1917
War Diary	Beauquesne	07/01/1917	07/01/1917
War Diary	Bus	08/01/1917	13/01/1917
War Diary	Courcelles	14/01/1917	16/01/1917
War Diary	Trenches	17/01/1917	18/01/1917
War Diary	Courcelles	19/01/1917	20/01/1917
War Diary	Trenches	21/01/1917	21/01/1917
War Diary	Mailly-Maillet	22/01/1917	24/01/1917
War Diary	Trenches	25/01/1917	25/01/1917
War Diary	Mailly-Maillet	26/01/1917	28/01/1917
War Diary	Trenches	29/01/1917	30/01/1917
War Diary	Bertrancourt	31/01/1917	31/01/1917
Heading	War Diary Of 15th Bn. Lancs Fusiliers 1st Of February 1917 To 28th Of February 1917 Vol 15		
War Diary	Bertrancourt	01/02/1917	01/02/1917
War Diary	Mailly Maillet	02/02/1917	04/02/1917
War Diary	Trenches	05/02/1917	08/02/1917
War Diary	Mailly-Maillet	09/02/1917	11/02/1917
War Diary	Louvencourt	12/02/1917	13/02/1917
War Diary	Herrisart	14/02/1917	15/02/1917
War Diary	Pierregot	16/02/1917	16/02/1917
War Diary	Villers Bocage	17/02/1917	19/02/1917
War Diary	Rivery	20/02/1917	20/02/1917
War Diary	Thennes	21/02/1917	22/02/1917
War Diary	Le Quesnel	23/02/1917	24/02/1917
War Diary	Trenches	25/02/1917	28/02/1917
Heading	War Diary Of 15th (s) Bn. Lancashire Fusiliers. From 1st March 1917 To 31st March 1917 Vol 16		
Heading	War Diary Of 15th (s) Battn Lanc Fus From 1/3/17 To 31/3/17		
War Diary	In Trenches	01/03/1917	02/03/1917
War Diary	Le Quesnel	03/03/1917	08/03/1917
War Diary	Bouchoir	09/03/1917	11/03/1917
War Diary	Trenches	12/03/1917	14/03/1917
War Diary	Le Quesnoy	15/03/1917	31/03/1917
Heading	War Diary Of 15th (s) Battn. Lancashire Fusiliers. From 1st April 1917 To 30th April 1917 Vol 17		
Heading	War Diary Of 15th (s) Battalion Lancashire Fusiliers From 1/4/17 To 30/4/17		
War Diary		01/04/1917	21/04/1917
Heading	War Diary Of 15th (s) Battn Lancashire Fusiliers From May 1st 1917 To May 31st 1917 Vol 18		
War Diary	Flez	01/05/1917	31/05/1917
Heading	War Diary Of 15th (s) Battn Lancashire Fusiliers From 1/6/17 To 30/6/17 Vol 19		
War Diary	Guillaucourt	01/06/1917	01/06/1917
War Diary	Caestre	02/06/1917	02/06/1917
War Diary	Noote-Boom	03/06/1917	30/06/1917
Heading	War Diary Of 15th (s) Battalion Lancashire Fusiliers. From 1/7/17 To 31/7/17 Vol 20		
War Diary	Ghyvelde	01/07/1917	05/07/1917
War Diary	Ribaillet	06/07/1917	18/07/1917
War Diary	Jean-Bart Camp	18/02/1917	27/02/1917

War Diary	Bray-Dunes		27/07/1917	31/07/1917
Heading	War Diary Of 15th (s) Battalion Lancashire Fusiliers From 1/8/17 To 31/8/17			
War Diary	Coxyde		01/08/1917	31/08/1917
Heading	War Diary Of 15th (s) Battn Lancashire Fusiliers. From 1-9-17 To 30-9-17 Vol 22			
War Diary	Coxyde		01/09/1917	12/09/1917
War Diary	Nieuport		12/09/1917	30/09/1917
Heading	War Diary Of 15th (s) Battn Lancashire Fusiliers From October 1st 1917 To October 31st 1917 Vol 23			
War Diary	Coxyde		01/10/1917	02/10/1917
War Diary	La-Panne		03/10/1917	04/10/1917
War Diary	Zuydcoote		05/10/1917	31/10/1917
Heading	War Diary Of 15th (S) Battn Lancashire Fusiliers November 1st 1917 To November 30th 1917 Vol 24			
War Diary	Eringhem		01/11/1917	10/11/1917
War Diary	Arneke		11/11/1917	11/11/1917
War Diary	Winnezeele		12/11/1917	12/11/1917
War Diary	School Camp		13/11/1917	22/11/1917
War Diary	Hospital Farm		23/11/1917	27/11/1917
War Diary	Irish Farm		28/11/1917	30/11/1917
Heading	War Diary Of 15th (s) Battn Lancashire Fusiliers From December 1st 1917 To December 31st 1917 Vol 25			
War Diary	In Trenches		01/12/1917	04/12/1917
War Diary	Irish Farm		10/12/1917	10/12/1917
War Diary	Wurst Farm		10/12/1917	13/12/1917
War Diary	In Trenches		13/12/1917	18/12/1917
War Diary	Hospital Fm		22/12/1917	23/12/1917
War Diary	Irish Farm		24/12/1917	29/12/1917
War Diary	Auden Fort		30/12/1917	31/12/1917
Heading	War Diary Of 15th (s) Battn Lancashire Fusiliers From 1st January 1918 To 31st January 1918 Vol 26			
War Diary	Auden Fort		01/01/1918	19/01/1918
War Diary	Hospital Farm		20/01/1918	31/01/1918
Heading	War Diary Of 15th (s) Bn Lancashire Fusiliers From 1-2-18 To 28-2-18 Vol 27			
War Diary			01/02/1918	28/02/1918
Heading	15th Battalion Lancashire Fusiliers March 1918			
Heading	War Diary Of 15th (s) Battalion Lancashire Fusiliers From 1-3-18 To 31-3-18 Vol 28			
War Diary			01/03/1918	31/03/1918
Heading	War Diary 15th Battn. The Lancashire Fusiliers. April 1918			
Heading	War Diary Of 15th Lancashire Fusiliers April 1st 1918 To April 30th 1918 Vol 29			
War Diary			01/04/1918	30/04/1918
Heading	15th (s) Battn Lancashire Fusiliers War Diary For Month Ending 31-5-1918 Vol 30			
War Diary			01/05/1918	31/05/1918
Heading	War Diary Of 15th (s) Bn Lancashire Fusiliers From 1st June 1918 To 30th June 1918 Vol 31			
War Diary			01/06/1918	31/07/1918
Heading	War Diary Of 15th (s) Battn Lancashire Fusiliers 1st August 1918 To 31st August			
War Diary			01/08/1918	31/08/1918

Type	Description	Start	End
Heading	War Diary Of 15th (s) Battn Lancashire Fusiliers From 1st September 1918 To 30th September 1918 Vol 34		
War Diary		01/09/1918	30/09/1918
Heading	War Diary Of 15th Lancashire Fusiliers From October 1st 1918 To 31st October 1918 Vol 35		
War Diary		01/10/1918	31/10/1918
Heading	War Diary Of 15th (s) Battn Lancashire Fusiliers. From November 1st 1918 To November 30th 1918 Vol 36		
War Diary		01/11/1918	30/11/1918
War Diary		01/12/1918	31/12/1918
Heading	15th Bn. Lancs. Fus. Jan-Oct 1919		
Heading	War Diary Of 15th Lancashire Fusiliers From 1-1-19 To 31-1-19 Vol 38		
War Diary		01/01/1919	31/01/1919
Heading	War Diary Of 15th (s) Battn Lancashire Fusiliers From 1-2-1919 To 28-2-1919 Vol 39		
War Diary		01/02/1919	28/02/1919
Heading	War Diary Of 15th (s) Battalion Lancashire Fusiliers. From 1st March 1919 To 31st March 1919 Vol 40		
War Diary	Bonn Germany	01/03/1919	31/03/1919
Heading	War Diary 15th (S) Battalion Lancashire Fusiliers From 1st April 1919 To 30th April 1919		
War Diary	Bonn Germany	01/04/1919	30/04/1919
War Diary	War Diary 15th (S) Lancashire Fusiliers. From May 1st 1919 To May 31st 1919		
Miscellaneous			
War Diary	Bonn Germany	01/05/1919	31/05/1919
Heading	War Diary Of 15th (s) Battalion The Lancashire Fusiliers. From June 1st 1919 To June 30th 1919		
War Diary	Bonn Germany	01/06/1919	30/06/1919
Heading	War Diary Of 15th (s) Batt The Lancashire Fusiliers. From July 1st 1919 To July 31st 1919		
War Diary	Bonn Germany	01/07/1919	31/07/1919
Heading	War Diary Of 15th (s) Battalion Lancashire Fusiliers. From 1st August 1919 To 31st, August 1919		
War Diary	Bonn	01/07/1919	30/07/1919
War Diary	Euskirchen	31/07/1919	31/07/1919
Heading	War Diary 15th (S) Battalion The Lancashire Fusiliers. From 1st September 1919 To 30th September 1919		
War Diary	Euskirchen	01/09/1919	01/09/1919
War Diary	Germany	01/09/1919	30/09/1919
Heading	War Diary 15th (S) Bn. The Lancashire Fusiliers. From October 1st 1919 To October 24th 1919		
War Diary			
War Diary	Euskirchen	01/10/1919	24/10/1919
Heading	WO95/2397(4)		
Heading	16th Bn. Lancs Fus. Nov 1915-1919 Oct		
Heading	War Diary Of 16 Lancashire Fusrs From Nov 21 To November 30th 1915		
Heading	16th Lancs Fus Vol I Nov 15		
War Diary	Eringhem	01/11/1915	28/11/1915
Heading	WO95/Box 2397		
War Diary	Codford Salisbury	21/11/1915	22/11/1915
War Diary	Boulogne	24/11/1915	24/11/1915
War Diary	Coulonvillers	27/11/1915	27/11/1915
War Diary	Flixecourt	28/11/1915	28/11/1915

War Diary	Coisy	30/11/1915	30/11/1915
War Diary	Codford Salisbury	21/11/1915	22/11/1915
War Diary	Boulogne	24/11/1915	24/11/1915
War Diary	Coulonvillers	27/11/1915	27/11/1915
War Diary	Flixecourt	28/11/1915	28/11/1915
War Diary	Coisy	30/11/1915	30/11/1915
Heading	16th Lancs Fus Vol 2		
Heading	War Diary Of 16 Lancs Fusrs From Dec To Dec 30th 1915		
War Diary	Albert La Somme	01/12/1915	12/12/1915
War Diary	E 3 Sector	15/12/1915	22/12/1915
War Diary	Albert E 3 Sector	23/12/1915	24/12/1915
War Diary	Albert	25/12/1915	28/12/1915
War Diary	Martinsart	29/12/1915	30/12/1915
Heading	16th Battalion Lancashire Fusiliers January 1916		
Heading	16th Lanc. Fusiliers Vol 3 Jan		
Heading	War Diary Of 16th Lancashire Fusrs. From Jan 1st To Jan 31st 1916		
War Diary	Martinsart 91 Sector	01/01/1916	05/01/1916
War Diary	Authuille	06/01/1916	06/01/1916
War Diary	Bouzincourt	10/01/1916	18/01/1916
War Diary	Martinsart	21/01/1916	21/01/1916
War Diary	G.I Subsect.	22/01/1916	26/01/1916
War Diary	Bouzincourt	27/01/1916	28/01/1916
Heading	16th Battalion Lancashire Fusiliers February 1916		
Heading	16th Lancs Fus. Vol 4		
War Diary	Bouzincourt	31/01/1916	12/02/1916
War Diary	Senlis	13/02/1916	29/02/1916
Heading	16th Battalion Lancashire Fusiliers March 1916		
Heading	16th Lan Fus 32nd Div Vol 5		
War Diary	F1. Subsector	01/03/1916	02/03/1916
War Diary	Albert	07/03/1916	10/03/1916
War Diary	G1 Subsector	11/03/1916	12/03/1916
War Diary	Authuille	13/03/1916	29/03/1916
Heading	16th Battalion Lancashire Fusiliers April 1916		
War Diary		01/04/1916	28/04/1916
Heading	16th Battalion Lancashire Fusiliers May 1916		
War Diary	Aveluy	02/05/1916	30/05/1916
Heading	1/16th Battalion Lancashire Fusiliers June 1916		
Miscellaneous	O O/c D.A.G's	30/06/1916	30/06/1916
War Diary	Aveluy	03/06/1916	30/06/1916
Heading	War Diary 16th Battn. The Lancashire Fusiliers. July 1916		
Miscellaneous			
Heading	War Diary 16th Lancashire Fusiliers 1st July 1916-31st July 1916		
War Diary	Authuille	01/07/1916	29/07/1916
Heading	16th Battalion Lancashire Fusiliers August 1916		
Heading	War Diary Of 16th Lancashire Fusiliers From 1st August 1916 To 31st August 1916 Vol 10		
War Diary	Haillicourt	05/08/1916	29/08/1916
War Diary	Cambrin	30/08/1916	31/08/1916
Heading	16th Battalion Lancashire Fusiliers September 1916		
Heading	War Diary Of 16 Lancashire Fusiliers From August 30th To September 29th 1916 Volume 11		
War Diary	Cambrin	30/08/1916	10/09/1916

War Diary	Cambrin Right Sub Section	10/09/1916	30/09/1916
Miscellaneous	Raid night of 10th/11th Septr. 1916. carried out by 16th (S) Bn. Lancashire Fusiliers.		
Miscellaneous	Recommended For Special Leave Owing To Good Work In Raid On Night 10th/11th Septr 1916	11/09/1916	11/09/1916
Miscellaneous	Equipment.	11/09/1916	11/09/1916
Miscellaneous	Raiding Party.		
Miscellaneous	C Form (Duplicate). Messages And Signals.	11/09/1916	11/09/1916
Miscellaneous	G.O.C., 1st Corps.	11/09/1916	11/09/1916
Heading	16th Battalion Lancashire Fusiliers October 1916		
Heading	War Diary Of 16 Lancashire Fusiliers For October 1916 Vol 11		
War Diary	Le Quesnoy	30/09/1916	31/10/1916
Heading	16th Battalion Lancashire Fusiliers November 1916		
Heading	War Diary. 16th Lancashire Fusiliers. November 1st To 30th. 1916		
War Diary	Rubempre	13/11/1916	26/11/1916
Miscellaneous	96th Infantry Brigade.	29/11/1916	29/11/1916
Heading	16th Battalion Lancashire Fusiliers December 1916		
Heading	War Diary Of 16 (s) Battn Lancashire Fusiliers For December 1916 Vol 14		
Miscellaneous	96 Inf Bde		
War Diary	Bonneville	01/12/1916	29/12/1916
Heading	War Diary Of 16 Lancashire Fusiliers For January 1917		
War Diary			
War Diary	Bonneville	06/01/1917	31/01/1917
Heading	War Diary Of 16 Lancashire Fusiliers For February 1917 (Volume 2)		
War Diary			
War Diary		02/02/1917	27/02/1917
Heading	War Diary Of 16th Bn. Lancashire Fusiliers. March 1917 Vol.2		
Heading	War Diary 16 Lancashire Fusiliers For March 1917 Vol 2		
War Diary			
War Diary	Warvillers	02/03/1917	25/03/1917
Heading	War Diary Of 16th Battn. Lancashire Fusiliers. From 1st April 1917 To 30th April 1917 Vol 18		
Miscellaneous	96 Inf Bde	30/04/1917	30/04/1917
Heading	War Diary Of 16 S. Batt Lancashire Fusiliers For April 1917 Volume 2		
War Diary	Douilly	01/04/1917	27/04/1917
Heading	War Diary Of 16 Lancashire Fusiliers For May 1917 Vol 19		
Miscellaneous	96 Inf Bde.	31/05/1917	31/05/1917
War Diary	Ennemain	01/05/1917	31/05/1917
Heading	War Diary Of 16 Lancashire Fusiliers For June 1917 Volume 2		
Miscellaneous			
War Diary	Caix	01/06/1917	26/06/1917
Heading	War Diary Of 16 Lancashire Fusiliers For July 1917		
War Diary	Gyvelde	01/07/1917	11/07/1917
War Diary	St Georges Sub Sector	11/07/1917	19/07/1917
War Diary	Kuhn Camp	21/07/1917	31/07/1917
Heading	War Diary Of 16 Lancashire Fusiliers For August 1917 Vol 22		

War Diary	Oost Dunkirk	01/08/1917	29/08/1917
Heading	War Diary Of 16 Lancashire Fusiliers For September 1917 Vol 23		
War Diary	Coxyde	01/09/1917	29/09/1917
Heading	War Diary Of 16 Lancashire Fusiliers From 1st October 1917 To 31st October 1917 Volume I Vol 24		
War Diary	La Panne	02/10/1917	26/10/1917
War Diary	O Mission	02/10/1917	29/10/1917
Heading	War Diary Of 16 Lan Fusiliers For November 1917 Vol 25		
Heading	WO95/Box 2397		
War Diary		29/11/1917	30/11/1917
Heading	Box WO95/2397		
Heading	War Diary Of 16th Lancashire Fusiliers 1st To 31 Dec 1917 Vol 26		
War Diary	Irish Farm	01/12/1917	02/12/1917
War Diary	Wurst Farm	03/12/1917	08/12/1917
War Diary	Trenches	09/12/1917	13/12/1917
War Diary	Irish Farm	14/12/1917	31/12/1917
Heading	War Diary Of 16th Lan Fus For January 1918		
War Diary	Licques Area	01/01/1918	17/01/1918
War Diary	Zouafques	18/01/1918	19/01/1918
War Diary	Dirty Bucket Camp	20/01/1918	21/01/1918
War Diary	Canal Bank	22/01/1918	25/01/1918
War Diary	Boesinghe Camp	26/01/1918	31/01/1918
War Diary	Bixschoote Area	01/02/1918	01/02/1918
War Diary	Houthulst Forest Sector	02/02/1918	18/02/1918
War Diary	Houthulst Forest Sector	18/02/1918	20/02/1918
War Diary	Area Bixschoote	21/02/1918	28/02/1918
Heading	16th Battalion The Lancashire Fusiliers March 1918		
Heading	War Diary 16th Battn Lancashire Fusiliers From 1st To 31st Of The Month Of March 1918 Vol 29		
War Diary	Abri Camp	01/03/1918	03/03/1918
War Diary	Renninghoe	04/03/1918	09/03/1918
War Diary	Baboon Camp	10/03/1918	10/03/1918
War Diary	In The Line (Houthulst Forest)	11/03/1918	27/03/1918
War Diary	Bridge Camp	28/03/1918	28/03/1918
War Diary	Lattre Quentin	29/03/1918	29/03/1918
War Diary	Adinfer Wood	30/03/1918	30/03/1918
War Diary	In The Line	31/03/1918	31/03/1918
Heading	War Diary 16th Battn. The Lancashire Fusiliers April 1918		
War Diary	Ayette South of Arras	01/04/1918	07/04/1918
War Diary	Ayette Sector South of Arras	08/04/1918	30/04/1918
War Diary	Barley	01/05/1918	10/05/1918
War Diary	In The Line	11/05/1918	11/05/1918
War Diary	Boisleux Au Mont	12/05/1918	20/05/1918
War Diary	Blairville	21/05/1918	24/05/1918
War Diary	In The Line Boisleux Au Mont	25/05/1918	31/05/1918
War Diary	Blaireville	01/06/1918	04/06/1918
War Diary	In The Trenches	05/06/1918	12/06/1918
War Diary	Blaire Ville	13/05/1918	16/05/1918
War Diary	In The Trenches	17/05/1918	24/05/1918
War Diary	Blaire Ville	25/05/1918	30/05/1918
War Diary	Blaireville	01/07/1918	07/07/1918
War Diary	La Bazeque	08/07/1918	18/07/1918

War Diary	Proven	19/07/1918	31/07/1918
War Diary	Proven	01/08/1918	07/08/1918
War Diary	Saiseval	08/08/1918	08/08/1918
War Diary	Domart	09/08/1918	09/08/1918
War Diary	Beaucourt	10/08/1918	10/08/1918
War Diary	Damery	11/08/1918	12/08/1918
War Diary	Ignaucourt	13/08/1918	13/08/1918
War Diary	Fouencamps	14/08/1918	17/08/1918
War Diary	Harbonnieres	18/08/1918	18/08/1918
War Diary	Vauvillers	19/08/1918	22/08/1918
War Diary	In The Line	23/08/1918	26/08/1918
War Diary	Vauvillers	27/08/1918	27/08/1918
War Diary	Ablaincourt	28/08/1918	29/08/1918
War Diary	Misery	30/08/1918	31/08/1918
War Diary	Berny	01/09/1918	06/09/1918
War Diary	Ennemain	07/09/1918	07/09/1918
War Diary	Monchy Lagache	08/09/1918	10/09/1918
War Diary	In The Line	11/09/1918	14/09/1918
War Diary	Corbie	15/09/1918	24/09/1918
War Diary	Tertry	25/09/1918	28/09/1918
War Diary	Vendelles	29/09/1918	29/09/1918
War Diary	Masny La Fosse	30/09/1918	30/09/1918
Heading	War Diary Of 16th Lan Fus For October 1918 Vol 36		
War Diary	In Trenches 500x NE Of La Baraque	01/10/1918	01/10/1918
War Diary	Fosse Wood	02/10/1918	03/10/1918
War Diary	Lehaucourt	04/10/1918	04/10/1918
War Diary	Vendelles	05/10/1918	05/10/1918
War Diary	Han Court	06/10/1918	18/10/1918
War Diary	Lehaucourt	19/10/1918	20/10/1918
War Diary	Bohain	21/10/1918	22/10/1918
War Diary	Busigny	23/10/1918	27/10/1918
War Diary	Becquigny	28/10/1918	31/10/1918
War Diary	Bazeul (Nr Le Calaise)	01/11/1918	01/11/1918
War Diary	Bazeul & Line	02/11/1918	03/11/1918
War Diary	Sambre Canal & Ground East of Canal	04/11/1918	04/11/1918
War Diary	La Folie	05/11/1918	10/11/1918
War Diary	L'Arbre Sec Petit Fayet (area)	11/11/1918	12/11/1918
War Diary	Avesnes	13/11/1918	13/11/1918
War Diary	Ramouses.	14/11/1918	16/11/1918
War Diary	Felleries	17/11/1918	19/11/1918
War Diary	Ranee	20/11/1918	23/11/1918
War Diary	Froidchapelle	24/11/1918	30/11/1918
War Diary	Froidchapelle	01/12/1918	11/12/1918
War Diary	Phillipville	12/12/1918	12/12/1918
War Diary	Avnehailles	13/12/1918	13/12/1918
War Diary	Mettet	14/12/1918	14/12/1918
War Diary	Gesves	15/12/1918	31/12/1918
Heading	16th Bn Lancs Fus. Jan-Oct 1919		
War Diary	Gesves	01/01/1919	31/01/1919
War Diary	Gesves Belgium	01/02/1919	06/02/1919
War Diary	Bonn A/Rh	07/02/1919	17/02/1919
War Diary	Bonn	18/02/1919	18/06/1919
War Diary	Menden	19/06/1919	30/06/1919
War Diary	Bonn	01/07/1919	10/08/1919
War Diary	Bonn (Germany)	11/08/1919	23/08/1919
War Diary	Bonn	24/08/1919	29/08/1919

War Diary	Bonn-Bruhl	30/08/1919	30/08/1919
War Diary	Bruhl	31/08/1919	31/08/1919
War Diary	Bruhl (Germany)	01/09/1919	22/09/1919
War Diary	Euskirchen	23/09/1919	24/09/1919
War Diary	Euskirchen (Germany)	25/09/1919	30/09/1919
War Diary	Euskirchen Germany	01/10/1919	31/10/1919

WDFS / 23972(2)

WDFS / 23972(2)

32ND DIVISION
96TH INFY BDE

2ND BN MANCHESTER REGT
~~FEB - DEC 1918~~
1918 FEB — 1919 MAR

FROM 14 DUF 32 DIV

WAR DIARY
INTELLIGENCE SUMMARY
(Erase heading not required.)

Army Form C. 2118.

Place	Date	Hour	Summary of Events and Information	Remarks and references to Appendices
	February			
EMILE CAMP	1st		Battalion in huts at EMILE CAMP. The Battalion marched off from EMILE CAMP at 1 p.m., relieving the 17th Bn H.L.I., in the Reserve Line at HET SAS. Relief was reported complete at 4-0 p.m. Working parties furnished Captain G.R.Thomas proceeded to England for a six months tour of duty.	G.
HET SAS.	2nd.		Battalion in Reserve Line at HET SAS. Practically the whole of the Battalion were engaged in furnishing parties for work on the Corps Line, carrying &c. Two wiring squads were tonight engaged in wiring on the Front Line Posts.	G. G.
- do -	3rd.		Battalion in Reserve Line at HET SAS. Working and carrying parties furnished by the Battalion.	
- do -	4th.		Battalion in Reserve Line at HET SAS. Working and carrying parties furnished by the Battalion. The Battalion was relieved by the 16th Bn H.L.I., relief being reported complete at 3 p.m. the Battalion (less working parties still out) then marched under Company arrangements to EMILE CAMP, being accommodated in huts. The working parties subsequently rejoined and the Battalion was reported complete at 9-0 p.m.	G.
EMILE CAMP.	5th.		Battalion in huts at EMILE CAMP. The day was spent in a general clean up and in overhauling clothes and boots. The G.O.C.,14th Infantry Brigade inspected the Battalion on the Football Ground at 5 p.m., and presented the ribbon of the 1914 Star to those present with the Battalion entitled to same. He then wished the Battalion "good-bye" on its being transferred from the	G.

WAR DIARY
or
INTELLIGENCE SUMMARY.
(Erase heading not required.)

Army Form C. 2118.

Instructions regarding War Diaries and Intelligence Summaries are contained in F. S. Regs., Part II. and the Staff Manual respectively. Title pages will be prepared in manuscript.

Place	Date	Hour	Summary of Events and Information	Remarks and references to Appendices
Continued	5th		14th to the 96th Infantry Brigade, and in so doing, expressed his thanks for the good work the Battalion had done in the past and his regret at it/ severing its connection with the 14th Infantry Brigade. Lieut Colonel E.Vaughan D.S.O., returned from Senior Officers Conference FLIXECOURT and resumed command of the Battalion.	E.V.
EMILE CAMP.	6th		Battalion in huts at EMILE CAMP. Bathing and inspections were carried out during the day. Lieut. R.B.Bennett and 119 Other Ranks joined the Battalion from the 23rd Battalion The Manchester Regiment, disbanded.	E.V
- do -	7th		Battalion in huts at EMILE CAMP. The Battalion moved off at 3-0 p.m., and proceeded by light railway to RUGBY CORNER relieving the 2nd Bn K.O.Y.L.I., and 1st Bn Dorset Rgt (parts of,) in the front line, HOUTHULST FOREST sector. "A" Company on the left and "B" Company on the right in the front line. "C" Company left support and "B" Company right support. "B" Company was shelled on the way up to the line causing casualties :- 3 O.R's Killed; 5 O.R's Wounded, everywhere else quiet. Relief (less "B" Company with whom no telephonic communication was established) was reported complete at 2.25 a.m. Relief was finally reported complete at 6-30 a.m.	E.V
HOUTHULST FOREST.	8th		Battalion in front line in same dispositions. Situation normal. Strengthening of posts and wiring of flanks carried out by companies in the Outpost Line, companies in support	

Army Form C. 2118.

WAR DIARY
or
INTELLIGENCE-SUMMARY.
(Erase heading not required.)

Place	Date	Hour	Summary of Events and Information	Remarks and references to Appendices
Continued.	8th		carrying up the necessary material.	
HOUTHULST FOREST.	9th		Battalion in front line. The enemy raided a post on the left company's front about 5-30 p.m. Bombs were thrown by the enemy into our post wounding the occupants. One of the men was afterwards reported missing and another died of wounds. Total casualties, 1 Died of Wounds, 1 Wounded, and missing, 4 Wounded (all other ranks).	6.
- do -	10th		Battalion in front line. Situation normal. Early in the morning a German entered our line on the left company's front and was taken prisoner. The enemy shelled the light railway in the vicinity of Battalion Headquarters at intervals during the day. The Left Company carried out a raid on one of the enemy posts in retaliation for the raid on the previous night. No prisoners however were captured or identifications secured. On return of the patrol one man was found to be missing; a search party immediately went out and finally discovered the man dead. All identifications were removed and the body left until it was possible to remove it.	6.
- do -	11th		Battalion in front line. Situation normal. The Battalion was relieved by the 16th Bn Lancashire Fusiliers, relief commencing at 5 p.m., and being reported complete about 1-15 a.m. On relief companies moved idependantly to ABRI WOOD Huts becoming Brigade Reserve.	6.

WAR DIARY
or
INTELLIGENCE-SUMMARY.
(Erase heading not required.)

Army Form C. 2118.

Place	Date	Hour	Summary of Events and Information	Remarks and references to Appendices
ABRI WOOD.	12th		Battalion in shelters at ABRI WOOD. Working parties furnished on Army Line under the supervision of the R.E.	6t
- do -	13th		Battalion in shelters at ABRI WOOD. Working parties furnished on Army Line under the supervision of the R.E. Captain A.McKenzie M.C., joined the Battalion and took over command of "A" Company, being transferred from the 23rd Bn The Manchester Regiment, disbanded.	6t
- do -	14th		Battalion in shelters at ABRI WOOD. Working parties furnished on Army Line under the supervision of the R.E.	6t
- do -	15th		Battalion in shelters at ABRI WOOD. Working parties furnished on Army Line under supervision of the R.E. The Battalion relieved the 15th Bn Lancashire Fusiliers in the Support System of the Forward Zone, relief commencing at 5 p.m., and being reported at 8 p.m. Battalion Headquarters at LA CHAUDIERE. Battalion placed under orders to be ready to move at 15 minutes notice.	6t
CORPS LINE.	16th		Battalion in shelters in Support System of Forward Zone. Working and carrying parties furnished.	6t
- do -	17th		Battalion in shelters in Support System of Forward Zone. Working and carrying parties furnished. Parties also employed salvaging material.	6t

Army Form C. 2118.

WAR DIARY
or
INTELLIGENCE-SUMMARY.
(Erase heading not required.)

Place	Date	Hour	Summary of Events and Information	Remarks and references to Appendices
CORPS LINE.	18th		Battalion in shelters in Support System of Forward Zone. Working, Carrying and Salvaging parties furnished. 2nd Lieut., A.T.Burton M.M. joined the Battalion from the 23rd Battalion The Manchester Regiment, disbanded.	6
- do -	19th		Battalion in shelters in Support System of Forward Zone. The Battalion was relieved by the 16th Lancashire Fusiliers. After relief the Battalion relieved the 15th Bn Lancashire Fusiliers in the front system of the Forward Zone (HOUTHULST FOREST SECTOR). "C" and "D" Companies in the Outpost Line and "A" and "B" Companies in Support. Battalion Headquarters at CALEDONIAN CLUB. Relief reported complete at 8-30 p.m.	6
HOUTHULST FOREST.	20th		Battalion in front system of Forward Zone - situation normal. Between 4-30 and 5 am the enemy shelled VELDHOEK - casualties 1 O.R Killed 2 O.R's Wounded. An enemy patrol attempted to raid the right post on the right company front but were driven off, 2 prisoners being captured. The enemy shelled Hill 20 in the early morning, 10.R. being wounded. Wiring of posts in the Outpost Line proceeded with. 2/Lieut., J.Berry joined the Battalion in the line from the 23rd Battalion The Manchester Regiment, disbanded.	6
- do -	21st		Battalion in Front System of Forward Zone. - situation normal. At 5 am the S.O.S., Signal went on the Belgian Divisional Front on our left - our artillery effectively replied.	

WAR DIARY
or
INTELLIGENCE-SUMMARY.
(*Erase heading not required.*)

Army Form C. 2118.

Place	Date	Hour	Summary of Events and Information	Remarks and references to Appendices
continued.	21st		Intermittent shelling went on throughout the day, otherwise everything else was quiet. A number of patrols went out during the night with the object of obtaining the suspected positions of enemy machine guns and the condition the of the enemy wire. Wiring of posts in the Outpost Line continued.	
HOUTHULST FOREST.	22nd		Battalion in Front System of Forward Zone.- situation normal. Intermittent shelling went on throughout the day. The enemy shelled in the vicinity of Battalion Headquarters from 11 am to 11-20 pm— enemy machine guns were active, LASALLE receiving special attention. Wiring of posts continued. 1 O.R. reported missing.	
- do -	23rd		Battalion in Front System of Forward Zone.- situation normal. Enemy artillery showed increased activity, Suez farm, VELDHOEK, and AJAX HOUSE receiving marked attention. There was also increased aerial activity, several enemy aeroplanes flying low over our lines. Two bombs were dropped on OWLS WOOD. Battalion was relieved by the 16th Bn Lancashire Fusiliers - relief commencing at 5-30 pm and being reported complete at 10 pm. During relief, enemy machine Guns were very active - Casualties 2 O.R's killed and 1 O.R. Wounded. After relief the Battalion proceeded to ABRI WOOD being in Brigade Reserve.	

Army Form C. 2118.

WAR DIARY
or
INTELLIGENCE-SUMMARY.
(Erase heading not required.)

Instructions regarding War Diaries and Intelligence Summaries are contained in F. S. Regs., Part II. and the Staff Manual respectively. Title pages will be prepared in manuscript.

Place	Date	Hour	Summary of Events and Information	Remarks and references to Appendices
ABRI WOOD.	24th		Battalion in shelters at ABRI WOOD. Usual inspections held and day spent generally in cleaning up - Bathing was commenced. Working parties found at night.	6
- do -	25th		Battalion in shelters in ABRI WOOD. Bathing was continued and working parties furnished.	6
- do -	26th		Battalion in shelters in ABRI WOOD. Bathing continued and working parties furnished.	6
- do -	27th		Battalion in shelters in ABRI WOOD. Relieved the 15th Bn Lancashire Fusiliers, relief commencing at 5 p.m. Dispositions on becoming No 2 Battalion of No 1 Brigade as follows :- B.H.Q., and "B" Company at LA CHAUDIERE. "A" Company at COLONELS FARM, "C" Company in CORPS LINE as permanent garrison, "D" Company in Corps Line. A raid was carried out by 7 officers and 119 O.R's under the Command of Captain W.Key. Zero hour 7-52 p.m. (See attached Operation Order No 21). 7 prisoners were taken and two Machine Guns and other booty, including shoulder straps cut from enemy dead, were brought in. Casualties inflicted on raiding party :- Lieut S.E.Hollins and 2/Lieut S.Surkitt Wounded. 2 O.R's Killed, 11 O.R's Wounded, 2 O.R's Missing. A wire was received from the G.O.C., 32nd Division congratulating the Raiding party on their brilliant exploit.	6
CORPS LINE.				
- do -	28th		Battalion in Support System of Forward Zone. Working Parties furnished on CORPS LINE.	

E Vaughan
Lieut Colonel,
Commanding 2nd Battalion The Manchester Regiment.

SECRET.   COPY No _____

2nd BATTALION THE MANCHESTER REGIMENT.

OPERATION ORDER No. 21.

Reference Maps Sheet No.20.N.W.   26th February 1918.
(BIXSCHOOTE) Edition 7A.d.
Special Map issued.
----

1.   The 2nd Battalion The Manchester Regiment, will carry
out a raid on the enemy's posts at MARACHAL FARM and in the
vicinity on the night of the 27th/28th February 1918., and
thoroughly search the ground within the area bounded by the
Artillery Barrage, as per special map, and destroy or capture all
enemy met with.

2. INFORMATION. MARACHAL FARM is composed of three buildings.
One low long concreted building running north and south, and two
ruined buildings West of it.
South of the FARM the ground is wet.

   Approaches. Road running North from COLOMBO HOUSE. This road
is reported to be in good condition, firm and dry for about 100
yards from our lines, afterwards there are a number of trees
felled across the road.
Road does not afford cover.
There are deep ditches full of water on either side of the road
and the ground on either side of the road is wet.
   At U.6.b.20.70 a road branches in an Easterly direction.
   Wire is reported along the side   of this road, and a
Machine Gun at U.6.b.50.75.
   There is a road at U.6.b.20.85 branching off in a westerly
direction. At this point there is a Machine Gun at the road
junction. The ground between COLOMBO HOUSE and MARACHAL FARM is
wet and full of shell holes.
   Trees along road running in a westerly direction from
U.6.b.20.85 are probably wired.

   OWL WOOD. Very thick and hard to move through on account of
fallen trees, undergrowth and shell holes. At U.6.a.85.60 there
is some loose wire among the trees. A breastwork is reported
here with a PILL BOX behind, unoccupied, but believed occupied at
night.
   About U.6.a.40.92 north of the road there are four PILL BOXES
unoccupied.

   Machine Guns. Suspected at MARACHAL FARM. U.6.b.24.87.,
U.6.b.80.90., U.6.b.80.82., U.6.b.95.50., U.6.b.90.40., U.6.a.60.72.,
O.36.d.7.1., O.36.d.90.42.

   Trench Mortars. Suspected North of MARACHAL FARM about
O.36.d.1.2.

3. OBJECT OF RAID.

   1.   To locate position of enemy's main line of resistance.

   2.   To find out what works the enemy is carrying out in OWL WOOD.

   3.   To capture all enemy found in the area raided.

   4.   To obtain identifications and bring back documents, maps,
        samples of food, and clothing and gas masks.

   5.   To secure Machine Guns, Trench Mortars and other booty.

Continued.

"2"

4. **AREA TO BE RAIDED.** The area to be raided will be that enclosed by a line drawn from U.6.b.7.6. to O.35.d.6.6. to O.36.c.4.5. to U.6.a.45.80 with MARACHAL FARM as centre. (This area will be referred to subsequently as MARACHAL FARM AREA).

5. **TROOPS ALLOTTED FOR RAID.** 6 Officers and 110 O.R's under the Command of CAPTAIN W.KAY, distributed as follows :-

No 1 party.
   1 Lewis Gun
   Cpl Cliffe
   O.R's 6.

No 2 Party.
   1 Lewis Gun.
   Cpl Monks.
   O.R's 6.

No 3 Party.
   Lieut.,R.B.Bennett.
   Sgt Metcalfe.
   O.R's 20.
   R.E's 2.with Bangalore Torpedoes.

No 4 Party.
   2/Lieut.,S.V.Brady M.C.
   Sgt Boyd.
   O.R's 20.
   R.E's 2 with Bangalore Torpedoes.

No 5 party.
   2/Lieut J.B.R.Thomas.
   Sgt Martin.
   O.R's 12.

No 6 Party.
   Lieut.,S.R.Hollins.
   Sgt Williams.
   O.R's 16.

No 7 Party.
   2/Lieut S.Burkitt.
   Sgt McElroy.
   O.R's 12.

No 8 Party.
   2/Lieut.,H.V.Parker.
   Sgt Sumner.
   O.R's 12.

At Zero minus 20 these parties will be formed up on the COLOMBO HOUSE - PANAMA HOUSE ROAD in above order, No 1 being on the right and near COLOMBO HOUSE. O.C.,Raiding Party will have his Headquarters in COLOMBO HOUSE and be in communication with Battalion Headquarters.

6. **DUTIES.** Line of advance, time of advance, the actual duty of each party and its moves on completion of its work.

    No 1 Party. Will move at Zero plus 5 minutes and proceed to U.6.b.24.27, taking up a position on the right of the main MARACHAL FARM ROAD. Their duty is to cover advance of raiders and open fire on any Machine Guns that may fire on the Right side of the main road, special attention being paid to Machine Guns that may be outside our own barrage on right flank. They will remain here until O.C.,Raiding Party orders them to retire.

    No 2 party. Will advance immediately in rear of No 1 Party and will form in a similar position to No 1 Party on the Left of the road, U.6.b.12.17. Their duty is to keep down all Machine Gun fire from the direction of MARACHAL FARM and the main road. They will not retire until ordered to do so by O.C.,Raiding Party.

    No 3 Party. Will advance at Zero plus 10 and move direct on MARACHAL FARM CROSS-ROADS keeping as close up to the barrage as possible. Should impassable wire be met with the Bangalore Torpedoes will be used and MARACHAL FARM rushed as soon as possible. This party will remain at MARACHAL FARM under orders of O.C.,Raid sending flanking parties down to the roads on each flank. O.C., this party will detail 4 men to take down prisoners to Brigade Headquarters.

    No 4 party. Will follow in immediate support of No 3 party and be ready to use the Bangalore Torpedoes if required and assist in the capture of MARACHAL FARM. Captain W.Kay will advance with this party and then form his Headquarters at MARACHAL FARM, as soon as it is taken.

(Continued)

"3"

On the capture of MARACHAL FARM this party will continue to advance down main road as far as the barrage and wheeling to the right will search all ground between there and the road running east of MARACHAL FARM. On reaching this road, the party will withdraw.

No 5 Party. Will move at 10 yards distance from No 4 party and proceed past MARACHAL FARM CROSS ROADS and endeavour to find and capture the Trench Mortar reported at 0.36.d.10.25. They will get into touch with No 7 party and search the ground in connection with them and withdraw with them.

No 6 Party. Will move at 10 yards distance of No 5 party and at U.6.b.80.68., will turn left and clear all ground in the area South of the MARACHAL FARM - LIASON FARM ROAD. They will withdraw on completing their work.

No 7 Party. Will advance at 10 yards distance of No 6 party and advance as far as the Box Barrage, when they will turn Left and search the ground within the area of the barrage and MARACHAL FARM - LIASON FARM ROAD getting into touch with No 5 party and on reaching the road they will withdraw.
Any prisoners they may collect they should bring with them and take them to Brigade Headquarters.

No 8 Party. Will advance immediately in rear of No 7 party and at U.6.b.23.75., will wheel to the Right and search all ground within the Barrage Area up to road running East from MARACHAL FARM. Any Prisoners they may collect, they will bring with them, and on reaching this road they will withdraw.

All parties withdrawing will pass AJAX HOUSE and use the CLARKES STREET Duckboard track and return to Battalion Headquarters at LA CHAUDIERE.

7. **IDENTIFICATION.** Each man will carry a cardboard disc showing his party number ie."No 1 of No 5 Party". A checking party under Captain Sloman will be established near AJAX HOUSE and each man as he passes will hand his disc to this officer who will have a full roll and check all who have passed.

8. **LINES OF ADVANCE.** Lines of advance of each party are shown on the small sketch map given to the Commander of each party and thoroughly explained to each man.

9. **ARTILLERY BARRAGE.** The raid will be carried out under an Artillery and Machine Gun Barrage.
The Artillery Barrage will begin at ZERO on a line about 250 yards North of the MARACHAL FARM - LIASON FARM ROAD and parallel to it.
It will creep forward to a line 200 yards South of the above road and be on the line at Zero plus 12.
One battery will remain all the time on the original starting line.
At Zero plus 12 the barrage will creep back again, resting finally as a protective barrage on line 0.36.c.45.25 to 0.36.d.00.45.
Orders re Machine Gun Barrage will be issued later.

10. **IDENTIFICATIONS.** One man in each party will be told off to collect identifications, documents etc., and to cut shoulder-straps off all dead.

11. **COMMUNICATION.** The Battalion Signalling officer will arrange to connect up AJAX HOUSE with Brigade Signalling officer and also to run a line to MARACHAL FARM immediately it is captured.
Lucas Lamp must also be taken in case of failure of line.

12. **MEDICAL.** Stretcher Bearers will follow No 4 party.

continued.

"4"

13. **DRESS.** Steel Helmets, rifles and fixed bayonets, magazines charged and twenty rounds in each bottom pocket of the tunic.
 Each man will carry **two** bombs.
 Box respirators will not be taken.
 Each man will carry his waterproof sheet rolled on his belt to assist in carrying wounded who must be brought back without fail.
 No papers, maps etc., or any marks of identification must be carried or worn by anyone.
 Wire cutters will be carried by 60 per cent of the men.

14. **PASSWORD.** Password will be "M.R".
 The Lancashire Fusiliers are patrolling OWLS WOOD and will on our retirement take up a position near MARACHAL FARM to deal with any returning enemy.
 Their password is "LANCS".

15. **REPORTS.** All parties on completion of their task must send a message to that effect to Capt. MAY at MARACHAL FARM and must without fail, bring back all their casualties.

16. **ROUTE.** When parties withdraw they will proceed direct to Battalion Headquarters at LA CHAUDIERE and report to the Adjutant who will check their names.

17. **FOOD.** Arrangements have been made for a hot meal both before and after the raid.

18. **RETURN OF PARTIES.** All parties must be south of MARACHAL FARM by Zero plus 70 minutes.

19. **SYNCHRONIZATION.** Watches will be synchronised at 6 p.m., on the 27th inst by the Signalling Officer.

20. **ZERO.** Zero hour will be notified later.

21. ACKNOWLEDGE.

E. Vaughan.
 Lieut.Colonel,
 Commanding 2nd Battalion The Manchester Regiment.

Issued at _____

Copies to:- 1. 36th Infantry Brigade.
 2. Commanding Officer.
 3. 16th Bn Lancashire Fusiliers.
 4 to 10 O.C., Raid & Officers.
 11. Signalling Officer.
 12. Intelligence Officer.
 13. Medical Officer.
 14 & 15 War Diary.
 16. File.

32nd Division.
96th Infantry Brigade

2nd BATTALION

THE MANCHESTER REGIMENT

MARCH 1 9 1 8

WAR DIARY or INTELLIGENCE SUMMARY

2 Manchesters Vol 44

Place	Date	Hour	Summary of Events and Information	Remarks and references to Appendices
	1/3/18		Battalion in Support system of forward zone. Battn H.Q. and Coys at LA CHAUDIERE. "B" company at COLONELS FARM. "C" and "D" companies in Coys Line. Working parties furnished for strengthening the Coys Line defence. Parties also furnished for carrying material forward and salvaging. C.O. & 2nd Lt Sergeant addressed the reading party at 11.30am at ABRI WOOD.	A.
	2/3/18		Battalion in Support system of forward zone. Working and carrying parties furnished for work on Coys Line defences.	A.
	3/3/18		Battalion in support system of forward zone. Relieved by 10th Argyll and Sutherland Highlanders. Relief commenced at 12noon and was complete at 3.30pm. The Battalion marched by platoons to CHARENTIER CROSS ROADS and were thence proceeded by light railway to TORRINGTON, thence marching to LA BERGERIE CAMP.	A.
	4/3/18		Battalion in shelters at LA BERGERIE CAMP. The day was spent in General cleaning up, exchanging of clothing and inspection of equipment.	A.
	5/3/18		Battalion in shelters at LA BERGERIE CAMP. At 10.45am the Divisional Commander inspected the Divl. Monthly Cups to the Battalion, having won same for passing	A.

WAR DIARY
or
INTELLIGENCE SUMMARY.
(Erase heading not required.)

Army Form C. 2118.

Place	Date	Hour	Summary of Events and Information	Remarks and references to Appendices
	5/3/18		Most point in the Division in capturing prisoners, machine guns, identifications etc. At 11.15 am the C.O. commander presented ribbons of the Military Medal to the following for Gallantry and devotion to duty during the raid on the night of Feby 27/28th 1918. No. 9561 Sgt. J.T. Metcalfe, No. 6255 Sgt. J. Medbury, No. 1738 Pte. C. Vizett, No. 2290 Pte. T.I. Wood. No. 26101 Pte. C. Roebuck and No. 2259 Pte. E. Jones.	R.
	6/3/18		Battalion in shelters at LABERGERIE CAMP. The whole of the Battalion employed working on the Army Battle Zone. Lieut Colonel E. Vaughan D.S.O. proceeded to the 4th Army Musketry School NORTBECOURT. Major N.T. Humphreys took over temporary Command of the Battalion.	B.F.
	7/3/18		Battalion in shelters at LABERGERIE CAMP. Working parties provided as for the 5th inst.	B.F.
	8/3/18		Battalion in shelters at LABERGERIE CAMP. Training carried out.	B.F.
	9/3/18		Battalion in shelters at LABERGERIE CAMP. The Battalion marched to ABRI WOOD arrived there at 4.15 p.m. and relieved the 11th Battn. Gordon Regt. Lieut Colonel E. Vaughan D.S.O. returned from 4th Army Musketry School and took over Command of the Battalion.	
	10/3/18		Battalion in shelters at ABRI WOOD. Two O.R's working on the Army Battle Zone.	B.

Army Form C. 2118.

WAR DIARY
or
INTELLIGENCE SUMMARY.
(Erase heading not required.)

Instructions regarding War Diaries and Intelligence Summaries are contained in F. S. Regs., Part II. and the Staff Manual respectively. Title pages will be prepared in manuscript.

Place	Date	Hour	Summary of Events and Information	Remarks and references to Appendices
	10/3/18		"C" and "D" Companies moved to Canal Banks at 4.15 pm	R.
	11/3/18		Battn. Hd. Qrs. "C" and "D" Coys in Shelters at ABRI WOOD. "A" and "B" Coys in Shelters at CANAL BANK. Nothing particular furnished on Army Battle Zone. Lieut. Colonel E. Vaughan M.O. and a party of 4 officers proceeded to reconnoitre the Forward Zone.	R.
	12/3/18		Battn. Hd. Qrs. "C" Coys "A" & "B" Coys in Shelters at ABRI WOOD. "C" and "D" Coys in Shelters at CANAL BANK. Nothing particular furnished as to the 11th inst.	R.
	13/3/18		Battn. Hd. Qrs. "A" & "B" Coys in Shelters at ABRI WOOD. "C" and "D" Coys in Shelters at CANAL BANK. Nothing particular furnished as for the 11th inst.	R.
	14/3/18		Battn. at ABRI WOOD in Shelters. The Battn. relieved the 5th R. Royal Scots of the 14th R. Left Bde., relief being reported complete at 10 pm. BHQ — MONDOVIE WOOD.	R.
	15/3/18		Battn. in Front System of Forward Zone. Enemy artillery was very active. A patrol under Lieut. M. Jackson was out during the night.	R.
	16/3/18		Battn. in Front System of Forward Zone. Enemy artillery was very active. Two O.R. being killed and 10 O.R. Wounded.	R.
	17/3/18		Battn. in Front System of Forward Zone — situation normal. The Battn. was	R.

WAR DIARY
or
INTELLIGENCE SUMMARY.
(Erase heading not required.)

Army Form C. 2118.

Place	Date	Hour	Summary of Events and Information	Remarks and references to Appendices
	17th		relieved by the 15th. Lanc. Gren., relief being complete at 9.30 p.m. The Battn. afterwards moved to the support system of Forward Zone.	
	18th		Battn. in support system of Forward Zone. Working parties provided for digging and revetting on the Corps Line.	G
	19th		Battn. in support system of Forward Zone. Working parties found for digging and revetting on the Corps Line.	G
	20th		Battn. in support system of Forward Zone. Tonight "B" Coy relieved "A" Coy at LANNES COPSE. Subsequently A and D Coys relieved "B"& "C" Coys of the 15th Lanc Gren. in the front system of the Forward Zone, and four time of relief such Coys came under the orders of O.C. 15th Lanc Gren. After the raid carried out by "D" Coy 15th Lanc Gren. they withdrew to CHAUNE FARM and STATUETTE FARM coming under orders of O.C 21/2 th the Manchester Regt.	G
	21st		Battn. (less A&D Coys) in support system of Forward Zone. Enemy artillery was unusually active in the vicinity of B.H.Q. during the afternoon. "B"&"C" Coys relieved two Companies of the 15th Lanc Gren. in front system of Forward Zone, relief being complete at 9.45 p.m. Gren. from 10.45 p.m to 12.30 a.m	D

WAR DIARY
or
INTELLIGENCE SUMMARY.
(Erase heading not required.)

Army Form C. 2118.

Place	Date	Hour	Summary of Events and Information	Remarks and references to Appendices
	21st		Enemy artillery shelled front and support area with H.E. and a percentage of shrapnel and sweeping gas shell. Casualties 6 O.R. wounded.	A.
	22nd		Battn. in front system of Forward Zone. Artillery again very active, otherwise everything quiet. Casualties 4 O.R. wounded. The usual patrols were out during the night.	A.
	23rd		Battn. in front system of Forward zone. Situation normal. Enemy artillery less active than on the previous day, only intermittent shelling taking place throughout the day. The usual patrols were out during the night. Casualties 1 O.R. wounded.	A.
	24th		Battn. in Front system of Forward zone — Situation normal. Artillery quiet during the day, but increased in activity during the afternoon. Several shells fell in the vicinity of B.H.Q. one hitting the runners hut but only 1 O.R. slightly wounded. The usual patrols were out during the night. H.Q. Coy relieved by two Companies 15th Lanc. Bros. H.Q. Coy afterwards proceeding to STATUETTE FARM and CHAUME FARM and here coming under the orders of 15th Lanc Bros. Casualties 4 O.R. wounded.	A.

WAR DIARY
or
INTELLIGENCE SUMMARY.

Army Form C. 2118.

(Erase heading not required.)

Place	Date	Hour	Summary of Events and Information	Remarks and references to Appendices
	25th		Battn (less A & D Coys) in Corps System of forward zone. Situation normal. Artillery very much quieter today. B and C Coys relieved by two Coys 18th Lanc Fusrs, relief being complete at 9.30 p.m. B and C Coys afterwards moved	
	26th		to LANNES COPSE and GOURBI respectively in Support System of forward zone. Battn in Support System of forward zone. Working parties found for working on Battn lines.	A
	27th		Battn in Support System of forward zone. The Battn was this morning relieved by 10th Bedevin Regt, relief being reported complete at 12.50 p.m. The Battn afterwards moved to WHITEMILL CAMP, ELVERDINGHE being accommodated in huts.	A
	28/29th		Battn at WHITEMILL CAMP. The Battn was this morning inspected by the Commanding Officer. The Battn today commenced its move to a new Army Area. Headquarters A B & C Coys entrained from ELVERDINGHE at 7.45 p.m. and were conveyed to PROVEN where they detrained. Leaving PROVEN at 11.45 p.m. the Battn arrived at SAVY at 7.30 a.m. on the 29th. The Battn then marched to HAUTEVILLE being accommodated in Billets. D Coy. left PROVEN at 5.30 a.m. on	A

WAR DIARY
or
INTELLIGENCE SUMMARY.
(Erase heading not required.)

Army Form C. 2118.

Place	Date	Hour	Summary of Events and Information	Remarks and references to Appendices
	30th		The Bn. eventually found the Battn. at HAUTEVILLE and the whole o/Battn. was reported present at 4am.	G.
			Battn. at HAUTEVILLE in Billets. The Battn. moved off at 2.40 p.m. and marched to ADINFER where they relieved the 2nd Bn. K.O.Y.L.I. being accommodated in trenches & dug outs. Casualties 1 O.R. wounded. Relief was reported Complete at 11.30 p.m.	G.
	31st.		Battn. at ADINFER. Battn. marched to AYETTE and took over portion of front line relieving the 1st Irish Guards. Relief was reported Complete at 12.15 a.m. Casualties 1 O.R. wounded	G.

Vaughan
Lieut. Colonel
Commanding 2nd Battn. The Manchester Regt.

96th Inf.Bde.
32nd Div.

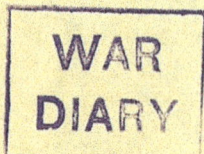

2nd BATTN. THE MANCHESTER REGIMENT.

A P R I L

1 9 1 8

Army Form C. 2118.

96/37
2 Manchester R.
Vol 45

WAR DIARY
or
INTELLIGENCE SUMMARY.

(Erase heading not required.)

Instructions regarding War Diaries and Intelligence Summaries are contained in F. S. Regs., Part II. and the Staff Manual respectively. Title pages will be prepared in manuscript.

Place	Date	Hour	Summary of Events and Information	Remarks and references to Appendices
	1918 Apl.	1.	Battalion at AYETTE - situation normal. Enemy snipers were very active. The Battalion was to-night relieved, the line which they held being taken over by the 5/6th Royal Scots, 16th H.L.I. and 2nd K.O.Y.L.I., relief being reported complete at 12.5 a.m. The Battalion then moved to the PURPLE LINE of Defence being accommodated in reserve trenches - B.H.Q. at QUESNOY FARM. Casualties:- 4 O.R. wounded.	Appx
		2.	Battalion in PURPLE LINE. Companies were engaged in strengthening and consolidating line of defence. Casualties:- 1 O.R. killed, 2 O.R. gassed, 2 O.R. missing and 1 O.R. wounded.	Appx
		3.	Battalion in PURPLE LINE. Companies engaged in consolidating and strengthening line of defence. Enemy artillery very active. Casualties:- 3 O.R. wounded.	Appx
		4.	Battalion in PURPLE LINE. Companies engaged in consolidating and strengthening line of defence. Enemy's artillery showed increased activity. The Battalion to-night relieved the 16th Lancs. Fusrs. in the Left sub-sector - "A" and "D" Companies in the line, "B" and "C" Companies in support. Relief reported complete at 10.25 p.m. The usual protective patrols were out during the night. Casualties:- 1 Officer (Lieut. R. B. Bennett) wounded.	Appx
		5	Battalion in the line - situation normal. At 10.30a.m. information was received that the Germans were about to attack. S.O.S. signal went up on the Left Brigade front but no further developments took place on the Battalion front. One of our patrols ("D" Company) which went out to-night brought in two prisoners. Casualties:- 6 O.R. wounded, 1 O.R. gassed.	Appx
		6	Battalion in the line - situation normal. Enemy artillery still very active but chiefly on the back areas. The usual protective patrols were out during the night. Casualties:- 1 Officer (2nd Lieut. T. S. Thomas) killed and 6 O.R. wounded.	Appx
		7	Battalion in the line - situation normal. Enemy artillery very active to-day, both on the front and back areas. To-night "B" and "C" Companies relieved "A" and "D" Companies. The usual protective patrols were out to-night. Casualties:- 1 O.R.killed, 10 O.R. wounded.	Appx

Army Form C. 2118.

WAR DIARY
or
INTELLIGENCE SUMMARY.
(Erase heading not required.)

Instructions regarding War Diaries and Intelligence Summaries are contained in F. S. Regs., Part II. and the Staff Manual respectively. Title pages will be prepared in manuscript.

Place	Date	Hour	Summary of Events and Information	Remarks and references to Appendices
	1918 Apl. 8		Battalion in the line - situation normal. Enemy artillery showed considerably less activity to-day. The usual protective patrols were out during the night. Casualties:- 3 O.R. wounded.	
	9		Battalion in the line - situation normal. Enemy artillery very active, a proportion of gas shells being sent over. The usual protective patrols were out during the night. Casualties:- 1 O.R. wounded 2 O.R. gassed.	
	10		Battalion in the line - situation normal. Scattered shelling of the front and back areas by the enemy's artillery continued. Battalion relieved to-night by the 15th Lancs. Fusrs., relief being reported complete at 1.25 a.m. After relief the Battalion moved to the PURPLE LINE being accommodated in reserve trenches. Casualties:- 2 O.R. Killed 7 O.R. wounded.	
	11		Battalion in PURPLE LINE. Companies engaged in strengthening line of defence. Marked activity on the part of the enemy's artillery. Casualties:- 3 O.R. wounded.	
	12		Battalion in PURPLE LINE. Companies engaged in strengthening line of defence, and in finding small working parties under R.E. Enemy's artillery very active on back areas. Casualties:- 8 O.R. wounded and 1 O.R. gassed.	
	13		Battalion in Purple Line. Working parties found for working under R.E. Companies engaged in generally strengthening line of defence. Enemy artillery showed its usual activity and in the early morning a number of gas shells were sent over on the Reserve Line. To-night the Battalion relieved the 16th Lancs. Fusrs. in the Right sub-sector, relief being reported complete at 3.20 a.m. Active patrolling was carried out until dawn. Casualties:- 3 O.R. wounded 2 O.R. gassed.

Major H. C. W. Theobald, D.S.O., to-day joined the Battalion. | |
| | 14 | | Battalion in the line - situation normal. About 7 a.m. this morning the enemy shelled very heavily the positions held by the Battalion and also in the vicinity of Battalion Headquarters - 2nd Lieut. B. McSherry being killed and Major N. W. Humphrys (2nd in Command) and 2nd Lieut. G. Handley being wounded. During the remainder of the day the enemy's artillery was unusually quiet. The usual protective patrols were out during the night. Total casualties:- 1 Officer killed, 2 Officers wounded, 4 O.R. wounded and 2 O.R. gassed. | |

WAR DIARY
or
INTELLIGENCE SUMMARY.

(Erase heading not required.)

Army Form C. 2118.

Place	Date	Hour	Summary of Events and Information	Remarks and references to Appendices
	1918 Apl.15		Battalion in the line. Situation normal. Enemy artillery unusually quiet to-day. Usual protective patrols out during the night. Casualties:- 1 O.R. killed 5 wounded. Major H. C. W. Theobald, D.S.O. to-day proceeded to take over the temporary command of the 15th Lancs. Fusrs.	
	16		Battalion in the line - situation normal. Enemy's artillery activity again much below normal. Inter-Company relief carried out to-night "B" Company relieving "A" Company and "C" Company relieving "D" Company. The usual protective patrols were out to-night. Casualties:- 5 wounded 3 gassed. The following Officers joined the Battalion in the line to-day;- Capt. F. O. Medworth, M.C., Lieut. R. E. Prouse, Lieut. G. Denison, Lieut. W. T. Williams-Green, 2nd Lieut. F. Brownson and 2nd Lieut. B. Burkett-Gottwaltz.	
	17		Battalion in the line - situation normal. Enemy shelled vicinity of Battalion Headquarters in the early morning - during the day below normal but increasing considerably during the night. Casualties:- 1 O.R. killed, 4 O.R. wounded and 1 O.R. gassed.	
	18		Battalion in the line - situation normal. Enemy artillery activity normal throughout the day. At 6 p.m. an intense bombardment by our artillery took place of the trench proposed to be raided that night. At 2 a.m. a party consisting of 3 officers and 20 O.R. from "A" Company and 20 O.R. from "C" Company raided a trench occupied by the enemy, the trench having been previously subjected to an intense bombardment for four minutes. The party entered the enemy trench from the North and South ends. After proceeding some little distance up the trench both parties met with strong opposition from bombs and M.G. fire and it was impossible for the raiding party to make further progress and they were compelled to withdraw without securing an identification which was their primary object. Casualties:- 1 officer (2nd Lieut. J. B. R. Thomas) killed, 2 Officers (Lieut. Hollins and 2nd Lieut. Berry) wounded, 5 O.R. killed, 15 O.R. wounded and 5 O.R. gassed. Lieut. Col. Vaughan proceeded to 109th Infy. Bde, Major Theobald taking over command of Batt.	
	19		Battalion in the line - situation normal. The enemy's artillery ativity was normal throughout the day. The Battalion was relieved to-night by the 15th Lancs. Fusrs, relief being reported complete at 11.45 p.m. After relief the Battalion moved to the PURPLE ZONE being accommodated in trenches. Casualties:- 1 O.R.killed, 1 O.R. wounded and 1 O.R. gassed.	

Army Form C. 2118.

WAR DIARY
or
INTELLIGENCE SUMMARY.

(Erase heading not required.)

Instructions regarding War Diaries and Intelligence Summaries are contained in F. S. Regs., Part II. and the Staff Manual respectively. Title pages will be prepared in manuscript.

Place	Date	Hour	Summary of Events and Information	Remarks and references to Appendices
	1918 Apl.20		Battalion in PURPLE ZONE - enemy artillery very active around QUESNOY FARM throughout the day. Casualties:- 1 O.R. wounded and missing (believed killed).	
	21		Battalion in PURPLE ZONE - situation normal. During the afternoon the enemy's artillery was very active, QUESNOY FARM and vicinity of Battalion Headquarters being shelled with 8" shells for more than two hours. During the remainder of the day only scattered and intermittent shelling took place. Casualties:- 2 O.R. wounded.	
	22		Battalion in PURPLE ZONE. Situation normal. Battalion to-night relieved the 16th Lancs. Fus. in the front line in the Left sub-sector, relief being reported complete at 1215 a.m. Casualties:- 2 O.R. wounded.	
	23		Battalion in the line - situation normal. Enemy artillery activity below normal. Usual protective patrols out during the night. 1 Officer (Lieut. J. W. Culley) gassed and 1 O.R. wounded.	
	24		Battalion in the line - situation normal. Enemy's artillery showed increased activity to-day. The usual protective patrols were out during the night. Casualties 2 O.R. wounded.	
	25		Battalion in the line - situation normal. Enemy artillery very active. Battalion Headquarters and vicinity being shelled at intervals throughout the day. Until relief the usual protective patrols were out. To-night the Battalion was relieved by the 2nd Batt. Scots Guards, relief commencing at 8 p.m. and being reported complete at 10.45 p.m. After relief the Battalion proceeded to BERLES AU BOIS being accommodated in billets. Casualties:- 1 O.R. killed, 5 O.R. wounded and 1 O.R. missing.	
	26		Battalion in billets at BERLES AU BOIS. The Battalion proceeded by route march to BARLY leaving BERLES AU BOIS at 9.30 a.m. and arriving at BARLY at 12 noon being accommodated in billets. The following Officers joined the Battalion to-day:- 2d Lieut. A. H. Bramley, 2nd Lieut. W. Mortiboy, 2nd Lieut. F. Hayward, 2nd Lieut. F. W. Mitchell, 2nd Lieut. H. R. Hill, 2nd Lieut. J. Tait.	

Army Form C. 2118.

WAR DIARY
or
INTELLIGENCE SUMMARY.
(Erase heading not required.)

Instructions regarding War Diaries and Intelligence Summaries are contained in F. S. Regs., Part II. and the Staff Manual respectively. Title pages will be prepared in manuscript.

Place	Date	Hour	Summary of Events and Information	Remarks and references to Appendices
	1918 Apl.27		Battalion in Billets at BARLY. The day was spent in generally cleaning up after the tour in the line, and in fitting new clothing, etc.	
	28		Battalion in Billets at BARLY. Church Parades. 2nd Lieut. H. Lawrence to-day joined the Battalion.	
	29		Battalion in Billets at BARLY. Training carried on according to programme. 2nd Lieut. W. Bramhall to-day joined the Battalion.	
	30		Battalion in Billets at BARLY. Training carried on according to programme.	

H.C. Theobald Major.

Commanding 2nd Battalion, The Manchester Regiment.

WAR DIARY
or
INTELLIGENCE SUMMARY.

(Erase heading not required.)

Army Form C. 2118.

2nd Manchester Regt

Place	Date	Hour	Summary of Events and Information	Remarks and references to Appendices
	1918 May 1		Battalion in Billets at BARLY. Training carried on according to programme. Afternoon devoted to a pool shoot and recreation.	[initials]
	2		Battalion in Billets at BARLY. Training similarly carried on - afternoon devoted to recreational sports.	[initials]
	3		Battalion in Billets at BARLY. Training carried on according to programme. Afternoon devoted to a pool shoot and recreational training. In view of the fact that the Brigade might have to move at very short notice (being in Third Army Reserve) a "Test Move" took place this evening. The warning order was received from Brigade at 10.15 p.m., and at 10.50 p.m., the Battalion was reported present and complete at the rendezvous position ready to move off.	[initials]
	4		Battalion in Billets at BARLY. Training carried on according to programme. Afternoon devoted to a pool shoot, Football and recreational training.	[initials]
	5		Battalion in Billets at BARLY. Church Parades. Capt. S. H. HOLLEY (Adjutant) to-day proceeded to the 96th Infantry Brigade, and Lieut. W. KAY, M.C., taking over the duties of acting Adjutant.	[initials]
	6		Battalion in Billets at BARLY. Training carried on according to programme. This afternoon the Corps Commander presented Medal Ribbons to Officers and men of the 32nd Division who had recently been awarded Military Honours at a special parade held at BAVINCOURT. The undermentioned attended from this Battalion as recipients of Ribbons:- 2nd Lieut. W. KAY, M.C. No. 1738, Private C. SYRETT.) " 276101, " E. ROEBUCK.) M.M. " 53091, " A. W. PASCOE.) One Officer and two N.C.Os. per Company, and four men per platoon, attended the parade as representing the Battalion. Recreational training carried on during the afternoon.	[initials]

Army Form C. 2118.

WAR DIARY
or
INTELLIGENCE SUMMARY.
(Erase heading not required.)

Instructions regarding War Diaries and Intelligence Summaries are contained in F. S. Regs., Part II. and the Staff Manual respectively. Title pages will be prepared in manuscript.

Place	Date	Hour	Summary of Events and Information	Remarks and references to Appendices
	1918			
	May 7		Battalion in Billets at BARLY. Training carried on as far as possible according to Programme but owing to rain training was to some extent interfered with. Recreational training carried on during the afternoon.	
	8		Battalion in Billets at BARLY. Training carried on according to Programme. The afternoon was devoted to Battalion Sports - pool shooting carried on as usual.	
	9		Battalion in Billets at BARLY. Training carried on according to Programme, which was watched during the greater part of the morning by the Battalion Commander. The afternoon was spent in recreational training, including a Battalion Boxing Competition at various weights.	
	10		Battalion in Billets at BARLY. Training carried on according to programme. Afternoon devoted to a pool shoot and recreational training.	
	11		Battalion in Billets at BARLY. Training carried on under Company arrangements. The rest of the day was devoted in generally preparing for the next tour of duty in the line.	
	12		Battalion in Billets at BARLY. Battalion left BARLY by bus at 7.30 p.m., and debussed on the outskirts of BLAIRVILLE. The Battalion then proceeded up the line and took over the Left sub-sector from the 2nd South Staffordshire Regiment, relief being reported complete at 1.30 a.m. Dispositions:- "C" and "B" Companies in the front line, "A" Company in reserve and "D" Company in defended locality.	
	13		Battalion in the Line. Casualties 6 O.R. wounded. Usual patrols out on the Battalion front - wiring carried on. Capt. F. O. MEDWORTH, M.C. (Commanding "C" Company) killed at 8.30 p.m.	
	14		Battalion in the Line. Casualties 3 O.R. wounded. Usual Patrols out and wiring carried on.	

WAR DIARY
or
INTELLIGENCE SUMMARY.
(Erase heading not required.)

Army Form C. 2118.

Place	Date	Hour	Summary of Events and Information	Remarks and references to Appendices
	1918			
	May 15		Battalion in the Line. Casualties 4 O.R. killed and 4 O.R. wounded. The Battalion was to-night relieved by the 15th Lancashire Fusiliers, relief being reported complete at 1.50 a.m. After relief the Battalion moved into Reserve - "A" and "D" Companies in the PURPLE SYSTEM, "B" and "C" Companies and Battalion Headquarters at BLAIRVILLE. Complete in Billets etc., at 3.50 a.m.	
	16		Battalion in Reserve. S.O.S. signal went up on the Left Divisional Front at 9.20 a.m., being subsequently cancelled at 9.30 a.m. Casualties 1 O.R. wounded. S.O.S. on the Right Brigade Front received at 11.25 p.m., being subsequently cancelled at 11.40 p.m.	
	17		Battalion in Reserve. Casualties 1 O.R. killed, 1 O.R. wounded.	
	18		Battalion in Reserve. A Patrol was found for reconnoitring the Front of the Right Sub-sector. Companies engaged in making knife rests. Practice S.O.S. signal sent up by Brigade on Right to judge visibility at 9.0 p.m. - signal was clearly seen from the PURPLE LINE SYSTEM. *Lieut. Colonel G.M. Robertson took over command of Battalion from Lieut. A.C.W. Theobald, D.S.O.*	
	19		Battalion in Reserve. Battalion relieved the 16th Lancashire Fusiliers in the Right sub-sector - "B" and "C" Companies in the line, "A" and "D" Companies in reserve. Relief reported complete at 12.50 a.m. After relief patrolling and wiring carried on.	
	20		Battalion in the line. Patrolling and wiring carried on.	
	21		Battalion in the Line. E.A. fairly active. Patrolling and wiring carried on. Casualties:- 2nd Lieut. B.W. SPROWELL wounded, 6 O.R. wounded.	
	22		Battalion in the Line. E.A. very active during the day, 13 E.A. crossing our lines and same were engaged by L.G. and A.A. fire. Patrolling carried on. Casualties:- 2 O.R. killed, 4 O.R. wounded.	

Army Form C. 2118.

WAR DIARY
or
INTELLIGENCE SUMMARY.
(Erase heading not required.)

Instructions regarding War Diaries and Intelligence Summaries are contained in F. S. Regs., Part II. and the Staff Manual respectively. Title pages will be prepared in manuscript.

Place	Date	Hour	Summary of Events and Information	Remarks and references to Appendices
	1918			
	May 23		Battalion in the Line. E.A. very active. Casualties:- 2 O.R. wounded. Inter-Company relief carried out to-night, "D" Company relieving "C" Company on the Right front and "A" Company relieving "B" Company on the Left front. Patrolling carried on.	
	24		Battalion in the Line. The usual Patrols were out to-night. Casualties:- 1 O.R. wounded.	
	25		Battalion in the Line. E.A. dropped bombs on the railway and were engaged by L.G. fire. Balloon dropped leaflets over the enemy's line about 3.15 p.m. The usual patrolling on the Battalion front carried on.	
	26		Battalion in the Line. E.A. still very active and vigorously engaged by L.G. fire. The usual Patrols were out to-night. Casualties:- 3 O.R. killed, 6 O.R. wounded.	
	27		Battalion in the Line. Between 2 a.m. and 4.30 a.m., Battalion Headquarters and vicinity were subjected to a heavy gas shell bombardment. The Battalion was relieved to-night by the 15th Lancashire Fusiliers, relief being reported complete at 12.45 a.m. After relief the Battalion moved into Reserve in the PURPLE SYSTEM - Battalion Headquarters at BLAIRVILLE. Casualties:- 6 O.R. wounded.	
	28		Battalion in Reserve. Bathing etc., carried on. Casualties:- 5 O.R. wounded. A practise manning of the Battle Stations in the Purple Line carried out at 8.45 p.m.	
	29		Battalion in Reserve. Casualties:- Nil.	
	30		ditto ditto	
	31		Battalion in Reserve. Casualties:- Nil. The Battalion to-night relieved the 16th Lancashire Fusiliers in the Left Sub-sector - "A" Company on the Right, "D" Company on the Left, "C" Company in Reserve and "B" Company in the Defended Locality. Relief reported complete at 12.30 a.m.	

Lieut. Colonel.
Commanding 2nd Battalion, The Manchester Regiment.

WAR DIARY
or
INTELLIGENCE SUMMARY.
(Erase heading not required.)

2 Manchesters Army Form 2118.

Vol 47

Place	Date	Hour	Summary of Events and Information	Remarks and references to Appendices
	1918 June 1		Battalion in the Line. Wiring carried on by the Front Line Companies and carrying parties by the other two Companies. The usual Patrols were out to-night and Listening Posts also established. Casualties - 1 OR killed, 7 OR wounded. Lieut J.N. MARSHALL. M.C. (Irish Guards) joined the Battalion to-day and took over the duties of Second-in-Command	Ans. 1
	2		Battalion in the Line. Wiring again carried on and working and carrying parties found. The usual Patrols were out and Listening Posts established. Casualties - 1 OR killed 4 OR wounded.	Ans. 1
	3		Battalion in the Line. Wiring carried on and working and carrying parties found. The usual Patrols were out and Listening Posts established. Casualties - 2nd Lieut B. BURKETT-GOTTWALTZ wounded. 5 OR killed and 7 OR wounded.	Ans. 1
	4		Battalion in the Line. The Inter-Company relief was carried out to-night. "B" Company relieving "A" Company and "C" Company relieving "D" Company, relief being reported complete at 11.35 p.m. The usual Patrols were out and Listening Posts established. Working and carrying parties also found. Casualties - Lieut J.E. GULLET wounded (accidentally). 1 OR killed and 11 OR wounded.	Ans. 1
	5		Battalion in the Line. At 2 p.m. this afternoon the enemy raided our front line	

WAR DIARY
or
INTELLIGENCE SUMMARY.
(Erase heading not required.)

Army Form C. 2118.

Place	Date	Hour	Summary of Events and Information	Remarks and references to Appendices
	1918 June 5		and succeeded in entering one of our Posts. It was subsequently reported that two of our men went missing together with one Lewis Gun. The remainder of the Garrison were either killed or wounded. The usual Patrols were out and Listening Posts established to-night. Carrying and working parties were also found. Casualties:- 1 OR killed. 6 OR. wounded and 4 OR wounded (gas).	Appx.?
	6		Battalion in the Line. The usual Patrols were out and Listening Posts established. A Patrol under 2nd Lieut MITCHELL went out to reconnoitre the enemy cap and trench from which front the enemy entered our Post the previous afternoon. This Patrol encountered strong enemy opposition and the whole of them became casualties - 2nd Lieut MITCHELL being afterwards reported as "missing". Casualties:- 2 OR killed 10 OR wounded and 5 OR wounded (gas).	Appx.?
	7		Battalion in the Line. The usual Patrols were out and Listening Posts established. A strong Patrol under 2nd Lieut BRAMLEY left our lines to-night to search for 2nd Lieut. MITCHELL who failed to return from patrol on the previous evening. The Patrol in question met with strong enemy opposition and bomb attacks in consequence of which the whole party became casualties, 2nd Lieut BRAMLEY being killed. Casualties:- 2 OR killed. 6 OR wounded and 4 OR wounded (gas).	Appx.?

WAR DIARY
or
INTELLIGENCE SUMMARY.

(Erase heading not required.)

Army Form C. 2118.

Place	Date	Hour	Summary of Events and Information	Remarks and references to Appendices
	1918 June 8		Battalion in the line. The usual patrols were sent out to-night. Battalion relieved by the 15th Battn. Lancs. Fus., relief being reported complete at 1.45 a.m. After relief the Battalion moved and occupied the positions vacated by the 15th Battn. Lancs Fus. on the Reserve Line. The Battalion was reported complete on the Reserve dispositions at 4.20 a.m. Battn. Headquarters at BLAIREVILLE. Casualties: 1 O.R. killed, 8 O.R. wounded.	Rwd.T.
	9		Battalion in Reserve. A party of 2 N.C.Os. and 15 O.R. found fatigue (interior ws Reserve) for cutting grass. Working parties found for working under C.R.E. "A" and "B" Companies bathed. Casualties - Nil.	Rwd.T.
	10		Battalion in Reserve. "C" and "D" Companies bathed. Working parties again found for work under the C.R.E. Casualties - Nil. 2nd Lieut. A.H. BRADLEY was to-day buried in the British Military Cemetery at BLAIREVILLE.	Rwd.T.
	11		Battalion in Reserve. Working parties found for work under C.R.E. Casualties - Nil.	Rwd.T.
	12		Battalion in Reserve. Casualties - Nil. The Battalion to-night relieved the 16th Lancs. Fusrs. in the Right Sub-sector. "A" Company on the Right Front Line. "D" Company Left Front Line. "C" Company Right Reserve and "B" Company Left Reserve. Relief was reported complete about 1.30 a.m. On relief Listening Posts were established by the Front Line	Rwd.T.

WAR DIARY
or
INTELLIGENCE SUMMARY.

(Erase heading not required.)

Army Form C. 2118.

Place	Date	Hour	Summary of Events and Information	Remarks and references to Appendices
	1918 Jan. 3		Companies	
	13		Battalion in the Line. Situation normal. Casualties:- Nil. Patrolling, wiring and work carried on.	[signature]
	14		Battalion in the Line. Situation normal. Casualties:- Lieut. W.J. Williams - Gun. N.C. wounded, 2 O.R. wounded. "D" Company sent out a Patrol of 1 Officer and 8 O.R. to endeavour to locate enemy posts in the vicinity of the Sugar Factory and Railway. "A" Company sent out a Patrol of 1 O.R. and 10 O.R. to endeavour to locate any enemy posts and investigate the shelters in front of our line. Strong Listening Posts were established so as to cover parties for the Patrols and the wiring parties which were also out.	[signature]
	15		Battalion in the Line. Situation normal. Casualties:- 2nd Lieut. E.J. LOWTHER (attached 96th T.M.B.) killed, 2nd Lieut. H.R. HILL wounded, 4 O.R. killed and 7 O.R. wounded. Patrols were again sent out from "D" and "D" Companies for the purpose of locating suspected enemy posts and T.M. emplacements and to investigate whether the enemy had any work in progress. Strong Listening Posts were established and were used. Wiring and digging carried on.	[signature]
	16		Battalion in the Line. Situation normal. Casualties:- Nil. 2nd Lieut. J. —	

WAR DIARY
or
INTELLIGENCE SUMMARY.
(Erase heading not required.)

Army Form C. 2118.

Place	Date	Hour	Summary of Events and Information	Remarks and references to Appendices
	1918 June		BRONFOSSEN (Inverness) now reported "Grand Sinks" Company relief carried out to-night. "C" Company relieving "D" Company in the Left Front Line and "B" Company relieving "A" Company in the Right Front Line. Relief reported complete at 10.15 p.m. Patrols from "D" and "B" Companies were again out for the purpose of obtaining information and if possible identifications. Listening Posts were established by "C" and "B" Companies.	
	17		Battalion in the Line. The usual Patrols were out to-night for the purpose of reconnoitring the Sugar Factory Posts etc proposed to be raided and also to observe for any movement and conditions of wire. Listening Posts were also established. Wiring and work carried on. Casualties: 1 OR killed, 1 OR wounded.	AmR
	18		Battalion in the Line. Situation normal. Two Patrols were out to-night to observe for enemy movement etc. Listening Post also established. Four hundred yards of double apron fencing was put along communication trench and wiring of gaps covered by chill and Lewis fire continued. Casualties: Nil.	AmR
	19		Battalion in the Line. Situation normal. A Raid was carried out by 4 officers and 76 OR under the command of Capt H SOMERVILLE M.C. Zero hour being at 1 a.m.	AmR

Army Form C. 2118.

WAR DIARY
or
INTELLIGENCE SUMMARY.
(Erase heading not required.)

Place	Date	Hour	Summary of Events and Information	Remarks and references to Appendices
	19/8 Ohm		(See attached Operation Order No. 1.) One wounded prisoner belonging to the 91st I.R. was taken but he died before he could be brought in. All identifications were taken from him. Casualties 2 OR wounded.	Gub.C.
	20		Battalion in the Line. Situation normal. Casualties. Lieut. R.W. CARROLL wounded, 19 OR wounded, 1 OR missing. The Battalion was to-night relieved by the 15th Lancs Fusrs, relief being reported complete at 2.35 a.m. After relief the Battalion moved into Reserve.	Gub.C.
	21		Battalion in Reserve. Bathing and general clean-up carried on. Casualties 4 OR wounded. At 10.30 to-night a post of N.Z. Signals were sent up by the Right Brigade which was seen from the Reserve positions. Working parties for grass cutting and work on new B.H.Q. found.	Gub.C.
	22		Battalion in Reserve. Nil. Working parties found for work on the new B.H.Q. Bathing also carried on. 2nd Lieuts BURROWS, GARTH and KING joined the Battalion to-day.	Gub.C.
	23		Battalion in Reserve. Casualties – 1 OR wounded. Bathing continued. Working parties found for grass cutting and work on new B.H.Q.	Gub.C.

Army Form C. 2118.

WAR DIARY
or
INTELLIGENCE SUMMARY.
(Erase heading not required.)

Place	Date	Hour	Summary of Events and Information	Remarks and references to Appendices
	1918 June 23		Battalion in Reserve. Casualties 1 OR wounded. To-night the Battalion relieved the 16th Lanc Fus in the left Sub-sector. Dispositions:- "D" Right Front, "A" Left Front, "B" Reserve and "C" in the Defended Locality. Relief reported complete at 12.18 a.m. Work and wiring carried out. The usual Patrols were out and Listening Posts established. Battalion in the Line. Situation normal. Casualties:- 2 OR wounded. To-night the	ChR
	25		Battalion took over the whole of the Brigade front relieving the 15th Lancs Fus. Relief was reported complete at 11.16 p.m. Dispositions:- "D" Company old Right Battalion front, "A" Company the old Left Battalion front. "B" Company was in support and "C" Company in the Defended Locality. The usual wiring and work was carried out. Patrols and Listening Posts were also out. The eliminating fighting of the Brigade Horse Transport in connection with the Divisional Corps Competitions was held this afternoon, with the result that the 2nd Battalion The Manchester Regiment was placed 1st. A telegram was subsequently received from the G.O.C. congratulating the Battalion on their contest achievement.	
	26		Battalion in the Line. Situation normal. Casualties:- 1 OR wounded. Battalion Headquarters to-night moved to their new Headquarters the taking over being reported complete at 11.5 p.m. Wiring and work carried out and the usual Patrols and	ChR

A6945 Wt. W14422/M1160 350,000 12/16 D. D. & L. Forms/C./2118/14.

Army Form C. 2118.

WAR DIARY
or
INTELLIGENCE SUMMARY.
(Erase heading not required.)

Instructions regarding War Diaries and Intelligence Summaries are contained in F. S. Regs., Part II. and the Staff Manual respectively. Title pages will be prepared in manuscript.

Place	Date	Hour	Summary of Events and Information	Remarks and references to Appendices
	1918 June			
	27		Listening Posts established. 2nd Lieut. B.R. COBLEY joined the Battalion to-day. Battalion in the Line. Situation normal. Casualties:- 2 OR wounded (1 remaining at duty). The usual "Patrols were out and Listening Posts established. Wiring and work also carried on.	Appx 1.
	28		Battalion in the Line. Situation normal. To-night an Inter-Company Relief took place. "B" Company relieving "A" Company and "C" Company relieving "B" Company. The usual Patrols were out and Listening Posts established. Wiring and work also carried on. Casualties:- 3 wounded (1 remaining at duty).	Appx 1.
	29		Battalion in the Line. Situation normal. The usual Patrols were out and Listening Posts established. Wiring and work carried on. Casualties:- Nil.	Appx 1.
	30		Battalion in the Line. Situation normal. The usual Patrols were out and Listening Posts established. Wiring and work carried on. Casualties:- Nil. 2nd Lieuts. R. Gregg and E.H. Murdock joined the Battalion today.	Appx 1.

Avel Nulas
Lieut. Colonel.
Commanding 2nd Battalion, The Manchester Regiment.

RAID OPERATION ORDER No. 1.
BY
Lieut., Colonel G.M. Robertson, D.S.O.
Commanding 2nd., Battalion The Manchester Regiment.
———oOo———

Ref maps: 51 B. 1.W.
51 C. 2.E.
Special Map issued.

Note: To be read in conjunction with Brigade Raid Orders & Batt'n preliminary instructions in possession of officers concerned.

1. 2nd., Battalion The Manchester Regiment in conjunction with the Battalion on the Left (16th Lan., Fus.,) will carry out a raid on enemy positions in the area enclosed by the line drawn through the following points:

   S.18.d.60.25. — S.18.b.80.75.
   T.18.b.36.75. — S.18.d.40.45.

   Operation will take place on the night June 19/20th, 1918.

2. **INFORMATION:**
   APPROACHES: Railway Bank running from Posts Nos., 9 & 10 in our lines making a slight bend northwards into the enemy's lines, where it strikes the rising ground at BOYELLES Railway Station. At S.18.d.42.40 is an elevated level crossing.

   The Bank affords cover to the raiders on the north side.

   SUSPECTED ENEMY POSTS:

   (a) Post about S.18.d.2.8.
   (b) BOY 10 on Railway about S.18.d.7.4.
   (c) Area S.24.b.35.05, following suspected:) Known to be about
   (1) BOY 16.) 200 yards south of
   (2) Machine Gun.) the Railway.
   (3) Post.)

3. **OBJECTIVES:**
   (a) To thoroughly search the ground as indicated on the attached map, and exterminate or capture all enemy met with.
   (b) Capture such M.Gs., T.Ms., etc., as may be encountered in that area, and obliterate their emplacements.
   (c) Gain identification and bring back documents, maps, samples of food and clothing, gas masks and any accoutrements.

4. **TROOPS ALLOTTED FOR THE RAID:** 4 Officers and 75 other Ranks under the Command of Captain R. Somerville, M.C., distributed as follows:

   No. 1 Party: 2/Lt., P.E.A. Kent.
   Corp'l J. Wilkinson.
   O.Rs., 11.

   No. 2 Party:
   (a) Sergt., J. Clay.) Covering
   6 O.Rs.) Party.
   (b) 2/Lt. E.J.Griffith.
   Corpl. Kirby,W.
   Corpl. Eyrett, C.
   O.Rs., 15.

   No. 3 Party: 2/Lt. Lawrence, H.
   Sergt. Savage, J.
   Sergt. Vance, J.
   O.Rs., 25.

   Main Covering
   Party: 2/Lt. C.D.Brace &

At zero minus 20 these parties will be in position in above order with the head of No. 1 party at point S.18.c.9.7. Parties in file south side of the Railway Bank.

The Covering Party to be in position astride the R'ly Bank and south of it about point S.18.d.15.55. This party will clear the field of all enemy to that point and deny the approach of any patrols. To be in position Zero minus 40.

O.C. Raiding party will have his headquarters at No. 8 Post, after he has supervised the forming up of the Raiding party. He will be in communication with Battalion Headquarters situate in dugout at S.18.a.20.52. The latter will be established Zero minus 60.

5. **BARRAGE**:

SEE TABLE ATTACHED.

6. **DUTIES**: As per Copy of Brigade Raid Scheme already issued and attached.

7. **LINES OF ADVANCE; & WITHDRAWAL**:

As per Map issued to O.C. Parties.

8. **IDENTIFICATIONS**: Two men in every 10 of the Parties will be detailed to collect identifications, documents etc., and to cut off shoulder straps from all dead. Men detailed for this shall each carry a sandbag.

9. **WITHDRAWAL**: No. 1 Party will withdraw on the north side of the Railway, and enter our trench at No. 10 Post. Nos. 2 & 3 Parties will withdraw on the south side of the Railway, and enter our trench between Nos. 7 & 10 Posts.

All Raiders will evacuate the line via No. 2 Front Line Post - RUTLAND LANE to the Double Company Headquarters.

None of the Raiders or men of the Battalion are to use NORTHUMBERLAND AVENUE after Zero. This to be left entirely for the use of Runners and evacuation of casualties.

10. **IDENTIFICATION**: Each Officer, N.C.O., and Man will hand in his ordinary identity discs to which will be attached a Green Raid Disc. The corresponding Red Raid Disc is the only mark of identification to be carried on the person.

A checking party under 2/Lt., Holmes will be established in No. 7 Post, and each man as he passes will hand his disc to this officer who will have a full roll and check all who have passed. A final check will take place at double Coy., Headquarters under Capt., A. McKenzie and C.S.Ms., A. & D Coys.

11. **COMMUNICATIONS**: All arrangements to be made between the Brigade and the Battalion Signalling Officers.

12. **MEDICAL**: Each man will carry his waterproof sheet rolled on his belt. Sheets will be used to carry wounded to No. 7 Post where first dressing will take place. Stretcher Bearers with stretchers will be posted here, who will convey men via NORTHUMBERLAND AVENUE AND GOAT TRENCH to the AID POST. The Battalion Medical Officer will help the M.O., at the Aid Post.

All wounded must be brought back.

13. **DRESS**: Steel Helmets, Rifles and Fixed Bayonets, magazines charged and 20 rounds in each bottom pocket.
Each man will carry 2 No. 5 Bombs.
No. 2 party will have 3 STOKES Bombs.
No. 3 party will have 6 -do-
50% of the Raiders will carry wire cutters. No papers, Maps etc., or any marks of identification must be carried or worn by any one.
PASSWORD: Will be "M.R."
Left Battalion Password will be: GOW---

3.

Para. 13 Cont'd:

>No. 2 party will have 3 Stokes Bombs.
>No. 3 party will have 6   -do-

30% of the Raiders will carry wire cutters.

No Papers, Maps etc., or any marks of identification must be carried or worn by any one.

14. PASSWORD: The Password will be "M.R."
Left Battalion Password will be "COWJUICE."

15. REPORTS: On completion of their task all parties must send the message to that effect to Capt., H. Somerville at No. 7 Post, and must, without fail, bring back all casualties.

16. FOOD: Arrangements have been made for a hot meal both before and after the raid.

17. RETURN OF PARTIES: All parties must be in our lines by ZERO plus 30. 45

18. ALL IN: O.C. Raid will send up the "ALL IN" signal immediately all parties are reported back.

19. SYNCHRONIZATION: Watches will be synchronised at 8 P.M., on the 19th Inst., at Double Company Headquarters by the Signalling Officer.

20. ZERO: Zero Hour will be notified later.

21. A C K N O W L E D G E.

[signature]

Lieut., Colonel,

Commanding 2nd., Battalion The Manchester Regiment.

18.6.18.

Issued at _____

Issued to:
1. 96th Infty Bde.
2. Commanding Officer.
3. Left Battalion.
4. Right Battalion.
5. O.C. Raid.
6. Raid Officers.
7.   -do-
8.   -do-
9.   -do-
10. Signalling Officer.
11. Intelligence Officer.
12. Medical Officer.
13. 2/Lt. Holmes, S.
14. Final Check.
15. War Diary.
16. File.

2nd., Battalion The Manchester Regiment.

Reference Raid Operation Order No. 1 para., 6:

DUTIES AS UNDER:

No. 1 Party will leave our line at S.18.a.55.20 and advance S. of the Railway Line as far as the level crossing at S.18.d.50.35 where it will turn North West and mop up the post located about S.18.d.5.6, and then return along the Railway to our line.

No. 2 Party follows No. 1 and searches for BOY 10 believed to be on the Railway about S.18.d.7.4., leaving a post on the level crossing to prevent it being cut off.

No. 3 Party follows No. 2 to the level crossing at S.18.d.5.4 where it turns S. and searches the area about S.24.b.35.85 for BOY 16, a M.G. and a post which are known to be about 200 yards S. of the Railway. This party will return by the same route.

Gilbert Robertson Lieut., Colonel,

18.6.18.

Commanding 2nd., Battalion The Manchester Regiment.

Army Form C. 2118.

2 Manchester Rgt

Vol 48

WAR DIARY
or
INTELLIGENCE-SUMMARY.
(Erase heading not required.)

Instructions regarding War Diaries and Intelligence Summaries are contained in F. S. Regs., Part II. and the Staff Manual respectively. Title pages will be prepared in manuscript.

Place	Date	Hour	Summary of Events and Information	Remarks and references to Appendices
	July 1918			
BOYELLES.	1st.		Battalion in Front Line. Dispositions:- "C" Coy., Right Front, "B" Coy., Left Front, "A" Coy in Reserve, "D" Coy, "STATION DEFENDED LOCALITY". Defensive Patrols and Listening Posts established. Casualties:- 2/Lieut., H. Garth, Wounded and 2 O.Rs., wounded. Battalion was relieved by 15th (S) Battalion Lancashire Fusiliers, relief being reported complete at 1.40 a.m., 2nd., inst. On completion of relief the Battalion became No. 3 Batt'n in Div'l Reserve, occupying positions evacuated by the 16th (S) Batt'n Lancashire Fusiliers S. of	Clerk R
BLAIREVILLE.	2nd.		BLAIREVILLE. Battalion reported complete in new position at 4 a.m. 2nd., inst. Batt'n in Div'l Reserve. Bathing carried out in morning and afternoon. General clean up. The Battalion Transport won the Div'l Transport Competition. Casualties Nil.	Clerk R
BLAIREVILLE.	3rd.		Batt'n in Div'l Reserve. Bathing resumed morning and afternoon. Refitting of clothing etc. carried out. "A" Coy., found working party of 40 Ors., for night work. "B" and "C" Coys., each found 80 O.Rs., for night work. Casualties Nil.	Clerk R
BLAIREVILLE.	4th.		Batt'n in Div'l Reserve. Bathing Continued. "B" Coy., found 1 N.C.O., and 12 O.Rs., for Grass Cutting. Casualties Nil.	Clerk R
BLAIREVILLE.	5th.		Battalion in Div'l Reserve. Bathing continued. "C" Coy., found 1 N.C.O. and 12 O.Rs., for Grass Cutting. Casualties Nil.	Clerk R

Army Form C. 2118.

WAR DIARY
or
INTELLIGENCE SUMMARY
(Erase heading not required.)

Instructions regarding War Diaries and Intelligence Summaries are contained in F. S. Regs., Part II. and the Staff Manual respectively. Title pages will be prepared in manuscript.

Place	Date	Hour	Summary of Events and Information	Remarks and references to Appendices
BLAIREVILLE.	6th.		Batt'n in Div'l Reserve. Batt'n relieved by 1st., Batt'n Grenadier Guards in the afternoon. On completion of relief Batt'n moved by Train from BLAIREVILLE to LA BAZEQUE, and took over billets evacuated by 3rd Batt'n Grenadier Guards. Batt'n accommodated in Tents, Shelters and Billets. Batt'n reported "All In" about 9.30 p.m. Captain G.R. Thomas rejoined the Batt'n. Casualties Nil.	C.u.R
LA BAZEQUE.	7th.		Companies held usual inspections of Kit, equipment etc. "A" Coy., found 1 N.C.O., and 20 O.Rs for work at Transport Lines. Casualties Nil.	C.u.R
-do-	8th		Companies completed inspections of Kit etc. Casualties Nil.	C.u.R
"	9th		Companies carried out training in accordance with Training Programme. A. Coy., on Range. Recreational Training carried out in the afternoon in accordance with programme. 2/Lieut., H. Emsley awarded the MILITARY CROSS. 2/Lieut., W.E.J.Hall, M.C., joined the Battalion. Casualties Nil.	C.u.R
"	10th		Companies carried out training in accordance with training programme. Afternoon Recreational training in accordance with programme. 40% of the Batt'n visited the Corps Transport Competition. Battalion Transport got 2nd., place in Corps Transport Competition - 1st., place lost by 1½ points. Batt'n Drums got 3rd place. Casualties Nil.	C.u.R

Army Form C. 2118.

WAR DIARY
or
INTELLIGENCE SUMMARY.
(Erase heading not required.)

Place	Date	Hour	Summary of Events and Information	Remarks and references to Appendices
LA BAZEQUE.	11th.		Battalion training carried out in accordance with Training programme. Pool Shoot carried out in accordance with programme. Lieut., R.W. Carroll and 2/Lieut., S. Holmes rejoined the Battalion from Hospital. Casualties Nil.	
	12th.		Training carried out in accordance with programme. Headquarters B. and C. Coys., bathed in the morning, followed by D and A. Coys., in the afternoon. "TEST TURN OUT" was carried out. The Battalion was present and ready to move off 36 minutes after receipt of order. The Batt'n was first in the Brigade. Casualties Nil.	
	13th.		Training carried out in accordance with Programme. Sports carried out in the afternoon according to programme. Casualties Nil.	
	14th.		Church Parades. The Corps Commander presented ribbons to O.Rs., of the Battalion at divisional Headquarters, BAVINCOURT. Casualties Nil.	
	15th.		Training carried out in accordance with programme. Recreational Training carried out in the afternoon in accordance with programme. Casualties Nil.	

Army Form C. 2118.

WAR DIARY
or
INTELLIGENCE-SUMMARY.
(Erase heading not required.)

Instructions regarding War Diaries and Intelligence Summaries are contained in F. S. Regs., Part II. and the Staff Manual respectively. Title pages will be prepared in manuscript.

Place	Date	Hour	Summary of Events and Information	Remarks and references to Appendices
LA BAZEQUE.	16th.		Training as per programme. A. Coy., and Headquarters Bathed at LA HERLIERE in the afternoon. 3rd Army Superintendent lectured on P.T. and B.T., on Training ground; 5 Officers and 33 N.C.Os., present. Practice attack with TANKS. Two platoons of "C" Coy., gave demonstration. Casualties Nil.	C.R.
	17th.		Training as per programme. Recreational Training carried out in the afternoon. Bathing resumed at LA HERLIERE. TANK Demonstration at 2.30 p.m. The following personnel was in attendance:- All Officers - All N.C.Os., All men of A. and C. Coys. Two platoons of "C" Company gave demonstration. Casualties Nil.	C.R.
	18th.		Battalion moved by bus to DOULLENS - from there by train to PROVEN. Headquarters, A.B. & C. Coys., moved off from LA BAZEQUE at 10 p.m. - arrived at DOULLENS about 12.15 a.m. "D" Coy., proceeded ahead in the afternoon as loading party for the Brigade.	C.R.
	19th.		Left DOULLENS at 3.20 a.m. arrived in PROVEN Area about 3.20 p.m. Battalion reported complete in billets about 8.30 p.m. Casualties Nil.	C.R.
PROVEN.	20th.		Battalion parade. Usual training carried out. All Officers & N.C.O. instructional parade. General clean up of billets, equipment etc. Casualties Nil.	C.R.

A6945 Wt. W14422/M1160 350,000 12/16 D. D. & L. Forms/C./2118/14.

WAR DIARY
or
INTELLIGENCE-SUMMARY.

(Erase heading not required.)

Army Form C. 2118.

Place	Date	Hour	Summary of Events and Information	Remarks and references to Appendices
PROVEN.	21st.		Battalion Church Parade. Officers proceeded to reconnoitre the Line. Casualties Nil.	[signature]
	22nd.		Battalion Training in accordance with programme. Recreational Training carried out in the afternoon. Officers proceeded to reconnoitre the Line. Casualties Nil.	[signature]
	23rd.		Battalion Training carried out in accordance with Training Programme. Recreational Training carried out in the afternoon. Officers proceeded to reconnoitre the Line. Casualties Nil. 2/Lieut., G. A. Moss, joined the Battalion.	[signature]
	24th.		Battalion Training carried out in accordance with Programme. Recreational Training carried out. Officers Versus W.Os., and N.C.O., Football. Result. Officers lost ½ Nil. Officers reconnoitred the Line. Casualties Nil.	[signature]
	25th.		Battalion Sports held on the Aerodrome GROUND, PROVEN. N.C.Os., reconnoitred the Line. Casualties Nil.	[signature]
	26th.		Army Commander's Inspection of 96th Infantry Brigade. Usual training carried out in accordance with programme. Recreational Training carried out in the afternoon. Bathing carried out at MENDINGHAM. Casualties Nil.	[signature]

Army Form C. 2118.

WAR DIARY
or
INTELLIGENCE SUMMARY.
(Erase heading not required.)

Instructions regarding War Diaries and Intelligence Summaries are contained in F. S. Regs., Part II. and the Staff Manual respectively. Title pages will be prepared in manuscript.

Place	Date	Hour	Summary of Events and Information	Remarks and references to Appendices
PROVEN.	27th.		Battalion Training in accordance with Programme. Recreational Training carried out. N.C.Os., reconnoitred the Line. 2/Lieut., William Coppack joined the Battalion. Casualties Nil.	C.u.B.
	28th.		Battalion Church Parades. Kit inspections carried out. Pay out. N.C.O., reconnoitred the Line. Casualties Nil.	C.u.B.
	29th.		Battalion Parade. Training in accordance with Training Programme. Recreational Training carried out - Inter-Company Football Matches. Officer and N.C.O., reconnoitred the Line. Casualties Nil.	C.u.B.
	30th.		Battalion Parade. Training in accordance with Programme. Recreational Training carried out. Officer and N.C.Os., reconnoitred the Line. Casualties Nil.	C.u.B.
PROVEN.	31st.,		Brigade carried out Practice of Manning Battle Positions West of POPERINGHE. Recreational training carried out. N.C.Os., reconnoitred the Line. Casualties Nil.	C.u.B.

Robert Martin, Lieut., Colonel,
Commanding 2nd., Battalion The Manchester Regiment.

Army Form C. 2118.

2 Manchester

Vol 49

WAR DIARY
or
INTELLIGENCE SUMMARY.

(Erase heading not required.)

Instructions regarding War Diaries and Intelligence Summaries are contained in F.S. Regs., Part II. and the Staff Manual respectively. Title pages will be prepared in manuscript.

Place	Date	Hour	Summary of Events and Information	Remarks and references to Appendices
Rouen	August 1st		Battalion found Working Parties for work with the Canadian Railway Troops on the Railway. Recreational training carried out in the afternoon. Officer and 1 N.C.O. reconnoitres the Line. Casualties Nil.	
do.	2nd		Battalion continued work on Railway. N.C.O. proceeded to reconnoitre the Line. Recreational training carried out. Casualties Nil.	
do.	3rd		Battalion continued work on Railway. N.C.O. proceeded to reconnoitre the Line. Recreational training carried out. Casualties Nil.	
do.	4th		Battalion Church Parade. At commemoration Service were held at TERDEGHAM. The following personnel were present from this Unit :— 1 Sergt. and 8 men from "C" Coy.— 8 men from "B" Coy. 2nd Lieut. H. Emeley M.C. was in charge of the 96th Infantry Brigade personnel. Officer and 2 N.C.O. proceeded to reconnoitre the Line. Attachments to Battalion of the 6th Division. Pay out. Casualties Nil. Battalion bathed at the Divisional Baths, MENDINGHAM.	
do.	5th		Battalion carried out training in accordance with Programme. Lecture delivered by Lieut. Colonel James, M.C., R.A.F. in Y.M.C.A. Hut, SCHOOL CAMP, on the Principles governing the employment of Aircraft in co-operation with other Arms. The following personnel were in attendance :— 2 Officers per Coy.— plus Offg. "B" & "D" Coys., 6 N.C.O.s per Coy. and one from Batt. H.Qrs. Battalion bathing at Divisional Baths, MENDINGHAM. Recreational training carried out in the afternoon. Casualties Nil. The Battalion sent one Cooker to represent the 32nd Division at EPERLEQUES. Divisional Horse Show at EPERLEQUES.	
do.	6th		Battalion held usual kit inspections.— Parade 10.30 a.m.— Drill Order.	

Army Form C. 2118.

WAR DIARY
or
INTELLIGENCE SUMMARY.
(Erase heading not required.)

Place	Date	Hour	Summary of Events and Information	Remarks and references to Appendices
Proven	August 6th		His Majesty the King inspected representatives of the Brigade at SCHOOL CAMP, PROVEN. The following personnel represented the Battn:- Capt L. Taylor and 20 O.R's. Dress:- walking out dress (kilts) no sidearms. Casualties Nil. Football carried out in the afternoon.	G.W.R
do.	7th		The Battalion moved from PROVEN by train about 11am, detraining at HANGEST 5.7pm, and marched to BRIQUEMESNIL, arriving there about 9pm. Casualties Nil.	G.W.R
Briquemesnil	8th		The Battalion moved by bus to BOVES - billeted in a field just outside the town. Casualties Nil.	G.W.R
Boves	9th		The Battalion marched and were billeted in a field between MEZIERES and BEAUCOURT.	G.W.R
	10th		The Battalion moved up at 11am into action, advancing in column of fours to LE QUESNEL, where Coy'd. extended into artillery formation, and attacked (in support to the 15th & 16th Bns. (Lancashire Fusiliers), PARVILLERS and DAMERY WOODS, over 3 miles, with slight casualties. Major J.A. Marshall M.O., 9Kh. Horsley, R.C. wounded. The day ended with the Battn. holding the outpost line. This was handed over to a Company Battn. of 15th & 16th Lancs. Fus. on the night Aug. 10/11th.	G.W.R
	11th		Still at DAMERY WOOD and PARVILLERS. Relieved by the Canadians on the evening of 11th inst. The Battn. withdrew to a field near LE QUESNEL. Casualties slight.	G.W.R

WAR DIARY or INTELLIGENCE SUMMARY

Army Form C. 2118.

Place	Date	Hour	Summary of Events and Information	Remarks and references to Appendices
Le Rucourt	August 12th		The Battn. moved from Le Rucourt to Igracourt. Arrived at Igracourt about 5.30 p.m. Battn. billeted in field. Casualties nil.	Ques R
Igracourt	13th		The Battn. moved from Igracourt to Fouencamps - billeted in field. Casualties nil.	Ques R
Fouencamps	14th		The Brigade was inspected by the Divisional Commander. A draft of 300 reinforcements joined the Battn. this day. Casualties nil.	Ques R
do.	15th		A draft of 40 casuals rejoined the Battn. Casualties nil.	Ques R
do.	16th		Divisional Commander inspected Brigade reinforcements. Casualties nil.	
do.	17th		The Battn. moved from Fouencamps, by bus, to Hartonnière. Casualties nil.	Ques R
			Billeted about 11.30 p.m. Battn. reported complete on arrival.	Ques R
Hartonnière	18th		The Battn. took over the line from the 23rd. Bn. Northumberland Regt. Completion of relief reported at 12.20 a.m. the 19th inst. Dispositions:- D Coy. Right Front Coy., A Coy. Left Support Coy., B Coy. Right Support Coy., C Coy. Left Support Coy. Casualties nil.	
	19th		Battn. dispositions on Aug 18 & 19 not shown. About 10.15 a.m. the enemy heavily shelled our front and support line system with all calibres and trench mortars. The intense mortar fire we had down 3 OR. They were killed by a party of our men and being strong hostile took place in the trench. Bombing parties were then reorganised and the enemy finally driven back from our front and support line system and our original line was completely restored. The enemy left 8 dead infront of our trenches and considerable casualties are known to have been inflicted upon him by our lewis guns, rifle fire and bombs. The approximate strength of the enemy raiders was 50 & 60 OR. on this frontage. Our casualties were 16 OR. killed, 153 OR. wounded, 27 OR. missing. 3rd W.E. Yorkshire in action during this raid. One prisoner passed through our hands. The usual patrols were sent out and improvement and consolidation of positions was carried out.	Ques R
	20th		Dispositions the same, with the exception that our B Coy. extended its left flank taking over posts previously occupied by one Coy. of the K.O.Y.L.I. This relief was reported complete about 11 p.m. Usual patrols were sent out, wiring parties worked along the front line system, and general improvements of posts were continued. Casualties 1 OR (accidentally wounded).	Ques R

WAR DIARY or INTELLIGENCE SUMMARY

Army Form C. 2118.

(Erase heading not required.)

Instructions regarding War Diaries and Intelligence Summaries are contained in F. S. Regs., Part II. and the Staff Manual respectively. Title pages will be prepared in manuscript.

Place	Date	Hour	Summary of Events and Information	Remarks and references to Appendices
	August 21st		Dispositions as for the 20th inst. Object:- To ascertain in certain portion of trench were in possession of the enemy. "D" Coy. posted a Lewis Gun on covering party. "B" Coy. placed one platoon at the disposal of "C" Coy. amid the completion of the operation. This operation was unopposed. Casualties. 2/Lt. E.J. Hall M.C. wounded. 4 O.R. wounded.	GwC
	22nd		The Battn. was relieved in the line by the 16th Rn. Lancs. Fus. Relief being reported complete about 1 a.m. 23rd inst. The Battn. took up the positions evacuated by the L.F. and the support line system. Casualties. 7 O.R. wounded.	GwP
	23rd		The 32nd Div. carried out a raid at 4.45 a.m. in conjunction with troops on the right. This was quite successful and all objectives were gained. Prisoners numbering 1195 O.R. and 36 Officers, together with booty, were captured. The following Officers joined the Battn. this day :- 2/Lt. Taylor L., 2/Lt. Borden 2/Lt; Fogaszberly, 2/Lt. Stanley, 2/Lt. Spencer also rejoined the Battn. this day. Casualties. 2 O.R. killed, 2 O.R. missing, reported wounded, since reported died of wounds. 8 O.R. wounded. 3 O.R. missing.	GwP
	24th		Battn. still in support, dispositions as for the 23rd inst. Casualties 1 O.R. killed, 2 O.R. wounded.	GwC
	25th		Battn. still in support, dispositions as for the 24th inst. In accordance with Brigade instructions C & D Coys. moved up in support of the 13th L.F. and A & B Coys in support of the 16th L.F. The usual patrols and covering parties were maintained. Casualties. 3 O.R. wounded.	GwC
	26th		Battn. in the line. Strong fighting patrols were sent forward by C. & D. Coys. CHAURIOU ALLEY. The objective was finally secured. Casualties. 1 O.R. killed. 4 O.R. wounded.	GwP
	27th		In continuation of involuntions dated 26th inst, the Battn. next objectives were as follows:- D. Coy.:- BLOCK HOUSE COPSE. C. Coy. Trench junction at S.21.E.05.80. B. Coy. OERTEL COPSE. A. Coy. in Reserve. All objectives were gained and Coys. pushed forward and prepared	GwC

WAR DIARY
or
INTELLIGENCE SUMMARY.
(Erase heading not required.)

Army Form C. 2118.

Place	Date	Hour	Summary of Events and Information	Remarks and references to Appendices
	August 27th		positions as follows:- D.Coy. HART COPSE, C.Coy. WILLIAM COPSE, B.Coy. Southern outskirts of VERMANDOVILLERS, A.Coy. in trench running almost due South from VERMANDOVILLERS. This line was the Battn. final objective gained. 30 enemy killed, 5 taken prisoners, and 1. M.G. captured. The Battn. outpost line only was relieved by the 16th Lancs. Fus.	G.L.R.
	28th		Dispositions:- B.Coy. Left front, C.Coy. Centre, D.Coy. Right front, A.Coy. Reserve. Two Platoons in line, one in support, and one in Reserve. The Battn. advanced from the above positions at 4.30 a.m., the First objective being SIREN'S ALLEY. The Battn. reached on to the Final objective, which was ground east of ABLAINCOURT. From the Final objective the Battn. line advanced slightly took dispositions as follows:- C.Coy. advanced from PYTNAGORE TRENCH and MAZANCOURT WOOD, and established their line in front of railway track. D.Coy. advanced their line on MIMOTHUNE ALLEY and MATOU, and occupied positions along the trench running through the station. A.Coy. remained in Reserve in GAMELLE TRENCH. B.Coy. as support Coy. occupied MATOU ALLEY from the junction with JUIL TRENCH. Casualties for 27/28th as follows:- Capt. Crossgate Smith & 2/Lt. A. McKenzie M.C., 2/Lt. Ingoodsley, 2/Lt. Starkey, wounded. 2/Lt. L. Taylor, killed in action; Capt. A. McKenzie M.C., 2/Lt. Ingoodsley, 2/Lt. Starkey, wounded. 4. O.R. killed in action, 26 O.R. wounded, 1 O.R. missing. The following is an extract from 96th Infantry Brigade Order No. 478, dated 27th August, 1918. - "The work of the 2nd Bn. Manchester Regt. today is beyond all praise. I am proud to have such a Battn. in my Brigade, and I thank all ranks for their splendid behaviour today. May good fortune attend them tomorrow."	G.L.R.
	29th		The Battn. advanced its line, occupying TROY, then South along the trench to great line. The advance was carried out by sections from the right, and formed up on the line:- BRIDGE T.16.d.3.7 and MITRE COPSE; the support Coy. astride the railway	

Army Form C. 2118.

WAR DIARY
or
INTELLIGENCE SUMMARY
(Erase heading not required.)

Instructions regarding War Diaries and Intelligence Summaries are contained in F. S. Regs., Part II. and the Staff Manual respectively. Title pages will be prepared in manuscript.

Place	Date	Hour	Summary of Events and Information	Remarks and references to Appendices
	August 29th		at the Station, conforming with the front line. The Reserve Coy. remained in artillery formation, its centre resting on ROAD - LOVELY HOUSE by the Station. The advance was carried out and objectives were gained without interference by the enemy by 8.15 a.m. The support Coy. coming round on the MINEY ALLEY took its right resting on the road and was at once pushed out to occupy MANGO COPSE, and another reconnoitring patrol advanced towards CIZANCOURT. The latter returned with information that the village was clear of enemy infantry, though they had seen a few mounted gunners galloping down the road through the village. It was immediately gained with the Border Regt. on the left and with the French on the right. During the afternoon the Battn. was relieved by the K.O.Y.L.I. and Coys. were withdrawn to reserve trenches. Casualties 3. O.R. wounded.	C in S
	30th		The Battn. moved from MISERY, owing to enemy shell fire and took up positions in BERNY. Casualties 10. O.R. killed, 11. O.R. wounded, 1. O.R. missing.	C in R
	31st		Battn. dispositions remained as for 30th inst. The day was spent in general clean up, inspections etc. Battn. parade and casualties nil.	C in R

Cecil T Beaton
Lieut. Colonel
Commdg. 2nd. Bn. The Hanoverian Regiment.

Army Form C. 2118.

Copy 96/32 Sept
2 Manchester Regt
Vol 50

WAR DIARY
or
INTELLIGENCE SUMMARY.
(Erase heading not required.)

Instructions regarding War Diaries and Intelligence Summaries are contained in F. S. Regs., Part II. and the Staff Manual respectively. Title pages will be prepared in manuscript.

Place	Date	Hour	Summary of Events and Information	Remarks and references to Appendices
	1918 SEPTEMBER			
BERNY	1st		Battalion still at BERNY. The day was devoted to reorganisation of Companies, platoons and sections, and still making up of all deficiencies. Casualties 1 O.R. wounded.	A.2.4%.
-do-	2nd		Dispositions same as the 1st. Several R.C. Church services were carried out. 1 O.R. killed. 1 O.R. 12 wounded.	A.2.4%.
-do-	3rd		Dispositions same as the 2nd. The day was devoted to completing the reorganisation of Coys. boundaries hit.	A.2.4 M
-do-	4th		Dispositions same as the 3rd inst. Training was carried out under company arrangements as follows. "A" Coy Bombing "B" Coy Lewis Gun "C" & "D" Coys Artillery formations & advancing as the undermentioned have been awarded the MILITARY MEDAL	A.2.4 M
			No 9226 C.S.M. Winterbottom A. " 1483 Sergt Saville E " 23248 Sergt Yates Jn " 270064 Private Lacey Jn " 299836 Private Cocking J The following have been awarded	
			No 51042 Cpl Stanley W " 11920 L/Cpl Humphreys G " 241652S Sergt. Barrett J.C. " 147952 Sergt Deus Gn " 46093 Sergt Fearnie A " 52556 Sergt Burks Gn MILITARY MEDAL	A.2.4%.

D.D. & L., London, E.C.
(A1c560) Wt W5500/P713 750,000 2/18 Sch. 32 Forms/C2118/16

Army Form C. 2118.

copy

WAR DIARY
or
INTELLIGENCE SUMMARY.
(Erase heading not required.)

Instructions regarding War Diaries and Intelligence Summaries are contained in F. S. Regs. Part II. and the Staff Manual respectively. Title pages will be prepared in manuscript.

Place	Date	Hour	Summary of Events and Information	Remarks and references to Appendices
BERNY	SEPT 4th contd		No.988 Sergt. Boardman 6. M.M., 27/6/01 S/Sgt. Rostock 6. M.M. Granatlie Hill.	L.L.M.
-do-	5		Dispositions same as the 4th Gunnery carried out as normal "A" "B" bays. Artillery formation - Deploying Etc. "C" bay - Lewis Gunnery. Officers proceeded to reconnoitre Artillery fire. "D" bay - Lewis Gunnery. Granatlie Hill.	L.L.M.
-do-	6		The Brigade Group moved from BERNY this morning. Head of column passing starting point at 6.30 A.M. Route:- FRESNES - MISERY - CROSSROADS - ST CHRIST - ENNEMAIN. The Battalion crossed the RIVER SOMME at point ST CHRIST at 9 A.M. and arrived in ENNEMAIN. Bathing was carried out, Granatlie Hill. Nothing in ENNEMAIN.	L.L.M.
ENNEMAIN	7		The Brigade Group moved from ENNEMAIN to MORCHY - LACACHE area this morning. Head of column passing starting point at 9 A.M. Route:- FOURQUES - DEVISE - and MORCHY - LAGACHE ROAD SOUTH of DEVISE WOOD. The Battalion arrived in the MORCHY-LAGACHE area about 10 A.M. and was billetted in a field in bivouacs. Bathing was carried out. Granatlie Hill. The undermentioned were attacked Gallantry Suid; 39475 Rifle Lovelace D, 29513 Rifle Boucault?	L.L.M.

(A10266) W1 W5904/P713 750/000 2/15 Sch. 82 Forms/C2118/16 D. D. & L., London, E.C.

WAR DIARY or INTELLIGENCE SUMMARY

Army Form C. 2118.

Place	Date	Hour	Summary of Events and Information	Remarks and references to Appendices
MONCHY-LAGACHE	SEPT 8th		Dispositions same as on the 4th. Special R.C. Service in the morning. The day was devoted to completing the reorganisation of companies & nothing was carried out. Casualties Nil.	Officers 8. O.R. Nil
do.	9th		Dispositions same as on the 8th. Battalions did Bathing & provided to reconnaissance the line. Bathing was carried out & refitting of clothing. The undermentioned men awarded the MILITARY MEDAL 300355 L/Cpl Mackie & 51295 Pte Brown J.W. 2664 Pte Kerry A. The following officer joined Battalion this day Capt G.M. BAXTER	Officers 8. O.R. Nil
do.	10th		Battalion moved from MONCHY-LAGACHE to VILHEVEQUE to support line positions. Battalion reported present in billets at 6.30 a.m. Chevalier Nil.	Officers Nil. O.R. Nil
VILHEVEQUE	11th		10th inst Dispositions during the day were the same as on the Commanding Officers reconnoitring at 6.0 a.m. cell company commanders reconnoitre the line The Battalion moved from its position at 11.0 p.m and took over the line in the MINETY/HIS area with dispositions as follows "A" Coy Right front. "B" Coy Left front, "C" Coy in Support "D" Coy in Reserve. Casualties Nil	Officers 8. O.R. Nil

Army Form C. 2118.

WAR DIARY
or
INTELLIGENCE SUMMARY.
(Erase heading not required.)

Instructions regarding War Diaries and Intelligence Summaries are contained in F. S. Regs., Part II. and the Staff Manual respectively. Title pages will be prepared in manuscript.

69/04

Place	Date	Hour	Summary of Events and Information	Remarks and references to Appendices
MARTEVILLE	SEPT 12th		The two front companies ("A" and "B") were ordered at 12.15 a.m. to attack their first objective on the outskirts of ST QUENTIN WOOD, which objective was gained at about 1.15 a.m. Patrols were immediately pushed forward into the wood, and the two leading companies pushed on further into their second objective, which was reached and lived enemy resistance at about 2.6 a.m. The Battalion frontage was finally established and outposts were put out on the eastern and northern outskirts of the wood. "D" company in reserve moved up into the new support position. "D" company remaining in reserve. Casualties killed O.R's 4, wounded O.R's 4, missing (believed prisoners of war) O.R's 1.	O.L.M.
-do-	13th		Dispositions same as on the 12th. Battalion attacked by the Loose Regiment Relay completely by 4.0 p.m. Battalion moved in the VILLEVEQUE and 4.30 p.m. companies were reported arrived in billets about 4.30 p.m. Casualties killed 1 O.R. Wounded 4 O.R's.	O.L.M.
VILLEVEQUE	14th	11.30 a.m.	The Battalion moved from the VILLEVEQUE area at 3.0 p.m. debusing at TERTRY at 3.0 p.m. for the GOTZBIE Caves - Battalion billeted in LA NEUVILLE area and was reported present in billets at 4.30 p.m. Casualties nil.	O.L.M.

WAR DIARY
or
INTELLIGENCE SUMMARY.

Copy

Place	Date	Hour	Summary of Events and Information	Remarks and references to Appendices
LA NEUVILLE	SEPT 15th		Dispositions the same as on the night of the 14th. It was not the day was devoted to a general clean up of kits, equipment etc. The Battalion paid out. The following officers joined the Battalion this day, 2nd Lt. Coleman, A., 2nd Lt. Yonckes, J. 2nd Lt. McDonald, A., 2nd Lt. Potts, A., Major J.L. Murphy and 2nd Lt. Owen Lugg rejoined the Battalion. Volunteers gave an Officers dance at 5.0 pm. The following awards were announced:- Major L.M. Marshall, M.C., Capt A. McKinzie both awarded MILITARY CROSS, Capt J. Taylor, 2nd Lt. G. Hayward both MILITARY CROSS, No 111/5 L. Cpl McEttuo M.M. awarded the DISTINGUISHED CONDUCT MEDAL, No 9035 A/Cpl W. Styrm M.M. awarded BAR to his MILITARY MEDAL.	A.L.M.
LA NEUVILLE	16th		Dispositions same as on the 15th inst. Conferences were held at Battalion on differences in kits etc. the Divisional commander inspected the Battalion on billets from 9 am to 2.0 pm. The Battalion completed nothing officers who proceeded to reconnoitre the training area.	A.L.M.

WAR DIARY
or
INTELLIGENCE SUMMARY.
(Erase heading not required.)

Army Form C. 2118.

copy

Place	Date	Hour	Summary of Events and Information	Remarks and references to Appendices
LA NEUVILLE	SEPT 14th		Dispositions same as on the 13th. Battalion training was carried out as under. 9.0 AM to 10 AM. Battalion drill. 10 - 10.30 A.M. A + B Coys - Physical training C and D Coys - Lewis Gun. 10.30 - 11.0 A.M. A + B Coys - Lewis Gun, C + D Coys - Physical training. 11.15 - 12 noon Platoon training. Gas drill also opening on platoons or squads during the morning's training. In the afternoon sports and company arrangements. Casualties 1 Officer accidentally injured (thrown off his charger) Capt. G.H. Bartlin of "A" Coy.	O.i.c. 4/.
-do-	15th		Dispositions the same as on the 14 inst. Battalion training carried out as under: "A" Coy on Range all day "B" Coy. " " " " 9.15 10 am Physical training "C" Coy - Lewis gun, "D" Coy Musketry. 10.30-11am Physical training, "B" Coy. Musketry, "D" Coy Physical training "B" Coy - Lewis Gun 10.15 10.30 am "B" Coy Lewis gun Musketry, "C" Coy - Physical training, "D" Coy - Lewis Gun. 11 to 12 noon Platoon training "C" Coy - Lewis gun. Musketry, "C" Coy Afternoon Compulsory sports under company arrangements	O.i.c. 4/.

Army Form C. 2118.

WAR DIARY
or
INTELLIGENCE SUMMARY.
(Erase heading not required.)

Place	Date	Hour	Summary of Events and Information	Remarks and references to Appendices
LA NEUVILLE	SEPT 18th		The Divisional Gas Officer gave a lecture at B.H.Q. at 9.15 P.M. followed by short demonstration. London Gazette 94, 7, 18, 2nd Lt. B.R. Gotley to be Temp Lieutenant 22.5.18 - Knoxvilles hill.	J.L.M.
LA NEUVILLE	19th		The dispositions were the same as on the 18th but the Rest of Battalion carried out training as under "G" Coy on Range - Rest of Battalion men on special outpost scheme in the afternoon. Knoxvilles hill.	J.L.M.
do.	20th		The dispositions were the same as on the 19th but the Battalion carried out training in accordance with training programme "A" but on the Range. The Divisional Gas Officer gave a lecture at B.H.Q. The undermentioned have been awarded the MILITARY MEDAL. No 2089 Sgt Taylor E, 37131 A/Cpl Surridge H, 1389 A/Cpl Earll A, 29713 Pte Thompson H, 27790 Pte Bolan H, 32594 Pte Cole A, 4391 Pte Chappell A, 3856 Pte Lane J.W. The undermentioned man has been awarded a BAR to his MILITARY MEDAL No 1410 Pte Drayton J. M.M. Knoxvilles hill.	J.L.M.

WAR DIARY
or
INTELLIGENCE SUMMARY.
(Erase heading not required.)

Army Form C. 2118.

Place	Date	Hour	Summary of Events and Information	Remarks and references to Appendices
LA NEUVILLE	SEPT 21st		Operations to be carried out as per training programme. "B" Coy Regimental numbers. The Divisional Baths were allotted to the Battalion from 1.0 p.m. to 6.0 p.m. The Battalion completed dusting. Casualties. Bruels killed.	G.L.M.
-do-	22nd		Dispositions the same as on the 21st inst. Lunch were arranged for as follows. b/4 & 6 at 9.0 a.m. Thoroughfare at 9.30 a.m. The Battalion buried out casualties hid. No.3108 Pte King A ("D" Coy) whilst in hospital extricated himself to an operation for the suspension of blood in a very urgent case of a wounded comrade.	G.L.M.
-do-	23rd		Dispositions the same as on the 22nd inst. Training was carried out as per training programme. "D" Coy on the range. The undermentioned Officer has been awarded a BAR to his MILITARY CROSS:- Capt H Somerville M.C. Capt A. R. Deysel awarded the MILITARY CROSS and No.240431 Pte A. Johnson awarded the DISTINGUISHED CONDUCT MEDAL	G.L.M.

Army Form C. 2118.

WAR DIARY
or
INTELLIGENCE-SUMMARY.

(Erase heading not required.)

Place	Date	Hour	Summary of Events and Information	Remarks and references to Appendices
LA NEUVILLE	Sept 24th		The Battalion moved from the CORBIE Area at 4.15 pm embussing at point on FOUILLY - VILLERS BRETTONEUX Road Ym. Detraining at 8.30 pm. Battalion marched via the TERTRY Area and was reported present in billets at 11.0 pm TERTRY Area Bouvellio Hill.	L.L.M.
TERTRY	25th		Dispositions were the same as on the night of the 24th inst. The Battalion carried out the training of practising infantry formation and general cleaning up. Bouvellio Hill.	L.L.M.
-do-	26th		The dispositions were the same as on the 25th inst. Rations training was carried out during the morning & in the auspices of the Brigadier General who is getting into attacking formation from mass of ranks and also in the attacking of a strong point. The Brigadier complimented the Battalion on the excellent method it had shewn in the recent engagements Bouvellio Hill.	L.L.M.

Army Form C. 2118.

copy

WAR DIARY
or
INTELLIGENCE SUMMARY.
(Erase heading not required.)

Instructions regarding War Diaries and Intelligence Summaries are contained in F. S. Regs., Part II. and the Staff Manual respectively. Title pages will be prepared in manuscript.

Place	Date	Hour	Summary of Events and Information	Remarks and references to Appendices
TERTRY	SEPT 27th		The dispositions were the same as on the 26th instant. Battalion training was carried out during the morning. Company sports were carried out, and general cleaning up.	J.L.M.
-do-	28th		Dispositions in the morning the same as on the 27th. Commanding officers conference at 10.0 a.m. In the evening the Brigade group moved to VENDELLES where the Battalion was huddled in TROUVUAES in a field. Head of column passed the starting point at 4.38 a.m. Battalion reported arrival at TROUVUAES at 9.50 P.M. Dinnerettes unl.	J.L.M.
VENDELLES	29th		Dispositions the same as on the night of the 28th. Officers marched to reconnoitre the line. Battalion marched at 2.30 a.m. for the line located the ST QUENTIN CANAL about 8.30 and stayed night in old German line of trenches about 3 kilometres east of CANAL. Dinnerettes unl.	J.L.M.

WAR DIARY
or
INTELLIGENCE SUMMARY

Army Form C. 2118.

copy

Place	Date	Hour	Summary of Events and Information	Remarks and references to Appendices
EAST OF MAGNY-LA-FOSSE BELLINGLISE	SEPT 30		Moved about 8.45 a.m. forwards thro' and North of Battalion Headquarters established on outskirts of village. Casualties 2 O.R. Killed, 18 O.R. wounded. Lt R.W. Sound, 2nd Lt B Parker, 2nd Lt A. McDonald D.C.M. wounded, 2nd Lt W. Longwork wounded but remained at duty.	J.L.M.

J.L. Murphy, Major

Commanding 2nd Bn. The Manchester Regt.

2nd Manchester

Army Form C. 2118.

Sep 1918. 96/32

WAR DIARY
or
INTELLIGENCE SUMMARY
(Erase heading not required.)

Place	Date	Hour	Summary of Events and Information	Remarks and references to Appendices
BERNY	SEPT 1st 1918		Battalion still at BERNY. The day was devoted to reorganization of Companies, Platoons and Sections, and the making up of all deficiencies. Casualties 1.O.R.W.	Chas T.
ditto	2nd		Dispositions same as the 1st. Special R.C. Church Service. Casualties 1.O.R.K.	Chas T.
ditto	3rd		Dispositions same as the 2nd inst. The day was devoted to completing the re-organisation of Coys. Casualties nil.	Chas T.
ditto	4th		Dispositions same as 3rd inst. Training was carried out under arrangements as follows:- "A" Coy - Bombing. "B" Coy - Lewis Gun. "C" Coy - Artillery formation. Deploying etc. The following have been awarded the MILITARY MEDAL:- No 9226 C.S.M. Mackinson A.J. 22548 Sergt. Yates H., 1483 Sergt. Lavelle P., 240064 Private Lacey B., 41462 Bandsr. Standry Jas., 14490 A/Cpl Dempsey B., 29936 Private Bostaey J., 376599 Sergt Savage P., 7492 Sergt Jones G., 17, 4693 Sergt Martin H., 52556 Sergt Burns., The following have been awarded BAR to MILITARY MEDAL:- 988 Sergt Rostankrans to M.M. 24601 A/Cpl Roebuck to M.M.	C.P.
ditto	5th		Dispositions same as 4th inst. Training was carried out as follows:- A+B Coys. Artillery formation. Deploying etc. "C" Coy - Bombing. "D" Coy Lewis Guns. Officers proceeded to reconoitre the line. Casualties nil.	C.P.

WAR DIARY or INTELLIGENCE SUMMARY

Army Form C. 2118.

Place	Date	Hour	Summary of Events and Information	Remarks and references to Appendices
BERNY	Sept 6th		The Brigade Group moved from BERNY this morning starting point at 6.30 a.m. column passing starting point at 6.30 a.m. Route: FRESNES - MISERY - CROSS ROADS - ST CHRIST - ENNEMAIN. The Battalion crossed the RIVER SOMME at front ST CHRIST at 9 a.m., and arrived in ENNEMAIN about 10.30 a.m. Battalion bivouaced at ENNEMAIN. Bathing was carried out. Casualties nil.	C.u.T
ENNEMAIN	7th		The Brigade Group moved from ENNEMAIN to MONCHY-LAGACHE area this morning. Route: FOURQUES - DEVISE - and ROAD SOUTH of DEVISE WOOD. The Battalion arrived in the MONCHY LAGACHE area about 10 AM and were bivouaced in a field in Battalion. The following were awarded Gallantry awards: Bathing was carried out. 28445 Pte Enalla D, 29513 Pte Cowper G.T. bivouaced nil.	C.u.T
MONCHY LAGACHE	8th		Dispositions same as on the 4th inst. General R.C. since the morning. The day was devoted to completing the re-organisation of companies and bathing was carried out. Casualties nil.	C.u.T
ditto	9th		Dispositions same as on the 8th inst. Officers proceeded to reconnoitre the line. Bathing and refitting of clothing carried out. The following were awarded the MILITARY MEDAL: 200255 L/Cpl Monk A, 31295 Pte Brown T.W, 2664 Pte Lenyh. The following these joined the Battalion this day CAPT C.D. BAXTER Casualties nil	C.u.T

WAR DIARY
or
INTELLIGENCE SUMMARY.
(Erase heading not required.)

Army Form C. 2118.

Place	Date	Hour	Summary of Events and Information	Remarks and references to Appendices
MONCHY LAGACHE	SEPT 10th		Battalion moved from MONCHY LAGACHE to VILLEVEQUE to support line positions. Battalion reported present in bivouacs at 6.20 p.m. No casualties this.	Cin C
VILLEVEQUE	11th		The dispositions during the day were the same as for the 10th inst. Commanding Officers conference at 6.0 p.m with all Company Commanders. Officers ordered to reconnoitre the line. The Battalion moved from its position at 11.0 p.m. and took over the line in the MARTEVILLE area with dispositions as follows:— "A" Coy: Right front, "B" Coy: Left front; "C" Coy in support, "D" Coy in Reserve. Casualties nil	Cin C
MARTEVILLE	12th		The two front companies ("A" & "B") went forward at 12.15 a.m. to attack their first objective on the outskirts of ST. QUENTIN WOOD, which objective was gained at about 1.15 a.m. Patrols were immediately pushed forward into the wood, and the two leading companies pushed on further into the wood to their second objective which was reached with little enemy resistance, at about 2.15 a.m. The Battalion frontage was finally established and outposts were sent out on the south and northern outskirts of the wood. "C" Company moved up into the new support position. "D" Company remaining in reserve. Casualties Killed:– Other ranks – 7. Wounded Other Ranks – 7; Missing Other Ranks 1. (Believed Prisoner of war.)	Cin C

D. D. & L., London, E.C.
(AS001) Wt. W1771/M2031 750,000 5/17 Sch. 52 Forms/C2–18/14

WAR DIARY
or
INTELLIGENCE SUMMARY.

(Erase heading not required.)

Army Form C. 2118.

Place	Date	Hour	Summary of Events and Information	Remarks and references to Appendices
MARTEVILLE	SEPT 13TH		Dispositions same as on the 12th. Battalion relieved by the 11th Battalion of the Essex Regiment. Relief complete by 4-0 P.M. Battalion moved to bivouacs in the VILLEVEQUE area, and companies were reported present in billets about 8.30 P.M. Casualties Killed 1.O.R. Wounded 4 O.R.	App
VILLEVEQUE	14th		The Battalion moved from the VILLEVEQUE area at 11.30 A.M. Detrussing at TERTRY at 3.0 P.M. to the CORBIE area. Detrussing at 6.45 P.M. Battalion billeted in LA NEUVILLE area and was reported present in billets at 7.30 P.M. Casualties Nil.	App
LA NEUVILLE	15th		Dispositions the same as on the night of the 14th inst. The day was devoted to general clean up of billets, equipment, etc. The Battalion paid out. The following officers joined the Battalion this day. 2nd Lt COLEMAN, A., 2nd Lt FOULKES J, 2nd Lt McDONALD, A., D.C.M., 2nd Lt POTTS, R, Major MURPHY, J.L., 2nd Lt OWEN, W.E.S. Honours awarded. Voluntary open air C.of E. service at 5.0 P.M. The following awards were published: Major MARSHALL, M.C., Capt A. McKENSIE M.C. both BAR to M.C., Capt L. TAYLOR, 2nd Lt F. HAYWARD, awarded M.C., No 1175 C.S.M. MUTTERS M.M. awarded the D.C.M., No 9025 A/Cpl. W. GLYNN, M.M. awarded BAR to his M.M. Casualties Nil.	App

WAR DIARY
or
INTELLIGENCE SUMMARY.
(Erase heading not required.)

Army Form C. 2118.

Place	Date	Hour	Summary of Events and Information	Remarks and references to Appendices
LA NEUVILLE	SEPT 16th		Dispositions same as on the 15th inst. Companies carried out checking of their deficiencies in kits etc. The divisional baths were allotted the battalion as follows: from 9 a.m. to 2.0 p.m. The Battalion completed bathing. Officers proceeded to reconnoitre the training area Bouzellies Hill.	CwP
ditto	17th		Dispositions same as on the 16th inst. Battalion training carried out as under:- 9 a.m. to 10 a.m. Battalion drill 10-10.30 a.m. "A" & "B" Coy Physical Training. "C" & "D" Coys Lewis gun. 10.30-11.0 a.m. "A"-"B" Coys Lewis gun "C"-"D" Coys Physical Training. 11 to 12 noon Platoon & Company drill. Coys also spring on platoons or squads during the mornings training. "C"-"D" Coys spring on platoons or squads during the mornings training drill also spring in the afternoon sports and bathing took place under company arrangements. 1 Officer accidentally injured (9 months of his casualties. – CAPT. G.V. BAXTER of "A" Coy.	CwP
LA NEUVILLE	18th		Dispositions the same as on the 14th inst. Battalion training carried out as follows "A" Coy on Range all day 9 to 10 a.m. Battalion drill, 10-10.30 a.m. "B" Coy Physical Training; "D" Coy Musketry "D" Coy Physical training. 10.30- 11 a.m. "B" Coy Lewis Gun; "C" Coy Musketry, "D" Coy Physical Training 11- 12 Platoon & Company Drill. – 12 to 12.30 "B" Coy Musketry; "C" Coy Physical Training "D" Coy Lewis Gun. Afternoon was compulsory sports under company arrangement. The Divisional Gas Officer gave a lecture at B.H.Q. at 2.15 a.m. followed by shot demonstrations *(continued)*	CwP

Army Form C. 2118.

WAR DIARY
or
INTELLIGENCE SUMMARY.
(Erase heading not required.)

Instructions regarding War Diaries and Intelligence Summaries are contained in F. S. Regs., Part II. and the Staff Manual respectively. Title pages will be prepared in manuscript.

Place	Date	Hour	Summary of Events and Information	Remarks and references to Appendices
LA NEUVILLE	18th (contd)		Posted from London Gazette 29.4.18 2nd Lt B. R. Lobley to be Temp. Lieut. 22.5.18 Bussallies Hill.	CnG
ditto	19th		The dispositions were the same as on the 18th inst. The Battalion carried out training as under. "C" Company on Range. Rest of the Battalion were on Special outpost scheme. Park in the afternoon. Bussallies Hill.	CnG
ditto	20th		The dispositions were the same as on the 19th inst. The Battalion carried out training in accordance with training programme. "A" Coy on the range. The Divisional gas officer gave a lecture at B.H.Q. The following have been awarded the Military Medal. 3069 Sergt Hayter s, 31781 A/Cpl Baden E, 1357 A/Cpl Leslie A, 29713 Pte Thompson J, 24790 Pte Guam b, 32594 Pte Dale H, 43671 Pte Chappell A, 2856 L/C Jarvis J V, The following man has been awarded Bar to his Military Medal:- 14110 Pte Hamilton J MM Bussallies Hill.	CnG
ditto	21st		Dispositions the same as on last 20th training was carried on as per training programme. "B" Coy on Range. The Divisional baths were allotted to the Battalion from 1-5 p.m. to 6-0 p.m. The Battalion completed bathing. Bussallies Hill.	CnG
ditto	22nd		Dispositions the same as on the 19th inst. Church services were arranged as follows:- C. of E. at 9-0 a.m., R.C. at 11-0 a.m. Hom-Com form at 9:30 a.m. The Battalion fend out. Bussallies Hill.	CnG

WAR DIARY
or
INTELLIGENCE SUMMARY.
(Erase heading not required.)

Army Form C. 2118.

Place	Date	Hour	Summary of Events and Information	Remarks and references to Appendices
LA NEUVILLE	SEPT 23rd		Dispositions the same as on Sept 22nd. Training was carried out as per training programme. "D" Coy on the range. The following Officers have been awarded a Bar to the MILITARY CROSS:- Capt. H. SOMERVILLE M.C. The undermentioned Officer has been awarded the MILITARY CROSS Lieut A.R. OLDFIELD. The following men has been awarded the DISTINGUISHED CONDUCT MEDAL No 404451 Pte A. JOHNSON. Sanvillie Hill.	GenP
ditto	24th		The Battalion moved from the CORBIE area at 4.15am embussing at point on FOUILLY - VILLERS BRETTONEUX Road in the TERTRY area. Debussing at 8.30 P.M. Battalion marched in TERTRY area and was reported present in billets at 11.0 P.M. Sanvillie Hill.	GenT
TERTRY	25th		Dispositions were the same as on the night of the 24th inst. The Battalion carried out the training & practising artillery formation and general cleaning up. Sanvillie Hill.	GenT
ditto	26th		The dispositions were the same as on the 25th inst. Battalion training was carried out during the morning under the auspices of the Brigadier General in getting into artillery formation from Mass and Column of route, and also in the attacking of a strong point. The Brigadier complimented the Battalion on the excellent work it had done and the recent operations. Sanvillie Hill.	GenT

WAR DIARY
or
INTELLIGENCE SUMMARY.
(Erase heading not required.)

Army Form C. 2118.

Place	Date	Hour	Summary of Events and Information	Remarks and references to Appendices
TERTRY	Sept 27th		The dispositions were the same as on the 26th inst. Battalion training was carried out during the morning. Inter company sports were carried out, and general cleaning up.	C in R
ditto	28th		Dispositions in the morning the same as on the 27th. Commanding Officers conference at 10.0 a.m. In the evening the Brigade Group moved to VENDELLES, where the Battalion billeted in bivouacs in field ahead of the column soused the starting point at 7.30 p.m. Battalion reported all in bivouacs at 9.30 p.m. Bivouacs lit.	C in R
VENDELLES	29th		Dispositions the same as on the night of the 28th. Battalion moved to accommodate the line. Bn marched at 2.30 p.m. in the line, crossed the ST QUENTIN CANAL about 8.30 p.m. and stayed night in the bivouacs.	Q in R C in R
E of BELLINGLISE	30th		Bivouacs about 3 Km east of Canal. Battalion moved to positions east of MAGNY LA FOSSE, B.H.Q on outskirts of village. Casualties 2 O.R. killed, 18 wounded. Lt. R. W Emmett 2 Lt. G Gorlin and Lt. A. Macdonald D.C.M. wounded. 2 Lt. 10 Lappan wounded but remained at duty. Battalion stayed the night in these positions.	C in R

Cuba Heath Lieut Colonel
Comdg 2nd Bn The Manchester Regiment

Vol 51

War Diary
- of -
2nd Manchester Regt.

From Oct 1st to 31st 1916

Army Form C. 2118.

WAR DIARY
or
INTELLIGENCE SUMMARY.
(Erase heading not required.)

Instructions regarding War Diaries and Intelligence Summaries are contained in F. S. Regs., Part II. and the Staff Manual respectively. Title pages will be prepared in manuscript.

Place	Date 1918	Hour	Summary of Events and Information	Remarks and references to Appendices
MAGNY-LA-FOSSE	September October 1st		Battalion still in the Line East of MAGNY-LA-FOSSE. The Battalion was ordered to attack enemy Line, capture and hold enemy system and SWISS COTTAGE on the Left Flank. Battalion moved into position and attacked at ZERO hour 4 p.m. with dispositions as follows: "A" Coy. & "D" Coy. in front. "C" & "B" Coys. in Support. "B" Coy. in Reserve. The front Coys. to "A" Coy. in Support held about 6.30 p.m. Left Objective (SWISS COTTAGE) The Right Objective was captured and held about 7 p.m. Approximately between 150 to 200 prisoners were captured. All Objectives gained were immediately consolidated and held. Casualties: 2nd Lieut R. GREGG, died of wounds; Capt. H. Somerville, M.C., 2nd Lieut F. Johnson, 2nd Lieut T. Heyward, M.C., 2nd Lt. R. Polk, 2nd Lieut A.N. Bowden, M.C., and Lt. A.T. Morris wounded. 4 O.R. Killed, 78 wounded, 7 Missing	A.L.M.
-do-	2nd		Dispositions same as the 1st inst.	
" "	3rd		Dispositions same as 2nd. Battalion relieved by 13th Batt. N.Y. & 3rd Belgs. and on completion of relief, moved back into dugouts on the Banks of the ST. QUENTIN CANAL near LEHAUCOURT. Battn reported complete in billets at 8.30 a.m. Casualties:- 23 O.R. Killed, Wounded O.R. 90. Missing 20 O.R. 2nd Lieut B.W. Sprowell, missing.	A.L.M.
LEHAUCOURT	4th		Dispositions same as 3rd inst. Battalion moved to LENDELLES AREA, and was reported present in Bivouacs about 6.30 p.m. Casualties Nil.	A.L.M.

Army Form C. 2118.

WAR DIARY or INTELLIGENCE SUMMARY.
(Erase heading not required.)

Place	Date	Hour	Summary of Events and Information	Remarks and references to Appendices
VENDELLES	October 5th	about 12.30 P.m.	Dispositions same as 4th. Battalion moved to HANCOURT — arrived in Billets. Casualties Nil.	J.L.M.
HANCOURT	6th		Dispositions same. The day was devoted to general clean up of Kit and Equipment; Reorganization of Coys. Platoons and Sections was carried out. Refitting of clothing was also carried out. The Divisional Bath wer allotted the Battn. Officers and Drums of the Battalion attended the funeral of the late Lieut Colonel A. Stowe, P.S.O. 4th Lancashire Fusiliers (Killed in action) Church Parades were carried out. Casualties Nil. Lieut Colonel G.M. Robertson, D.S.O. awarded "bar" to his "D.S.O."	J.L.M.
do	7th		Dispositions same as 6th inst. Training was carried out under Company arrangements. The Battalion completed Bathing. Casualties Nil.	J.L.M.
do	8th		Dispositions same as 7th inst. Training carried out under Coy. arrangements. 2nd Lieut A.W. Bowden awarded the Military Cross. No. 322448 Sergt. M Fisher, M.M. awarded the Distinguished Conduct Medal. Casualties Nil. Major J.K. Murphy assumed command of the Battn. in the absence of Lieut Colonel Robertson, D.S.O. to United Kingdom on Leave.	J.L.M

WAR DIARY
or
INTELLIGENCE SUMMARY

Army Form C. 2118.

Place	Date	Hour	Summary of Events and Information	Remarks and references to Appendices
HANCOURT	October 9th		Dispositions same as the 8th inst. Training was carried out — Route march and deployment. Casualties Nil.	J.L.M.
do	10th		Battn. dispositions same as the 9th. The Battn. went on a Route march carrying out deployment. The following Officers joined the Battalion this day: 2nd Lieut. D.J. Taylor, 2nd Lieut. G.E. Overton, Q.E.M. and 2nd Lieut R.E. Winder. 2nd Lieut J.T. Baugh rejoined from hospital. The following were awarded the Military Medal. No. 23806 L/Cpl. W. Collins and No. 44496 Pte. A.E. Miller. Casualties nil.	J.L.M.
"	11th		Dispositions same as 10th. Training carried out in vicinity of Billet. No. 9131 Corpl. A.E. Heap awarded the Distinguished Conduct Medal.	J.L.M.
"	12th		Dispositions same as 11th. Route march and deployment carried out. Major J.M. Marshall M.C. rejoined the Battalion from leave. Casualties Nil.	J.L.M.
"	13th		Dispositions same as 12th. Training carried out in accordance with programme. The following officers joined the Battn. this day; 2nd Lieut G.M. Semple, 2nd Lieut J. Balla. R.S.P. 2nd Lieut P.S. Grice, 2nd Lieut J. Kirk, 2nd Lieut S. Smith. Casualties Nil.	J.L.M.

Army Form C. 2118.

WAR DIARY
INTELLIGENCE SUMMARY.
(Erase heading not required.)

Place	Date	Hour	Summary of Events and Information	Remarks and references to Appendices
HANCOURT	October 14th		Dispositions same as 13th inst. Training carried out in accordance with Training programme. "The PEDLERS" entertained the troops. Lieut R.W. Carroll rejoined the Battalion from Hospital. Casualties Nil.	S.L.M.
" "	15th		Dispositions same as 14th inst. Training carried out in accordance with Training programme. Casualties Nil.	S.L.M.
" "	16th		Dispositions same as 15th inst. Battalion Training :- ROUTE MARCH - practicing consolidation. Casualties Nil.	S.L.M.
" "	17th		Dispositions same as 16th. Training carried out in accordance with Training Programme. Casualties Nil.	S.L.M.
" "	18th		Dispositions same as 17th inst. Battalion moved by Route to LEAHCOURT. Arrived in Billets about 2pm. Casualties Nil.	S.L.M.
LEAHCOURT	19th		Dispositions same as 18th inst. Companies devoted the day to general clean up. Casualties Nil.	S.L.M.

WAR DIARY

INTELLIGENCE SUMMARY

Army Form C. 2118.

Place	Date	Hour	Summary of Events and Information	Remarks and references to Appendices
LEAMCOURT	October 20th.		Disposition same as 19th inst. Battalion moved by Route to BOHAIN at 8 am. Arrived and reported present in Billets at 1.30 pm. Casualties Nil.	S.L.M.
BOHAIN	21st		Disposition same as 20th. The day was devoted to general clean up, Drill, etc. The under mention was awarded the "Distinguished Conduct Medal" No. 18929 Pte. L. Kenny. The following were awarded a Bar to the Military Medal:- No. 3400 C.S.M. Hammond, M.M. and No. 22248 Sergt. M. Fisher, D.C.M.M.M. The under were awarded the Military Medal:- No. 34509 Sergt. S. Wilkes. " 245264 Pte. J. Roe. " 245252 " S. Higginson " 18696 " W. Redman. " 9819 C.S.M. J.F. Mulroney. " 24855 Sergt. F. Williams. " 245341 Cpl. A.E. Tozer. " 31902 L/Cpl. J. Atkinson No. 41394 L/Cpl. J. Crabbe. " 352369 Pte. F. Boleman " 430449 " H. Minton. " 298824 " W.G. Hardy. " 301115 " F.E. Cliffe. " 1146 " J. Banford. " 91/33 " P. Moran. " 249923 " E. Coleman. " 56001 " S. Cock. " 47432 " W. Coate. " 9319 " H. Poole.	S.L.M.

WAR DIARY
or
~~INTELLIGENCE SUMMARY~~
(Erase heading not required.)

Army Form C. 2118.

Place	Date	Hour	Summary of Events and Information	Remarks and references to Appendices
BOHAIN	October 21st Cont'd		The Divisional Commander presented Medal Ribands to Officers and O.Rs of the Battalion. Casualties Nil.	J.L.M.
" "	22nd		Dispositions same as 21st. Battalion moved by Route to BUSIGNY — arrived and complete in Billets at 4 pm. Casualties Nil.	J.L.M.
BUSIGNY	23rd		Dispositions same as 22nd. Battalion carried out cleaning up of Billets equipment etc. Officers proceed to reconnoitre Route to LE SOUPLET. Battalion paid and 2nd Lieut W. Crawford joined Battalion this day. Casualties Nil. Battalion gone out	J.L.M.
BUSIGNY	24th		Disposition same as 23rd. Battalion training carried out under Coy arrangements during morning. Battalion bathed in afternoon. 2 Lt A. Coleman rejoined Battalion from hospital 85 O.R. reinforcements joined Battalion.	J.L.M.
BUSIGNY	25th		Dispositions same as 24th. G.O.C. Division inspected reinforcements who joined 24th Training carried out under Coy arrangement Lieut J.V. Brady rejoined Battalion from 6 months duty at home. Casualties Nil.	J.L.M.

WAR DIARY
or
INTELLIGENCE SUMMARY.
(Erase heading not required.)

Army Form C. 2118.

Place	Date	Hour	Summary of Events and Information	Remarks and references to Appendices
BUSIGNY	October 26th		Disposition same as 25th. Battalion training carried out under Coy arrangements. Guard provided for Coy's headquarters.	J.L.M.
BUSIGNY	27th		Disposition same as 26th. Battalion Church Parade. Battalion took over Billets in BUSIGNY vacated by 15th Lancashire Fusiliers, arrived and relied ground in Billets 1-30 p.m. Capt Taylor rejoined Battalion from Rest. Casualties Nil.	J.L.M.
BUSIGNY	28th		Dispositions same as on the 27th. Battalion training carried out under Coy arrangements. Battalion paid out. 7 Officers M.O.R. proceeded to reconnoitre Right Bn. 16th Brigade, 6th Divisional Front. Casualties nil.	J.L.M.
BUSIGNY	29th		Dispositions same as on the 28th. Battalion moved by Route to ST SOUPLET, arrived & complete in Billets at 7.0 p.m. Casualties nil.	J.L.M.

Army Form C.2118.

WAR DIARY
or
INTELLIGENCE SUMMARY.
(Erase heading not required.)

Place	Date	Hour	Summary of Events and Information	Remarks and references to Appendices
	Oct			
St. SOUPLET	30th		Dispositions same as the 29th. Battalion relieved right Battalion 16th Infantry Brigade (2nd K.S.L.I.). "B" and "C" companies in front line, "D" Company in support and "A" Company in reserve. Relief complete at 4 p.m. Casualties nil	J.L.M.
DITTO	31st		Dispositions same as the 30th. Front line Companies reconnoitred ground in front during day but were unable to establish posts. Casualties nil	J.L.M.

J. L. Gregory Major
Comdg. 2nd Bn. Manchester Regt.

2 Manchester Regt Army Form C.2118.

Vol 52

WAR DIARY
or
INTELLIGENCE SUMMARY.
(Erase heading not required.)

Place	Date	Hour	Summary of Events and Information	Remarks and references to Appendices
POMMEREUIL	1918 NOVEMBER 1st		See attached report.	Ref
-do-	2nd		Dispositions same as the 1st. See attached report.	Incl
-do-	3rd		Dispositions same as the 2nd. See attached report.	Incl
-do-	4th		Dispositions same as the 3rd. See attached report.	Ref
-do-	5th		Dispositions same as the 4th. See attached report.	Incl
SAMBRETON	6th		Battalion in billets. The day was devoted to general clean up of equipment, clothing etc. Re-organisation of companies was carried out. Louvuières Hill.	Ref

WAR DIARY or INTELLIGENCE SUMMARY

Army Form C. 2118.

Place	Date	Hour	Summary of Events and Information	Remarks and references to Appendices
SAMBRETON	Nov. 7th		Dispositions same as the 6th instant. Training was carried out during the morning under company arrangements.	AF
do.	8th		Dispositions same as the 7th instant. Training was carried out under company arrangements. Major J. F. Murphy was awarded the "Distinguished Service Order". Capt W. Ray M.C. awarded second bar to the "Military Cross". Capt. L. Taylor M.C. awarded bar to the "Military Cross". The following officers were awarded the "Military Cross":— 2/Lt J. Goulden, 2/Lt Y. Johnson, 2/Lt J. Burrows, 2/Lt J. Webb. Sergt. Sharp and L/C R.B. Birtley no. 11745 & Pte B.W. Martin D.C.M.M.M. awarded the "Military Cross". Pte J. Granville L/C —	AF
do.	9th		Dispositions same as the 8th instant. Training was carried out under company arrangements. Battalion was in the afternoon.	AF
do.	10th		Dispositions same as the 9th instant. Battalion was out the day to cleaning up. Lt. Col. S. W. Roberts D.S.O. assumed command from 2nd Lt. J. T. Dunn during "10 Distinguished Divide order" on his return from leave.	AF

WAR DIARY
or
INTELLIGENCE SUMMARY

Army Form C. 2118.

Place	Date	Hour	Summary of Events and Information	Remarks and references to Appendices
SAMBRETON	Nov 11th		Dispositions same as the 10th instant. Battalion moved by Route to PRISCHES, passing the starting point at 11.15 a.m. Battalion reported present in Prischés at 1.30 p.m. The cessation of hostilities was finally concluded at 11.0 am.	QMS
PRISCHES	12th		Dispositions same as evening of the 11th instant. The day was devoted to cleaning up of equipment, billets &c. Bivouacs hill.	QMS
-do-	13th		Dispositions same as the 12th instant. Battalion moved by Route to AVESNES, passing the starting point at 2-10 p.m. Battalion reported present in billets at 4.0 p.m. Battalion paid out. Bivouacs hill.	QMS
AVESNES	14th		Dispositions same as evening of the 13th instant. The Brigade moved by Route to FERRIÈRES, passing the starting point at 1.45 p.m. Battalion reported present in billets at 3.30 p.m. Bivouacs hill.	QMS

WAR DIARY
or
INTELLIGENCE SUMMARY.
(Erase heading not required.)

Army Form C. 2118.

Place	Date	Hour	Summary of Events and Information	Remarks and references to Appendices
FELLERIES	Nov 15th		Dispositions same as evening of the 14th instant. The day was spent in the cleaning up of rifles, equipment etc, also refitting of clothing. No 9025 Sergt. E. Lynn M.M. awarded "LA MEDAILLE MILITAIRE" brevetière No	RwR
-do-	16th		Dispositions same as the 15th instant. Training was carried out under Company arrangements. Lance Corporal Major J. Murphy proceeded to the United Kingdom to wing French Regimental Colours.	RwR
-do-	17th		Dispositions same as the 16th instant. The following church services were arranged for:- C of E. Dinner 10·30 am, R.C. Dinner at 11·0 am, then Communion at 10·30 am. Casualties Nil	RwR
do	18th		Dispositions same as the 17th instant. Training were carried out under Company arrangements. Casualties Nil	RwR

WAR DIARY
or
INTELLIGENCE SUMMARY.
(Erase heading not required.)

Army Form C. 2118.

Place	Date	Hour	Summary of Events and Information	Remarks and references to Appendices
FELLERIES	19th		Dispositions same as on evening of the 18th instant. Brigade Group moved by route to LIESSIES on Battalion forming starting point at 11.0 a.m. and were reported complete in Sillik at 1.30 p.m. Major R.L. Wegeth M.C. 1/4 Battalion to assume command of the 1/5 Battalion Lancashire Fusiliers	[initials]
LIESSIES	20th		Brigade Group moved by Route to RANCE. Battalion forming starting point at 9.47 a.m. and were reported complete in Sillers at 4.30 p.m. Casualties nil.	[initials]
RANCE	21		Dispositions same as evening of 20th instant. Battalion were employed in clearing up of equipment Sillis etc. the battalion were employed in clearing up the roads under the supervision of the C.R.E. Casualties nil.	[initials]

WAR DIARY
or
INTELLIGENCE SUMMARY.

(Erase heading not required.)

Army Form C. 2118.

Place	Date	Hour	Summary of Events and Information	Remarks and references to Appendices
RANCE	Nov 22nd		Dispositions same as the 21st instant. Battalion carried out the cleaning up of the roads round the C.R.E. Bruxelles Rd. Battalion parades out.	
-ditto-	23rd		Dispositions same as the 22nd instant. Battalion completed the task of cleaning of roads. Casualties nil.	
-ditto-	24th		Dispositions same as the evening of the 23rd instant. Brigade group moved by route to FROIDCHAPELLE. Battalion guard starting point at 9.30 a.m., and were present in billets at 11-0 a.m. Casualties nil. Battalion reported present.	
FROIDCHAPELLE	25		Dispositions same as the 24th instant. Parades were carried out under Company arrangements during the morning. Casualties nil.	

Army Form C. 2118.

WAR DIARY
or
INTELLIGENCE SUMMARY.
(Erase heading not required.)

Instructions regarding War Diaries and Intelligence Summaries are contained in F. S. Regs., Part II. and the Staff Manual respectively. Title pages will be prepared in manuscript.

Place	Date	Hour	Summary of Events and Information	Remarks and references to Appendices
FROIDCAPELLE	Nov 26		Dispositions same as the 25 instant. Parades were carried out union company arrangements during the morning. Casualties Nil.	Ref
ditto	26		Dispositions same as the 26th instant. Battalion carried out the cleaning the roads. The following men awarded the MILITARY MEDAL:- No 43074 Sergt. E. Ainsdale No 2813 Corpl. E. Thinkle No 252156 Acpl. Y. Smith No 297/636 Pte H. Mullworth No 34086 Pte C. Back No 302396 Pte C.H. Birchwell No 361177 Pte H. Birks No 415175 Pte J. Wordehouse Casualties Nil. No 351125 Sergt. C. Bancroft No 40021 Corpl. W. Pidcom No 50137 Acpl. R.G. Hunter No 626637 Pte D.W. Jones No 302396 Pte W. Needham No 245324 Acpl. W. Jordan No 520514 Pte F. Ridmore No 60548 Sergt Bay No 351177 Cpl. Q.S. Hull No 251702 Acpl. H. Bridge No 332521 Pte E.B. Salin No 398440 Pte W. Styham No 303061 Pte W. Reed No 352550 Cpl. J. Munn No 16910 Pte W. Bluester No 303332 Pte J.B. McCarty	Ref

Army Form C. 2118.

WAR DIARY
or
INTELLIGENCE SUMMARY.
(Erase heading not required.)

Instructions regarding War Diaries and Intelligence Summaries are contained in F. S. Regs., Part II. and the Staff Manual respectively. Title pages will be prepared in manuscript.

Place	Date	Hour	Summary of Events and Information	Remarks and references to Appendices
FROID CAPELLE	Nov 28th		Dispositions same as on the 29th instant. Battalion carried out with the cleaning of rifles. Battalion sent out Bowallies hill.	and
ditto	29th		Dispositions same as on the 28th instant. "B" Coy carried out cleaning of rifles. "A", "C" and "D" Companies carried out the following training Company arrangements. The following officers joined the battalion this day: 2/Lt W. B. Brown, 2/Lt F. Sidey, 2/Lt Officer, 2/Lt A. G. Hodgetts, 2/Lt F. J. O'Grady, 2/Lt J.W. White, 2/Lt A. Smith, Bowallies hill.	and
ditto	30th		Disposition same as on the 29th instant. Battalion carried out a Route march during the morning. Bowallies hill	and

Cecil Stockin
Lieut. Colonel.
Commanding 2nd Bn. the Manchester Regiment

To be attached to War Diary for November.

2nd Battalion The Lancaster Regiment.

Headquarters,
    76th Infantry Brigade.

REPORT ON OPERATIONS FROM 30-10-18 TO 6-11-18.

The Brigade relieved the 18th Infantry Brigade in the line west of the OISE CANAL, North of ORS on the night 30th/31st October 1918. It was understood the Battalion would take part in an attack over and beyond the Canal at an early date. It was essential that the time prior to 'Z' day should be used to full advantage; consequently the following points were kept prominently in view.

    (a) Reconnoitre approaches to Canal.
    (b) Crossings of Canal.
    (c) Detailed nature of country beyond Canal.
    (d) Location of Machine Gun Posts beyond Canal.
    (e) Probable line of enemy S.O.S.

In order to bridge the Canal it was essential that all enemy west of the Canal be removed. Days prior to zero were spent in strong deliberate patrolling and in inisheting all ranks with every possible detail. Patrols on the nights 30th/31st and 31st Oct/1st Nov., reported enemy this side of the Canal, but only as alarm posts, not permanently held, and not intended as resistance points.
The night 1st/2nd Nov., was spent in an organised clearance of the west bank of the Canal. This was completely done by 1700, November 2nd, when the last enemy post was raided at dusk and exterminated. The only persons remaining alive were four who were taken prisoners, three machine guns along with them.

November 3rd passed without incident, the enemy were carefully observed and their posts approximately noted east of the Canal.

Strong active patrolling took place on the night November 3rd/4th prior to zero at 0545, November 4th.

The Battalion attack was to take place with two companies in the line, one in support and one in Reserve. The Canal was to be bridged by Royal Engineers after the initial 5 minute's barrage which was to fall on the East bank of the Canal. During the ensuing half hour stationary barrage the bridging would be done, the Canal crossed, companies re-formed along the Battalion area, and preparations completed for advancing with the barrage to the YELLOW, BLUE and RED final line.

Orders were issued for cases of emergency, definite Officers and personnel were to superintend.

    (1) The initial forming up.
    (2) The crossing by the bridge.
    (3) The re-forming on the east bank.
    (4) The liaison with flanking Units.
    (5) The minute co-operation with the Barrage Table.
    (6) The communications.
    (7) The stragglers Posts.

The following happened.

    (1) The initial forming up without incident.
    (2) Preliminary 5 minute's barrage with all personnel ready to dash forward.
    (3) The attempt to bridge the Canal under most terrific machine gun fire, heavy trench mortar fire, and spasmodic artillery fire. The R.E's in throwing over the bridge worked in a magnificently gallant manner but were decimated with perishing fire.

(continued)   /The

the bridge was actually thrown across and two platoons immediately rushed over, establishing themselves on the Eastern bank to cover other troops. It was at this time that an enemy shell knocked the bridge away and no further crossing of troops was possible. Repeated endeavours were made to get across but the fire from the opposite bank was intensely destructive.

(4) All personnel were methodically withdrawn under cover on the Western bank. Double runners were despatched to both flanking bridges to ascertain if a passage was possible elsewhere. The entire situation was promptly reported to Advanced Brigade Headquarters.

It was learned that the Northern flank bridge was not across but that the Right Brigade had effected a crossing at OMI Church.

(5) The original Support and Reserve Companies proceeded <u>immediately</u> to this bridge with orders as under.

   (a) To cross rapidly and turn sharply Left pushing Northwards.

   (b) To brook no opposition and to turn Eastwards on reaching original objective line.

   (c) To push forward as rapidly as possible to the YELLOW LINE and to keep abreast of, and liaison with the Right Brigade.

   (d) To detail a special party for North flank protection where the enemy were strongly resisting at DE LA MOTTE FARM. This party was to effect a junction with the Lancashire Fusiliers where they should have crossed the Canal but was unable to give more than flank protection owing to withering fire.

(6) These Companies reached the YELLOW LINE before noon, but the Left Company swung back its Northern flank as there were many hostile posts in that direction. The two remaining Companies were brought into frontal and flank support and reserve with definite instructions to reinforce wherever necessary and to again endeavour to assist the Lancashire Fusiliers at their crossing point.

(7) As the Lancashire Fusiliers were unable to cross, they came round by OMI Bridge with definite orders to attack DE LA MOTTE FARM and protect our flank.

(8) Under orders from Brigade the advance on the BLUE LINE was begun and the objective reached at 1900. Orders were then issued to push on to the RED LINE which would have been done but for the following reasons.

   (a) No further advance was made by the 14th Infantry Brigade.

   (b) The night was intensely dark and the country thick.

   (c) The Left flank was woefully exposed. The men rested during the night for a few hours on a line approximately 500 yards East of the BLUE LINE.

(9) The move to the RED LINE was continued at dawn and posts were there established and consolidated by 0645. Touch was maintained with the 14th Infantry Brigade. The 97th Infantry Brigade passed through at a later hour.

(continued) /The

The following points were noticed,

    (a) The enemy barrage fell East of our forming up point.
    (b) Spasmodic fire was kept up on the Canal.
    (c) The enemy intended to hold this line to the bitter end.
    (d) Once routed out of his defences he resolved his policy into one of fighting rearguard.

Casualties were,

    3 Officers Killed.
    5 Officers Wounded.
    22 Other Ranks Killed.
    81 Other Ranks Wounded.
    18 Other Ranks Missing.

Captures were,

    About 80 prisoners.
    At least 30 Machine Guns.
    One Battery 77mm Field Guns.
    One 5.9 Gun.

The captures are entirely approximated.

November 6th : The Battalion is comfortably billeted in the CAMBRETCH area.

[signed] Robertson
Lieut., Colonel,
6/11/18. Commanding 2nd Battalion The Manchester Regiment.

WAR DIARY
INTELLIGENCE SUMMARY

2 Manchester
Army Form C. 2118.
Vol 5-2

Place	Date	Hour	Summary of Events and Information	Remarks and references to Appendices
FROIDCHAPELLE	DEC 1918 1st.		Dispositions same as 30th ultimo. Major J.C. Murphy, D.S.O., and Escort returned from the United Kingdom with the Regimental Colours. The Battalion paraded to meet the Colours. In accordance with programme one company carried out Bathing. The following Officers rejoined the Battalion this day. Major A.J. Scully, M.C.; Lieut. J. Barratt, M.C.; 2nd Lieut. F.T. Brownson; 2nd Lieut. G. Van Heck. Casualties Nil.	G.R.M.M.
" "	2nd		Dispositions same as 1st. Bathing carried out. Casualties Nil.	A.J.S.
" "	3rd		Dispositions same as 2nd. Training carried out in accordance with programme. Bathing carried out. Casualties Nil.	A.J.S.
" "	4th		Dispositions same as 3rd inst. Training carried out in accordance with programme. Inspections of Kit, Equipment etc. Casualties Nil.	A.J.S.
" "	5th		Dispositions same as 4th inst. Training carried out in accordance with programme. Bathing carried out. Casualties Nil.	A.J.S.
" "	6th		Dispositions same as 5th. Training carried out in accordance with programme. Bathing carried out. Casualties Nil.	A.J.S.

WAR DIARY

INTELLIGENCE SUMMARY.

(Erase heading not required.)

Army Form C. 2118.

Instructions regarding War Diaries and Intelligence Summaries are contained in F.S. Regs., Part II. and the Staff Manual respectively. Title pages will be prepared in manuscript.

Place	Date	Hour	Summary of Events and Information	Remarks and references to Appendices
FROIDCHAPELLE	7th		Dispositions same as 6th inst. Battalion Ceremonial Parade. Training carried out in accordance with programme. Bathing carried out. Casualties Nil.	Capt R.G.G?
"	8th		Dispositions same as the 7th inst. Church parades carried out. Casualties Nil.	Capt R
"	9th		Dispositions same as 8th inst. Training carried out in accordance with programme. Bathing carried out. Casualties Nil.	Capt R
"	10th		Dispositions same as 9th inst. Training carried out in accordance with programme. Bathing carried out. Casualties Nil.	Capt R
"	11th		Dispositions same as 10th inst. Day was devoted to the cleaning up of Billets, equipment etc.	Capt R
"	12th		Dispositions same as 11th inst. Battalion moved by route to PHILIPPEVILLE passing starting point at 09/15. Bn. reported present in Billets at 2.30 p.m. Casualties Nil.	Capt R
PHILIPPEVILLE	13th		Dispositions same as evening of 12th. Bn. moved by route to STAVE. Bn. reported present in Billets at 14.00. Casualties nil.	Capt R

Army Form C. 2118.

WAR DIARY

INTELLIGENCE SUMMARY.

(Erase heading not required.)

Instructions regarding War Diaries and Intelligence Summaries are contained in F. S. Regs., Part II. and the Staff Manual respectively. Title pages will be prepared in manuscript.

Place	Date	Hour	Summary of Events and Information	Remarks and references to Appendices
STAVE	14th		Dispositions same as evening of 13th. Bn. moved by Route to Yvoir-sur-MEUSE. Bn. passed starting point at 0947 — reported present in billets at 1500 — Casualties nil.	C.R.M/B.L.
ASSESSE	15th		Dispositions same as evening of 14th. Bn. moved by Route to ASSESSE, passing starting point at 0900. Bn. reported present in Billets at 1330. Casualties Nil.	C.R.B.
"	16th		Dispositions same as 15th inst. Companies at disposal of Company Commanders for cleaning up billets, equipment etc. Casualties Nil. Capt W. Ray, M.C. awarded The Distinguished Service Order. Capt R. Taylor M.C. 2nd Bar to Military Cross. Capt A.R. Oldfield M.C. awarded bar to Military Cross. 2nd Lieut G.M. Semple awarded the Military Cross.	C.R.B.
"	17th		Dispositions same as 16th. A/B. Coys employed on cleaning Roads. C & D Coys at disposal of Company Commanders for cleaning up of billets etc. Casualties nil.	C.R.B.

WAR DIARY

INTELLIGENCE SUMMARY

Army Form C. 2118.

Place	Date	Hour	Summary of Events and Information	Remarks and references to Appendices
ACHEUX	18th		Dispositions same as 17th inst., "A and B. Coys", working on Road Clearing. "A and B. Coys" at disposal of Company Commanders. The following Officers rejoined the Battn. today:- Lieut. A. Robertson, 2nd Lieut. N. Coppack, 2nd Lieut. J. D. O'Toole. Casualties Nil.	Ref
" "	19th		Dispositions same as 18th inst. "A and B. Coys" attended a lecture delivered by Captain Dennys, Australian Corps, in the Cinema Hall. Casualties Nil.	Ref
" "	20th		Dispositions same as 19th inst. "A and B. Coys" on Road Clearing, "C and D Coys" at disposal of Company Commanders. Bathing carried out. Casualties Nil.	Ref
" "	21st		Dispositions same as 20th inst. "C and D Coys" Road Clearing. "A and B Coys" attended Lecture by Mr. A. C. VINEGAR, in the Cinema Hall. Subject :- "Dr. JEKYLL and MR. HYDE." Bathing carried out. Inter-Company football in accordance with Sports Programme. Casualties Nil.	Ref
" "	22nd		Dispositions same as 21st inst. Church Parade. Major T. P. Murphy, D.S.O., awarded BAR to "The Distinguished Service Order". Lieut J. C. Pearce, awarded the Military Cross. The following were awarded "The Distinguished Conduct Medal":- No. 9025 Sergt W. Flynn, M.M. No. 1483 Sergt E. Lovell M.M. No. 8648 Corpl. J. Snape. No. 57993 Pte. W. E. Southern. No. 46695 Pte. W. Garrod. Casualties Nil.	Ref

Army Form C. 2118.

WAR DIARY

(Erase heading not required.)

Instructions regarding War Diaries and Intelligence Summaries are contained in F. S. Regs., Part II. and the Staff Manual respectively. Title pages will be prepared in manuscript.

Place	Date	Hour	Summary of Events and Information	Remarks and references to Appendices
ASSESSE	23rd		Dispositions. Training carried out in accordance with Programme. Bathing carried out. Casualties Nil.	
" "	24th		Dispositions same as 23rd inst. General Holiday. Casualties Nil.	
" "	25th		Dispositions same as 24th inst. General Holiday Xmas Day. Casualties Nil.	
" "	26th		Dispositions same as 25th inst – General Holiday – Casualties Nil.	
" "	27th		Dispositions same as 26th inst. Training carried out in accordance with programme. "A" and "B" Coys attended a lecture in the Cinema Hall on "EDUCATION ACT" – delivered by Mr. H. FARRANDS. Inter Companies Rugby Football match in the afternoon. Casualties Nil.	
" "	28th		Dispositions same as 27th. Training carried out in accordance with programme. Bathing carried out. Casualties Nil.	

WAR DIARY

Army Form C. 2118.

Place	Date	Hour	Summary of Events and Information	Remarks and references to Appendices
ASSEVE	Dec. 29th		Dispositions same as 28th inst. Church Parades. Casualties Nil.	
"	30th		Dispositions same as 29th inst. Training carried out in accordance with Programme. Sports carried out in the afternoon in accordance with Programme. Casualties Nil.	
"	31st		Dispositions same as 30th inst. Battalion Parade in accordance with Programme. Battn Football Team played 15th Lancashire Fusiliers in "The Regimental Team" Divisional League Competition. Result:- "The Regimental Team" won, 4-1. 2nd Lieut J. KIRK late of this Battalion awarded the "VICTORIA CROSS" for conspicuous bravery during operations North of ORS, France, on November 4th 1918.	

Alec Blackra
Lieut Colonel
Commandg 2nd Battn The Manchester Regiment

LANCASHIRE DIVISION
(LATE 32ND DIVN)
96TH INFY BDE (2ND LANCS INFY BDE)

2ND BN MANCHESTER REGT
JAN - MAR 1919

2 Manchesters

WAR DIARY
~~INTELLIGENCE SUMMARY~~

(Erase heading not required.)

Army Form C. 2118.

Instructions regarding War Diaries and Intelligence Summaries are contained in F. S. Regs., Part II. and the Staff Manual respectively. Title pages will be prepared in manuscript.

Place	Date	Hour	Summary of Events and Information	Remarks and references to Appendices
	1919			
ASSEVE	Jan 1st		Dispositions same as 31st ultimo. General holiday.	
"	2nd		Dispositions same as 1st inst. Training carried out in accordance with programme. Sports in afternoon in accordance with programme.	
"	3rd		Dispositions same as 2nd inst. Training in accordance with programme. Sports in afternoon in accordance with programme.	
"	4th		Dispositions same as 3rd inst. Training in accordance with programme. Sports in afternoon in accordance with programme.	
"	5th		Dispositions same as 4th inst. Training in accordance with programme.	
"	6th		Dispositions same as 5th inst. G.O.C. delivered a speech to the Battalion. Regimental Team played 16th Lancashire Fusiliers – Reg'tl team won 3–1. Lieut. Colonel G.M. Roberts, D.S.O. assumed command of 96th Infantry Brigade in the absence of the G.O.C.	
"	7th		Dispositions same as 6th inst. Corps Commander inspected the Battalion area. Sports carried out in afternoon in accordance with programme.	
"	8th		Dispositions same as 7th inst. Training carried out in accordance with programme. Route March. Sports carried out in afternoon.	

Army Form C. 2118.

WAR DIARY
INTELLIGENCE SUMMARY.
(Erase heading not required.)

Instructions regarding War Diaries and Intelligence Summaries are contained in F. S. Regs., Part II. and the Staff Manual respectively. Title pages will be prepared in manuscript.

Place	Date	Hour	Summary of Events and Information	Remarks and references to Appendices
ASSEVILLERS	9th		Dispositions same as the 8th inst. Battalion Route march. Sports carried out in the afternoon in accordance with programme.	JLM
" "	10th		Dispositions same as the 9th inst. Training carried out in accordance with programme. Sports carried out in accordance with programme.	JLM
" "	11th		Dispositions same as 10th inst. Companies at disposal of Company Commanders. Sports carried out in the afternoon. Capt W. Ray, 2SOMC, and 2nd Lieut. Winder, Coleman and Jones proceeded to U.K. for demobilization.	JLM
" "	12th		Dispositions same as 11th inst. Church Parades.	JLM
" "	13th		Dispositions same as 12th inst. Divisional General presented Medal Ribands. Lieut Col Robinson D.S.O. proceeded to U.K. to take staff appointment. No horse drawn at Aldershot. Sports carried out in the afternoon in accordance with programme.	JLM
" "	14th		Dispositions same as 13th inst. Battalion Route March. Sports carried out in accordance with programme.	JLM
" "	15th		Dispositions same as on 14th inst. Training in accordance with programme. Sports held in the afternoon.	JLM
" "	16th		Dispositions same as 15th inst. Battalion Route March. Sports carried out in afternoon.	JLM

WAR DIARY

(Erase heading not required.)

Army Form C. 2118.

Place	Date	Hour	Summary of Events and Information	Remarks and references to Appendices
ASSESSE	1919. Jan 17		Dispositions same as 16th. Commanding Officers inspection. Sports carried out in the afternoon	O.L.M.
"	Jan 18		Dispositions same as 17th. Adjutants parade. Sports held in afternoon in accordance with programme	O.L.M.
"	Jan 19		Dispositions same as 18th. Church Parade. Sports carried out in afternoon in accordance with programme	O.L.M.
"	Jan 20		Dispositions same as 19th. Battalion Route March. Sports carried out according to programme in afternoon	O.L.M.
"	Jan 21		Dispositions same as 20th. Companies at disposal of Company Commanding for Physical Training etc in accordance with programme. Sports carried on in afternoon	O.L.M.
"	Jan 22		Dispositions same as 21st. Commanding Officers Parade. Sports in afternoon	O.L.M.
"	Jan 23		Dispositions same as 22nd Adjutants parade. Sports in afternoon.	O.L.M.
"	Jan 24		Dispositions as 23rd. H.R.H. The Prince of Wales visited the Battalion about 1115 including spoke with many of the [illegible] inspected men [illegible] Lieut [illegible] 2/4 S.M. Bn [illegible] M.C. D.C.M. &c. before leaving the battalion he personally inspected the adjutant Lieut [illegible] L.M.M. M.M. L.M. asked for the L.M. complimented them in their fine turnout. He [illegible] asked for the L.M. & congratulated him	O.L.M. [illegible]

WAR DIARY
INTELLIGENCE SUMMARY
(Erase heading not required.)

Army Form C. 2118.

Place	Date	Hour	Summary of Events and Information	Remarks and references to Appendices
ASSEVILLE	Jan 24/Cont.		On the arrival, appearance of the Headquarters Guard is to be departed from the	QM
			battalion when he proceeded to the 96th Infantry Bde. Headquarters where he	
			was entertained by the General Staff.	
"	Jan 25	10	Dispositions as on 24th. C.O. inspection of Kilts, Kit and equipment	QM
			Sports held in the afternoon according to programme.	
"	Jan 26		Dispositions same as on 25th. Church Parade. Inspection of Parade by Col (CPBG)	QM
			S.M.McPherson. 10.50 promoted to rank RSM. Majority No9347 CSM Newman awarded DCM.	
			No 9003? OptnStaff RSM TRSM? Snow & 69M? Mullaney awarded Neurmerous Swedish	
"	Jan 27	10	Dispositions as on Jan 26. Battalion occupied in Inter-Company Sports in afternoon.	QM
"	Jan 28	10	Dispositions as on Jan 27. Lt Col. G.G. Stapledon took Command of Battalion & May. Crampton O/C	QM
			of disposal of Company ammunition. Sports held in afternoon	
"	Jan 29		Dispositions same as on Jan 28. C.O. speak. Sports in the afternoon.	C23.
"	Jan 30		Dispositions same as on Jan 29. Adjutants Parade. Companies at disposal of Company commanders	C23.
			afterwards. Sports held in afternoon. Spoke hilden the	
"	Jan 31		Dispositions as on Jan 30. Battalion Route March. Spoke hilden the	US.
			afternoon according to programme.	C23.

WAR DIARY

Army Form C. 2118.

Instructions regarding War Diaries and Intelligence Summaries are contained in F.S. Regs., Part II. and the Staff Manual respectively. Title pages will be prepared in manuscript.

(Erase heading not required.)

Place	Date	Hour	Summary of Events and Information	Remarks and references to Appendices
ASSESSE	Feb. 1		Battalion at ASSESSE. Dispositions same as January 31st. Commanding officers inspection of Billets Kit and Equipment. Sports held in the afternoon in accordance with the programme.	
ASSESSE	Feb. 2		Dispositions Same as February 1st. Church Parades. Sports in the afternoon according to programme.	
ASSESSE	Feb. 3		Dispositions same as February 2nd. Companies at the disposal of Company Commanders. Sports held in the afternoon in accordance with the Sports Programme.	
ASSESSE	Feb. 4		Dispositions Same as February 3rd. Battalion employed in general clean up of Billets and Equipment prior to move to BONN area.	
FIELD	Feb. 5		Battalion commences move to BONN area. Marches to NAMUR and Billets for the night in the CAVALRY BARRACKS NAMUR.	
NAMUR	Feb. 6	Noon	Battalion entrains for the BONN AREA with the exception of B. Company which remained behind to load for the Brigade Group.	
FIELD	Feb. 7		The Battalion detrained at BEUEL and marched to BONN. The Battalion is Billeted in the ARTILLERY BARRACKS BONN.	
BONN	Feb. 8		Battalion in the ARTILLERY BARRACKS, BONN. Companies at the disposal of Company Commanders for general clean up of Billets and Equipment.	
BONN	Feb. 9		Dispositions Same as on February 8th. Companies at the disposal of Company Commanders. Major J.L. MURPHY D.S.O. proceeded to U.K. on Leave.	
BONN	Feb. 10		Dispositions Same as on February 9th. Companies at the disposal of the Company Commanders. Commanding Officers inspection of the Barracks.	
BONN	Feb. 11		Dispositions Same as on February 10th. Companies at the disposal of Company Commanders for P.T. etc. Sports held in the afternoon in accordance with the Sports Programme.	
BONN	Feb. 12		Dispositions same as on February 11th. Commanding Officers Parade. Sports held in the afternoon in accordance with the programme.	
BONN	Feb. 13th		Dispositions same as February 12th. Adjutants Parade. In the afternoon the Battalion was visited by General Sir. H.S. RAWLINSON Bart. G.C.B.; G.C.V.O.; K.C.M.G. and Staff.	
BONN	Feb. 14		Dispositions Same as February 13th. Companies at the disposal of Company Commanders for Company and Platoon Drill P.T. etc. Sports held in the afternoon in accordance with the programme.	
BONN	Feb. 15.		Dispositions Same as on February 14th. Companies at the disposal of the Company Commanders Commanding Officers inspection of Kit Billets Cookhouses and Cookers. A lecture was delivered to the Battalion at 17.30 hours on the "Relations of Italy and Great Britian" by the Chevalier SAMBUCETTE.	
BONN	Feb. 16t		Dispositions same as on February 15th. No Church of England Parade. Sports held in the afternoon in accordance with the Sports Programme.	

WAR DIARY

INTELLIGENCE SUMMARY

(Erase heading not required.)

Army Form C. 2118.

Instructions regarding War Diaries and Intelligence Summaries are contained in F.S. Regs., Part II. and the Staff Manual respectively. Title pages will be prepared in manuscript.

2nd BATTALION, THE MANCHESTER REGIMENT.

Place	Date	Hour	Summary of Events and Information	Remarks and references to Appendices
BONN	Feb. 17		Dispositions Same as on February 16th. Lewis Gun Classes held under 2/Lieut. F. BROWNSON Companies at the disposal of Company Commanders. Sports held int the afternoon according to the Sports Programme.	
BONN	Feb. 18		Dispositions Same as on February 17th. Lewis Gun Classes under 2/Lieut. F. BROWNSON. Training in accordance with the Training Programme. Sports held in the afternoon.	
BONN	Feb. 19		Dispositions Same as on February 18th. Companies at the disposal of Company Commanders for P.T. etc. Lewis Gub Classes held under 2/Lieut. F. BROWNSON. Sports carried out in the afternoon in accordance witht the sports programme.	
BONN	Feb. 20		Dispositions Same as on the 19th. February Companies at the disposal of the Company Commanders Lewis Gun Classes under 2/Lieut. F. BROWNSON. Sports held in the afternoon.	
BONN	Feb. 21		Dispositions Same as on February 20th. Battalion Route March The educational classes marched in rear of the Battalion. Sports held in the afternoon in accordance with the Sports Programme.	
BONN	Feb. 22		Dispositions Same as on February 21st. Companies at the disposal of the Company Commanders Commanding Officers inspection of Barracks Kit and Equipment. Sports held in the afternoon.	
BONN.	Feb. 23		Dispositions Same as on the 22nd. February. C. of E. Service held in the UNIVERSITY CHURCH BONN. Sports held in the afternoon in accordance with the Sports programme.	
BONN	Feb. 24		Dispositions Same as on February 23rd. Companies at the disposal of Company Commanders for Platoon Drill etc. Sports held in the afternoon.	
BONN	Feb. 25		Dispositions Same as on February 24th. Battalion Route March. Educational Classes march in the rear of the Battalion. Sports held in the afternoon.	
BONN	Feb. 26		Dispositions Same as on February 25th. Commanding Officers inspection and Parade. Lewis Gun Classes under 2/Lieut. F. BROWNSON. Sports held in the afternoon in accordance with programme	
BONN	Feb. 27		Dispositions Same as on February 26th. Battalion Route March. Educational Classes march in rear of the Battalion Sports held in the afternoon.	
BONN	Feb. 28		Dispositions Same as on February 27th. Companies at the disposal of Company Commanders for Company Platoon and Section Drill. P.T. and Bathing. Sports held in the afternoon in accordance with sports programme.	

WAR DIARY

INTELLIGENCE SUMMARY

(Erase heading not required.)

Army Form C. 2118.

2nd Battalion The Manchester Regiment.

Title pages March 1919.

Place	Date	Hour	Summary of Events and Information	Remarks and references to Appendices
Bonn, Germany.	1st		Dispositions same as Febry.,28th. Commanding Officer's inspection of Billets,Kits, and Barracks. Companies at disposal of Company Commanders.	as
	2nd		Dispositions same as 1st March.,1919. Church Parades. Sports held in afternoon.	as
	3rd.		Dispositions same as 2nd March.,1919. Companies at disposal of Company Commanders for Scrubbing of equipment, cleaning clothes and Guard Drill. Sports held in afternoon.	as
	4th.		Dispositions same as March 3rd 1919. 1040 hours Guards mount on KAISERPLATZ. 1450 Guard Mount on BONN Bridge. Army Commander,General Plumer watched the relief of BONN Bridge Guard found by this Battalion and inspected the Barracks occupied by the Battalion immediately afterwards.	as
	5th.		Dispositions same as March 4th 1919. Guard mounts on KAISERPLATZ. Cinema views taken, Sports held in the afternoon.	as
	6th.		Dispositions same as March 5th 1919. Army Commanders congratulations on Battalion of smart, clean and soldierlike turnout of Guards mounting over BONN. Strength of Guards 7 Officers 2 Warrant Officers 188 Other Ranks. Captain F. HAYWARD,M.C. rejoined Battalion and assumed duties of 2nd in Command. 2nd Lieut. HOPKINSON took over duties of Sports Officer.	as
	7th.		Dispositions same as March 6th 1919. Training in accordance with programme. Sports held in afternoon.	as
	8th.		Dispositions same as March 7th 1919. Guards and Picquets mount on KAISERPLATZ. Balance of Companies at disposal of Company Commanders.	as
	9th.		Dispositions same as March 8th 1919. Church Parades. Captain S.H. HOLLEY,M.C. rejoined the Battalion from Detachment.	as
	10th.		Dispositions same as March 9th 1919. Guards and Picquets mount on KAISERPLATZ. Balance of Companies at disposal of Company Commanders. Battalion paid out. Captain A.Robertson proceeded on Leave to U.K.	as
	11th.		Dispositions same as March 10th 1919. Guards and picquets mount on KAISERPLATZ. Balance of Companies at disposal of Company Commanders.	as
	12th.		Dispositions same as March 11th.1919. Guards and Picquets mount on KAISERPLATZ. Balance of Companies at disposal of Company Commanders.	as
	13th.		Dispositions same as March 12th 1919. Commanding Officers parade. Companies at disposal of Company Commanders.	as
	14th.		Dispositions same as March 13th.1919. Divisional General's farewell speech,and inspection of Battalion followed by Brigadier's inspection. Sports held in afternoon in accordance with Sports programme.	as
	15th.		Dispositions same as March 14th 1919. Training in accordance with Training Programme.	as

Army Form C. 2118.

WAR DIARY
or
INTELLIGENCE SUMMARY.

2nd Battalion The Manchester Regiment.

Sheet -2-

(Erase heading not required.)

March 1919.

Instructions regarding War Diaries and Intelligence Summaries are contained in F.S. Regs., Part II. and the Staff Manual respectively. Title pages will be prepared in manuscript.

Place	Date	Hour	Summary of Events and Information	Remarks and references to Appendices
Bonn, Germany.	16th		Dispositions same as March.15th 1919. Church Parades. Sports held in the afternoon.	as
	17th		Dispositions same as March 16th 1919. Companies at disposal of Company Commanders for physical training etc. Battalion is ordered to reduce to CADRE. in readiness to proceed to United Kingdom. Retainable men and Volunteers to be split up amongst 51st,52nd and 53rd Battns. Manchester Regiment. Major J.L.Murply,D.S.O. rejoined Battalion from Leave.	as
	18th		Dispositions same as March 17th 1919. 6 Officers and 86 O.RS. despatched to 53rd Bn.Manchester Regiment.6 Offrs. and 105 O.RS. posted to 51st Bn.Manchester Regt. 7 Offrs. 86 O.RS posted to 52nd Batt'n.Manchester Regiment. Cadre of Battalion and remainder of Battalion marched from Barracks to Corps Reception Camp with Colours unfurled. Colour Coy. "B" Company.	as
	19th		Dispositions same as 18th March 1919. Companies at disposal of Company Commanders for Baths, etc.	as
	20th		Dispositions same as 19th March 1919. Companies at disposal of Company Commanders for physical training. Battalion paid out.	as
	21st		Dispositions same as 20th March.,1919. Lieut.Taylor and 32 O.RS. despatched to Corps Concent. Camp for demobilization.	as
	22nd		Dispositions same as 21st March.1919. All Leave and Demobilization stopped owing to Labour Trouble in U.K. Companies at do sposal of Company Commanders.	as
	23rd.		Dispositions same as 22nd March 1919. Balance of Battalion at disposal of Company Commanders for cleaning equipment,billets and Baths.	as
	24th		Dispositions same as 23rd March.,1919. Companies at disposal of Company Commanders for physical training. Sports held in the afternoon.	as
	25th		Dispositions same as 24th March.,1919. Leave and Demobilization to commence again to-morrow. Labour Trouble Settled. Balance of Battalion Bathed.	as
	26th		Dispositions same as 25th March.1919. Lieut.J.Bullen,D.C.M.,2/Lieut.F.Ashworth and 99 O.RS. to Corps Concentration Camp for Demobilization. Remainder of Battalion marched to Station to give them a Send off.	as
	27th		Dispositions same as 26th March.,1919. 28 O.R. despatched to Corps Demobilization Camp for demobilization. Balance of Bn. marched to Station to give them a send off.	as
	28th		Dispositions.Dispositions same as 27th March.,1919. 27 O.RS. despatched to Corps Concentration Camp for demobilization. Balance of Battalion marched to Station to give them a send off.	as
	29th		Dispositions same as 28th March 1919. 25 O.R. despatched to Corps Concentration Camp for Demobilization. Balance of Battalion marched to Station to give them a send off. Baths.	as
	30th		Dispositions same as 29th March 1919. 23 O.R. despatched to Corps Concentration Camp for Demobilization. Balance of Battalion marched to Station to give them a send off.	as
	31st		Dispositions same as 30th 1919. CADRE reported ready to proceed to United Kingdom. Cleaning of equipment etc.	as

Commanding 2nd Bn MANCHESTER Lieut. Colonel.

32ND DIVISION
96TH INFY BDE

15TH BN LANCS FUS.
SEPT ~~DEC~~ 1915 - DEC 1918
1919 OCT.

96th Brigade.

32nd Division.

15th BATTALION

LANCASHIRE FUSILIERS

JANUARY 1 9 1 6

96/32

15th Lancers: Pers:
Vol I

121/7894

I.T.
5 Mark

M Davies

32nd KLH
Sep 14 – Dec 15.

Army Form C. 2118

WAR DIARY
or
INTELLIGENCE SUMMARY
(Erase heading not required.)

Instructions regarding War Diaries and Intelligence Summaries are contained in F.S. Regs, Part II. and the Staff Manual respectively. Title Pages will be prepared in manuscript.

Place	Date	Hour	Summary of Events and Information	Remarks and references to Appendices
Salford	13/9/14	–	Formation of Battⁿ. Commenced by Lt. Montagu Bedlow M.P.	
Conway	28.12.14		Moved to Conway	
Catterick	24.6.15		Moved to Catterick	
Codford	13.8.15		Moved to Codford	
Boulogne	22.11.15		Arrived for foreign service and went to Rest Camp – 29 Officers and 925 other Ranks	
Longpré	23.11.15		Entrained at 9.30 for Longpré	
Maison Roland	24.11	2.0 am	Detrained and marched to Maison Roland to Billets.	
"	25.11		In Billets	
"	26.11		In Billets. Strength – 29 Officers 925 other Ranks	
"	27.11		Marched to BOURON to Billets	
Bouron	28.11		" " POULAINVILLE to Billets	
Poulainville	29.11		In Billets	
-do-	30.11		" Marched to ALBERT to Billets	
Albert	1.12.15		Billets	
Albert	2.12		" "	
Albert	3.12		" "	

WAR DIARY
or
INTELLIGENCE SUMMARY
(Erase heading not required.)

Army Form C. 2118

Place	Date	Hour	Summary of Events and Information	Remarks and references to Appendices
ALBERT	4.12.15		In Billets	
"	5.12		"	
"	6.12		"	During this period the Batt.n went
"	7.12		"	through Course of instruction in Trench
"	8.12		"	Warfare in Sector E.1. 55th Brigade.
"	9.12		"	These Regts instructed us 7th Royal West Kent
"	10.12		"	& 7th Buffs.
"	11.12		"	
"	12.12		"	
"	13.12		"	
"	14.12		"	
"	15.12		Marched to trenches. Sector E.I. Becourt	
Becourt	16.12		Relieved the 7th Buffs in the trenches	
"	16.12		In the Trenches. Sector E.I. Becourt	
"	17.12		"	
"	18.12		"	
"	19.12		"	
"	20.12		Relieved by the 7th Queens and marched to Albert to Billets	
Albert	21.12		In Billets	
"	22.12		"	

WAR DIARY
or
INTELLIGENCE SUMMARY
(Erase heading not required.)

Army Form C. 2118

Place	Date	Hour	Summary of Events and Information	Remarks and references to Appendices
Albert	23.12.15		In Billets	
"	24.12		Marched to trenches section E.3. La Boiselle, relieved the 16th (S) Battn. Lan. Fus.	
La Boiselle	24.12		In the trenches	
"	25.12		" " " ⎫ Batt⁰ was very lucky to escape with only 1 man killed and 2 slightly wounded —	
"	26.12		" " " ⎬ 19th (S) Lan Fus. shared the trenches with us.	
"	27.12		" " " ⎪	
"	28.12		" " " ⎭	
"	29.12		Relieved by the 8th Suffolk Regt and marched to Albert to Billets	
Albert	29.12		In Billets. Marched to Hénencourt to Billets.	
Hénencourt	30.12		In Billets	
"	31.12		" " Strength — 28 Officers, 914 Other Ranks	

J.H. Lloyd Lieut. Colonel
Comm.dg 15th (S) Batt. Lan Fus.

15th Lawes, Pro:
Vol. 2

WAR DIARY
or
INTELLIGENCE SUMMARY
(Erase heading not required.)

Army Form C. 2118

Place	Date	Hour	Summary of Events and Information	Remarks and references to Appendices
Hénencourt	1/1/16		In Billets	
"	2/1/16		Marched to Authuille. In Brigade Reserve.	
Authuille	3/1/16		In Brigade Reserve	
"	4/1/16		" " "	
"	5/1/16		" " "	
"	6/1/16	10.30am	Relieved by the 16th Lancashire Fusiliers. Marched to the trenches. G.I. In the trenches. The 16th Northumberland Fusiliers were on our left, and the Kings Own Yorkshire Light Infantry on our right	
"	7/1/16		" " "	
"	8/1/16		" " "	
"	9/1/16		" " "	
"	10/1/16	4.30pm	" " " Relieved by the 1st Dorset Regt. Marched to Hénencourt to Billets	
Hénencourt	11/1/16		In Billets	
"	12/1/16		" "	
"	13/1/16		" " Reinforcement from England of 19 men arrived	
"	14/1/16		" " Strength of Battn is as follows:— 28 Officers "A" Coy. = 231. "B" Coy. = 229. "C" Coy. = 228. "D" Coy. = 240. Total 928 O.R.	

WAR DIARY
or
INTELLIGENCE SUMMARY

Army Form C. 2118

Place	Date	Hour	Summary of Events and Information	Remarks and references to Appendices
Hennencourt	15/1/16		In Billets. Additional reinforcement from England of 15 men arrived. Strength now is:- 28 Offrs. 943 O.R.	
"	16/1/16		"	
"	17/1/16		"	
"	18/1/16		" Marched to the trenches. G.1. relieved the 2nd Manchester Regt.	
"	19/1/16		In the trenches.	
"	20/1/16		"	
"	21/1/16		" Relieved by the 16th Lan. Fus. Marched to Billets in Div. Res.	
Frévincourt	22/1/16		In Div Reserve. relieved the 16th Lan. Fus.	
"	23/1/16		"	
"	24/1/16		"	
"	25/1/16		"	
"	26/1/16		" relieved by the 2nd Manchester Regt. Marched to Hennencourt to Billets.	
Hennencourt	27/1/16		In Billets.	
"	28/1/16		"	
"	29/1/16		"	

Army Form C. 2118

WAR DIARY
or
INTELLIGENCE SUMMARY

(Erase heading not required.)

Instructions regarding War Diaries and Intelligence Summaries are contained in F. S. Regs., Part II. and the Staff Manual respectively. Title Pages will be prepared in manuscript.

Place	Date	Hour	Summary of Events and Information	Remarks and references to Appendices
HENNENCOURT	30-1-16		for Billets	
"	31-1-16		" "	

J.H.Lloyd Lieut. Colonel.
Commdg 15th (S) Bn. Lancashire Fusiliers

96th Brigade.

32nd Division.

15th BATTALION

LANCASHIRE FUSILIERS

FEBRUARY 1916

Army Form C. 2118

21
15th Lancs: Fus:
Vol: 3

J.T.
6 sheets

Davis

Place	Date	Hour		Remarks and references to Appendices
Hannescourt	1-2-16		In Billets	
"	2-2		"	
"	3-2		"	
"	4-2		"	
"	5-2		"	
"	6-2		" Marched to	
Authuille	7-2		In Brigade Reserve	H.L.I. in Brigade Reserve
"	8-2		"	
"	9-2		"	
"	10-2		"	
"	11-2		"	
"	12-2		" Return	
Millencourt	13-2		In Billets	Marched to Millencourt to Billets
"	14-2		"	
"	15-2		"	
"	16-2		"	
"	17-2	12.45pm	" Marched to	
Aveluy	17-2	3pm	In the trenches relie	
	18-2		In the trenches	
	19-2			

Army Form C. 2118

WAR DIARY
or
INTELLIGENCE SUMMARY
(Erase heading not required.)

Instructions regarding War Diaries and Intelligence Summaries are contained in F. S. Regs., Part II. and the Staff Manual respectively. Title Pages will be prepared in manuscript.

Place	Date	Hour	Summary of Events and Information	Remarks and references to Appendices
Hennencourt	1-2-16		In Billets	
"	2-2		" "	
"	3-2		" "	
"	4-2		" "	
"	5-2		" "	
"	6-2		" Marched to Authuille, relieved the 17th H.L.I. in Brigade Reserve	
Authuille	7-2		In Brigade Reserve	
"	8-2		" "	
"	9-2		" "	
"	10-2		" "	
"	11-2		" "	
"	12-2		" " Relieved by the 7th West Yorks. Marched to Millencourt to Billets	
Millencourt	13-2		In Billets	
"	14-2		" "	
"	15-2		" "	
"	16-2		" "	
"	17-2	12.45a	" " Marched to the trenches. F.L. Aveluy	
Aveluy	17-2	3 pm	In the trenches relieved the 17th H.L.I.	
"	18-2		In the trenches	
"	19-2		" "	

Army Form C. 2118

WAR DIARY
or
INTELLIGENCE SUMMARY
(Erase heading not required.)

Instructions regarding War Diaries and Intelligence Summaries are contained in F. S. Regs., Part II. and the Staff Manual respectively. Title Pages will be prepared in manuscript.

Place	Date	Hour	Summary of Events and Information	Remarks and references to Appendices
Aveluy	20-2		In the trenches. The 16th Northumberland Fusiliers were on our left	
"	21-2		" and the 7th Suffolk Regt on our right.	
"	22-2		"	
"	23-2		"	
"	24-2	2 pm	" relieved by 16th Lan Fus, marched to Albert, to Billets.	
Albert	24-2	5 pm	In Billets. In Brigade Reserve	
"	25-2		" "	
"	26-2		" "	
"	27-2		" "	
"	28-2		" "	
"	29-2		" "	

JH Lloyd Lieut Colonel
Commdg 15th (S) Battn Lancashire Fusiliers

96th Brigade.

32nd Division.

15th BATTALION

LANCASHIRE FUSILIERS

MARCH 1 9 1 6

15 Jan Feb
32 164

Ham

H.T.
Schultz

WAR DIARY
or
INTELLIGENCE SUMMARY
(Erase heading not required.)

Instructions regarding War Diaries and Intelligence Summaries are contained in F. S. Regs., Part II. and the Staff Manual respectively. Title Pages will be prepared in manuscript.

Place	Date	Hour	Summary of Events and Information	Remarks and references to Appendices
Albert	1-3-16		In Brigade Reserve. Strength of Battn. now is :- 30 Officers + 912 O.R.	
"	2-3	3·0 pm	" marched to trenches sector F.1. Aveluy. relieved the 16th Lan. Fus.	
Aveluy	2-3	5·0 pm	In the trenches. F.1. The 16th Northumberland Fus. were on our left and	
"	3-3		" " " the 1st Suffolk Regt. on our right.	
"	4-3		" " "	
"	5-3		" " "	
"	6-3	3·0 pm	" " relieved by the 15th H.L.I. Marched to Aveluy.	
"	6-3	9·30 pm	Relieved the Duke of Wellington Regt. in G.1. Trenches. Authuille.	
Authuille	6-3	12 M.N.	In the trenches. G.1.	
"	7-3		" " "	
"	8-3		" " "	
"	9-3		" " " relieved by the 16th Lan. Fus. Marched to Authuille.	
"	10-3		In reserve.	
"	11-3		" "	
"	12-3	7·0 pm	" " marched to trenches, relieved the 2nd Innis. Fus. in F.2.	
"	12-3	11·0 pm	In the trenches F.2.	
"	13-3		" " "	

Army Form C. 2118

WAR DIARY
or
INTELLIGENCE SUMMARY
(Erase heading not required.)

Instructions regarding War Diaries and Intelligence Summaries are contained in F. S. Regs., Part II. and the Staff Manual respectively. Title Pages will be prepared in manuscript.

Place	Date	Hour	Summary of Events and Information	Remarks and references to Appendices
Authuille	14-3		In the trenches. F.2.	
"	15-3		" " " "	
"	16-3	8.0 PM	" " relieved by the 16th Lan. Fus. marched to BOUZINCOURT.	
Bouzincourt	16-3	10.0 PM	" " Billets	
"	17-3		" " "	
"	18-3		" " "	
"	19-3		" " "	
"	20-3	7.30 PM	" " marched to the trenches. Relieved the 16th Lan Fus. in F.2.	
Authuille	20-3	10.0 PM	" " the trenches. F.2.) The 16TH NORTHUMBERLAND FUSRS were on our left and the	
"	21-3		" " " "	
"	22-3		" " " "	19TH LANCASHIRE FUSILIERS on our right.
"	23-3		" " " "	
"	24-3	9.0 PM	" " " " relieved by the 16th LAN FUS. marched to AUTHUILLE.	
"	24-3	11.0 PM	" " Relieved the 2ND R. INNIS. FUS. in reserve.	
"	25-3		" " In reserve.	
"	26-3		" " "	
"	27-3		" " "	
"	28-3	4.30 PM	" " marched to the trenches	

WAR DIARY
or
INTELLIGENCE SUMMARY
(Erase heading not required.)

Place	Date	Hour	Summary of Events and Information	Remarks and references to Appendices
Authuille	28-3	10·4pm	In the trenches relieved the 2nd R. Innis. Fus. in G.1.	
"	29-3		" " " "	
"	30-3		" " " "	
"	31-3		Strength of Battn. now is:— A. Coy. 225 B " 217 C " 205 D " 233 880 + 8 not on coy rolls Total. 32 Officers + 888 Other Ranks	

J H Lloyd Lieut Colonel
Commanding 15th (S) Bn. Lan. Fus.

96th Brigade.

32nd Division.

15th BATTALION

LANCASHIRE FUSILIERS

APRIL 1916

WAR DIARY
or
INTELLIGENCE SUMMARY

Army Form 2118

1/5th Lan. Fus.
1 of 5

XXXII

5.T.
2 sheets

Place	Date	Hour	Summary of Events and Information	Remarks and references to Appendices
Authuille	1-4-16		In the trenches G.1.	
"	2-4		" " " "	
"	3-4	12 M.N.	" " " relieved by the 1st DORSET REGT. marched to BOUZINCOURT to Billets	
BOUZINCOURT	4-4		In Billets. marched to MERVAUX to Billets	
MERVAUX	5-4		" "	
"	6-4		" "	
"	7-4		" "	
"	8-4		" "	
"	9-4		" "	
"	10-4		" "	
"	11-4		" "	
"	12-4		" "	
"	13-4		" "	
"	14-4		" "	
"	15-4		" "	
"	16-4		" "	
"	17-4		" "	
"	18-4		" "	
"	19-4		" "	
"	20-4		" "	
"	21-4		" "	
"	22-4		" "	Auch

WAR DIARY
or
INTELLIGENCE SUMMARY.
(Erase heading not required.)

Army Form C. 2118

Place	Date	Hour	Summary of Events and Information	Remarks and references to Appendices
MERVAUX	23.4		In Billets. Marched to WARLUY to billets.	
WARLUY	24.4		" " Marched to AVELUY. "	
AVELUY	24.4		Relieved the 2nd Manchester Regt in Reserve.	
"	25.4		" " " " In Reserve.	
"	26.4		" " " "	
"	27.4		" " " "	
"	28.4		" " " Marched to the trenches. C.L.	
HAUTHUILLE	29.4		In the trenches { The 16th North'd Fus. are on our right and the 11th Royal Irish Rifles on our left.	
"	30.4		" " " "	

J. Millard Lieut-Colonel
Comdg 15th (S) Bn. Lan Fus.

96th Brigade.
32nd Division.

15th BATTALION

LANCASHIRE FUSILIERS

M A Y 1 9 1 6

Appendices attached:-
    Raid carried out 5/6th May.

WAR DIARY or INTELLIGENCE SUMMARY

(Erase heading not required.)

Army Form C. 2118

13" Lon Fus
XXII Vol 6

6.T.
3 sheets

Place	Date	Hour	Summary of Events and Information	Remarks and references to Appendices
AUTHUILLE	1.5.16		In the trenches. C.2	
"	2.5		" relieved by 16th (S) Bn. Lon. Fus. Proceeded to dugouts	
HUTHUILLE	3.5		Blackhorse Bridge Authuille and formed Brigade Reserve	
"	4.5		In Brigade Reserve. On the night of 5/6 a party of 4 officers + 50 O.R. made a successful raid on the German trenches capturing 5 prisoners. Our casualties were 2 off + 3 O.R. killed + 5 O.R. wounded.	Sam
"	5.5		"	
"	6.5	10.30 pm	" relieved by 1st Dorset Regt. Marched to Bouzincourt to billets	
BOUZINCOURT	6.5	12 mn	In billets	
"	7.5		"	
"	8.5		"	
"	9.5		"	
"	10.5		"	
"	11.5		"	
"	12.5		"	
"	13.5		" Marched to Senlis to billets.	
SENLIS	14.5		"	
"	15.5		"	
"	16.5		"	

Army Form C. 2118

WAR DIARY
or
INTELLIGENCE SUMMARY
(Erase heading not required.)

Instructions regarding War Diaries and Intelligence Summaries are contained in F. S. Regs., Part II. and the Staff Manual respectively. Title Pages will be prepared in manuscript.

Place	Date	Hour	Summary of Events and Information	Remarks and references to Appendices
SENLIS	14·5		In billets. Marched to Contay to billets.	
CONTAY	18·5		In billets	
"	19·5		" "	
"	20·5		" " Strength of Battn now is :-	
			A Coy = 210	
			B " " 207	
			C " " 216	
			D " " 216	
			749 O.R.	
			32 Officers + 749 O.R.	
CONTAY	21·5		In Billets	
"	22·5		" " On 28/5/16 Major General Rycroft Comdg. 32nd Div. attended Church Parade after which he presented the following decorations.	
"	23·5		" " Major. E.E. Maclaren Military Cross	
"	24·5		" " 10628 Sgt J. Pollitt D.C.M	
"	25·5		" " 10657 L/Cpl. J. Harbour Military Medal	
"	26·5		" " Three Awards were made in connection with the raid on night of 5-6 May 1916.	
"	27·5		" " The following Units were on parade. —	
"	28·5		" " 16th Northumberland Fus.	
"	29·5		" " Marched to BOUZINCOURT to Billets	15th Lancashire Fus.
				2nd R. Inniskilling Fus.
				96/1 Bde. M.G. Coy.
				96/1 T.M. Battery.

Army Form C. 2118

WAR DIARY
or
INTELLIGENCE SUMMARY
(Erase heading not required.)

Instructions regarding War Diaries and Intelligence Summaries are contained in F. S. Regs., Part II. and the Staff Manual respectively. Title Pages will be prepared in manuscript.

Place	Date	Hour	Summary of Events and Information	Remarks and references to Appendices
BOUZINCOURT	30-5-16		In Billets. March to Trenches. (AUTHUILLE) G.I.	
AUTHUILLE	31-5-16		In Trenches.	

J M Lloyd
Lieut. Colonel. Commdg.
15th (S) Battn Lancashire Fusiliers.

Raid carried out by 15th Lanc. Fusiliers on
the night of 5th/6th May 1916.

Narrative.

1. Scheme for Raid marked "A" attached.

2. On the night of 5th/6th May 15th Lancashire Fusiliers were located in Reserve dug outs 900x behind the nearest front line trenches.

3. Leading groups of party arrived at point of exit from our trenches at 11.0 p.m.

   At 11.30 p.m. Scouts who had been out in No mans land reported all clear.

   11.40 p.m. Bangalore Torpedo taken out and tape layers started laying out tape, going out through a previously prepared exit in our wire.

   Groups advanced along tape as previously arranged at 10 yards distance at 12 m.n. when our bombardment started they had pushed forward 130 yards in front of our front line.

   12.20 a.m. Head of column was within 60 yards of where our Artillery were dropping shells in the enemy's line. The accuracy of our fire inspired confidence to the column none of whom had before been in a similar situation.

   12.25 a.m. Bangalore torpedo brought up and placed in wire but failed to explode.

   12.30 a second torpedo which had been brought up was fired and this caused the original dud torpedo to explode. The result was a clean cut of about 10 yards in length through concertina wire and apron fencing, behind this were some knife rests but a way was found round this and through some inferior wire which was simply trampled down.

   12.33 a.m. enemy trench entered and a couple of prisoners were captured and sent back to our line.

The various parties went about their prearranged tasks
meeting with little opposition. Dug outs were entered but
removal of prisoners owing to a sort of passive resistance
on their part was very difficult. A few were taken and
bombs thrown into several dug outs. The dug outs were much
damaged by our Artillery. In one dug out which was entered
all the occupants were wounded and as the British Army is
not composed of low class Huns no bombs were thrown.
The enemy made rather a poor attempt at a counter attack,
this was driven off by a short and vigorous counter bombing
on our part.
Everyone was clear of the enemy trenches at the scheduled
time.

Notes.

a/. The night was very dark and stormy progress was difficult, but as soon as our bombardment started the light of the explosions made progress easy.

b/. The enemy counter bombardment which did not start properly till 12.45 a.m. was placed on our trenches opposite our point of entry into their trenches.

c/. The casualties known to have been inflicted on the enemy are given as 20, and the dugouts which were bombed were not empty and the bombs exploded.

d/. The tape was coloured dark brown and white to make it less conspicuous from the enemy trench.

e/. The protection afforded by the steel helmet was exemplified in several instances.

f/. The enemy finally located the point of our attack by what looked like Very lights which did not ignite properly. These were fired, probably from Reserve Trenches, from each flank of the threatened area. They were fired so as to form an arch.

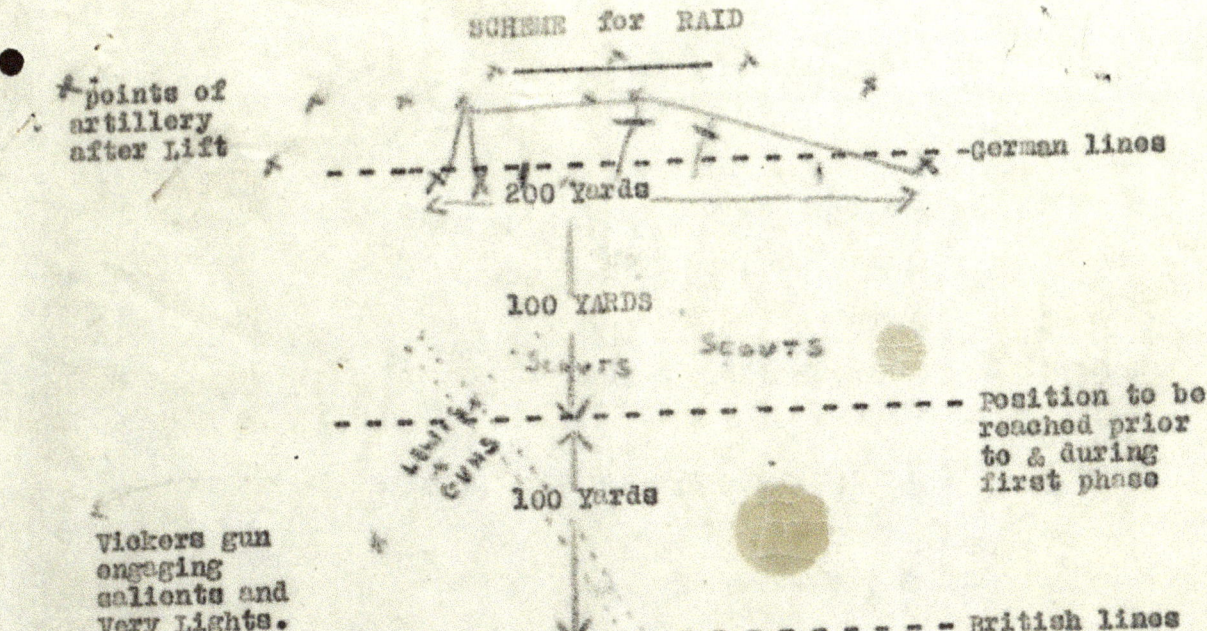

SCHEME for RAID

The General Idea is as follows:— Zero time 12 midnight

Hrs.	Min.	Sec.	
0	0	0	Start bombardment on Right Flank of the position to be attacked
0	5	0	Start bombardment on Real point
0	10	0	Start bombardment on Left flank
0	24	30	Lift bombardment on Real point
0	25	0	Continue bombardment round Real point

Barrage

After this ½ minute pause — Raiders go in

| 0 | 45 | 0 | Raiders start coming out if they have not already started back with prisoners or other prizes |
| 0 | 60 | 0 | Cease fire |

The Special Idea for Infantry:—

The party will consist of 10 groups —

in each group   4 persons

Total:— 40

Scouts, Vickers & Lewis
              guns:— 18 persons

Grand total   58

(1)

Detail of groups:-

		Off	Sgts	Men
Group 1	Advanced patrol		1	3
" 2	Leader and tape layers	1		3
" 3	Torpedo		1	3
" 4	Sentry tacklers & Blockers	1		3
" 5	" " "		1	3
" 6	Dugouts and Snatchers		1	3
" 7	" "	1		3
" 8	" "		1	3
" 9	" "		1	3
" 10	Bell ringers and clearing out party - bring up the rear coming back, after counting every one out.	1		3

(Reinforced by the torpedo men 1sgt 3 men)

..................;

Movements and dispositions.

Advanced patrol parties out and watchers.

Groups go out of trench in order, and take up positions towards half-way or thereabouts as circumstances allow - the head of the Column pushing as near as out preliminary bombardment will permit.

(During this bombardment 2" trench mortar places 15 bombs as near the spot of entry as possible. This will guide leader and help to keep direction)

At 0. 25. 0 leaders guides torpedoes to point of entry - sets torpedo and retires.

at 0. 26. 0 torpedo explodes.

Group 4 now finds itself at the head of the tape and rushes in.

Group 5 follows in.

The remaining groups are now coming along the tape in rear, and push in outer trench, and seize prisoners, or any objects of military importance.

A group is to be satisfied if it can secure and bring away 2 prisoners or a machine gun, and having obtained such success will at once withdraw reporting to the clearing officer (Group 10) who remains at the exit with his party on guard.

Group 10 commences bell-ringing and trench clearing at 0. 45½ 0 or sooner as circumstances dictate.

The O. C. Group 10 is in charge of the retirement He is to act offensively if necessary with his party to cover the retirement.

The Vickers gun is to engage enemy on our left flank

and the Lewis guns are to stop any counter attack from that flank.

The leader is to explore and send back 3 messengers, at 5 minutes intervals, from the time of entry reporting progress.

A pass-word will be given and told to our troops holding trenches so that anyone getting back off the tape line can shout it out on approaching our line.

96th Brigade.
32nd Division.

1/15th BATTALION

LANCASHIRE FUSILIERS

JUNE 1916::

WAR DIARY or INTELLIGENCE SUMMARY

(Erase heading not required.)

Army Form C.2118

Place	Date	Hour	Summary of Events and Information	Remarks and references to Appendices
AUTHUILLE	1-6-16		In trenches G.I. Sector.	
	2-6-16		" " G.I. "	
	3-6-16		" " G.I. "	
	4-6-16		" " G.I. " proceeded to Dugouts CRUCIFIX CORNER, AVELUY.	
AVELUY.	5-6-16		In reserve	
"	6-6-16		" "	
"	7-6-16		" " Marched to trenches (AUTHUILLE.) G.I.	
AUTHUILLE	8-6-16		In trenches G.I. Sector.	
"	9-6-16		" " G.I. "	
"	10-6-16		" " G.I. "	
"	11-6-16		" " G.I. "	
"	12-6-16		" " G.I. "	
"	13-6-16	MIDNIGHT	" " G.I. " Marched to WARLOY to Billets.	
WARLOY.	14-6-16	4.0AM.	In Billets WARLOY.	
"	15-6-16		" " "	
"	16-6-16		" " "	
"	17-6-16		" " "	
"	18-6-16		" " "	
"	19-6-16		" " "	
"	20-6-16		" " "	

Army Form C. 2118

WAR DIARY
or
INTELLIGENCE SUMMARY
(Erase heading not required.)

Copy

Instructions regarding War Diaries and Intelligence Summaries are contained in F. S. Regs., Part II. and the Staff Manual respectively. Title Pages will be prepared in manuscript.

Place	Date	Hour	Summary of Events and Information	Remarks and references to Appendices
WARLOY	21-6-16		In Billets WARLOY.	
"	22-6-16		" " "	
"	23-6-16		" " "	
"	24-6-16		" " "	
"	25-6-16		" " "	
"	26-6-16		" " "	
"	27-6-16		Marched to BOUZINCOURT to BILLETS.	
BOUZINCOURT.	27-6-16		at BOUZINCOURT.	
"	28-6-16		" " "	
"	29-6-16		" " "	
"	30-6-16		" Marched to trenches G.2. SECTOR.	

Original sent 1st July.

M Murphy Lieut Colonel.
Commdg 15th (S) Battn Lancashire Fusiliers

96th Inf.Bde.
32nd Div.

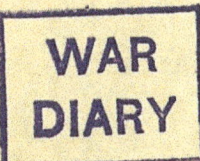

15th BATTN. THE LANCASHIRE FUSILIERS.

J U L Y

1 9 1 6

Attached:

Maps.

5.

WAR DIARY
or
INTELLIGENCE SUMMARY

(Erase heading not required.)

Army Form C. 2118.

96/32 July

Vol 8

CONFIDENTIAL
WAR DIARY
15th Lancashire Fusiliers

1st July 1916 — 31st July 1916

ORIGINAL

WAR DIARY or INTELLIGENCE SUMMARY

Army Form C. 2118

Place	Date	Hour	Summary of Events and Information	Remarks and references to Appendices
THIEPVAL Sub sector	1 July	1.0 am	Batt: arrived and took up positions for Attack.	
		7.30 am	Zero time. Batt: attacked as ordered. Disposition of Companies was as follows:-	

A Coy under command of Captain A LEE WOOD formed the Right half of attacking line —
C Coy   "   "   "   Lieut C. H WRIGHT   "   Left   "   "   "   "
B Coy   "   "   "   Captain G. Y. HEALD   — Support to A Coy
D Coy   "   "   "   Captain E. C. MacLAREN —   "   " C Coy.

2nd Lt. NOYES, FREEMAN and CLEGG led platoons of A Coy —
2nd Lt. DONNITER, JACKSON.   "   "   "   of C Coy —
2nd Lt. LODGE & AIRD led platoons of B Coy —
2nd Lt. ROBINSON, WRONG, HAMPSON, AUDNER led platoons of D Coy —
Lieut CROSSLEY, MARTYN, MARRIOTT, P J SMITH were all wounded almost immediately — and Capt. A LEE WOOD killed.

All the men got forward some considerable distance, and either fell before or after reaching the German lines. Certain Officers, NCO's and men penetrated the line and passed into the third line trench probably, where it is almost certain they were seen later by our own aeroplanes — in an isolated position. It is presumed that they gave a good account of themselves, and hoped that some were taken prisoners probably after being wounded, and received first treatment. After a leading line or two had got up to the front line French, lagging dropped up practice. The Germans continued the front line, crows in from

WAR DIARY or INTELLIGENCE SUMMARY

Army Form C. 2118

our Right, and overcame the mopping up parties - It is probable that one or two mopping up parties had been wiped out on the way over. When the later lines followed on it was found that the German front line was occupied - It was known that the earlier lines had penetrated - All attempts to get forward by the later lines resulted in the instant killing or wounding of the party moving forward. It was shown by 9.0 am that further efforts in this direction were only useless waste of life. By this time only the Adjutant and Lewis Gun Officer, and some 20 or 30 men remained as a collected body under the C.O. In the course of the next 3 or 4 hours, three were withdrawn to more sheltered positions, and individuals gradually collected, until by evening some 120 N.C.O's and men had been got together, including stretcher bearers. The result at 8.0 pm was 3 Officers, and 150 men, remaining out of a total of 24 Officers, and 600 odd who attacked in the morning -

Casualties ultimately worked out as follows:-

	Officers	Other Ranks
Killed	2	17
Wounded	4	144
Missing	15	288
	21	449

Army Form C. 2118

WAR DIARY
or
INTELLIGENCE SUMMARY
(Erase heading not required.)

Instructions regarding War Diaries and Intelligence Summaries are contained in F. S. Regs., Part II. and the Staff Manual respectively. Title Pages will be prepared in manuscript.

Place	Date	Hour	Summary of Events and Information	Remarks and references to Appendices
The Bluffs on River ANCRE	2 July		Batt. Remained here, and marched away in evening to Reserve position	
MARTINSART WOOD	3 July		Having spent night of 2/3/7. Moved back to rest at WARLOY	
WARLOY	4 July		to Rest Billets	
WARLEY	5 July		March in evening to LEALVILLERS	
LEALVILLERS	6 July		In Rest Billets Bequmin?	
LEALVILLERS	7 July		March in evening to HEDAUVILLE	
HEDAUVILLE	8 July		" " " to Senlis	
SENLIS	9 July		" " " Reserve Trenches S.E. Bouzincourt	
Reserve Trenches S.E. Bouzincourt	10 July		Resting —	
	11 July		Marched to old front line opposite Ovillers which we now partly in possession of. No troops — so that our old front line was empty now. Our support line —	
Ovillers	12 July		Remained in Support. Collected equipment, buried dead.	

Army Form C. 2118

WAR DIARY
or
INTELLIGENCE SUMMARY
(Erase heading not required.)

Instructions regarding War Diaries and Intelligence Summaries are contained in F. S. Regs., Part II. and the Staff Manual respectively. Title Pages will be prepared in manuscript.

Place	Date	Hour	Summary of Events and Information	Remarks and references to Appendices
OVILLERS	13 July		Remained in Support. Collected equipment, buried dead	
OVILLERS	14 "		"	
OVILLERS	15 "		Buried in all — 5 Officers and 81 O.R. — T. various regiments belonging to 2 & 3 divisions — 8", 25", 30".	
			March in evening to SENLIS.	
SENLIS	16.7.		Bivouac near Bonqueval — Senlis Road.	
"	17.7		Marched to HALLOY	
HALLOY	18.7		" BUNQUE MAISON.	
BUNQUE MAISON	19.7		" CROISETTE	
CROISETTE	20.7		" BOYAVAL	
BOYAVAL	21.7		" WESTREHAM	
WESTREHAM	22.7		Rested in billets	
"	23.7		"	
"	24.7		"	

1875 Wt. W593/826 1,000,000 4/15 J.B.C. & A. A.D.S.S./Forms/C. 2118.

Army Form C. 2118

WAR DIARY
or
INTELLIGENCE SUMMARY
(Erase heading not required.)

Instructions regarding War Diaries and Intelligence Summaries are contained in F.S. Regs., Part II. and the Staff Manual respectively. Title Pages will be prepared in manuscript.

Place	Date	Hour	Summary of Events and Information	Remarks and references to Appendices
WESTREHEM	25.7		In billets at Rest.	
"	26.7		March to MARLES LES MINES	
MARLES-LES-MINES	27.7		In billets at Rest. annual training	
"	28.7		" " "	
"	29.7		– Moved to HAILLICOURT	
HAILLICOURT	30.7		In billets training – Reinforcement { 99 men E. Lancashire Regt. 75 " 2 North Lancs Regt 174	
"	31.7		The Strength of Battn now is:- A Coy - 214 B Coy - 92 C " - 107 D " - 146 553 + 5 = 558 Total (Asson Bde) O.R.	

Officers - 27 - O.R.

JM Lloyd Lieut. Colonel
Comdg [illegible] Fusiliers

MAPS.

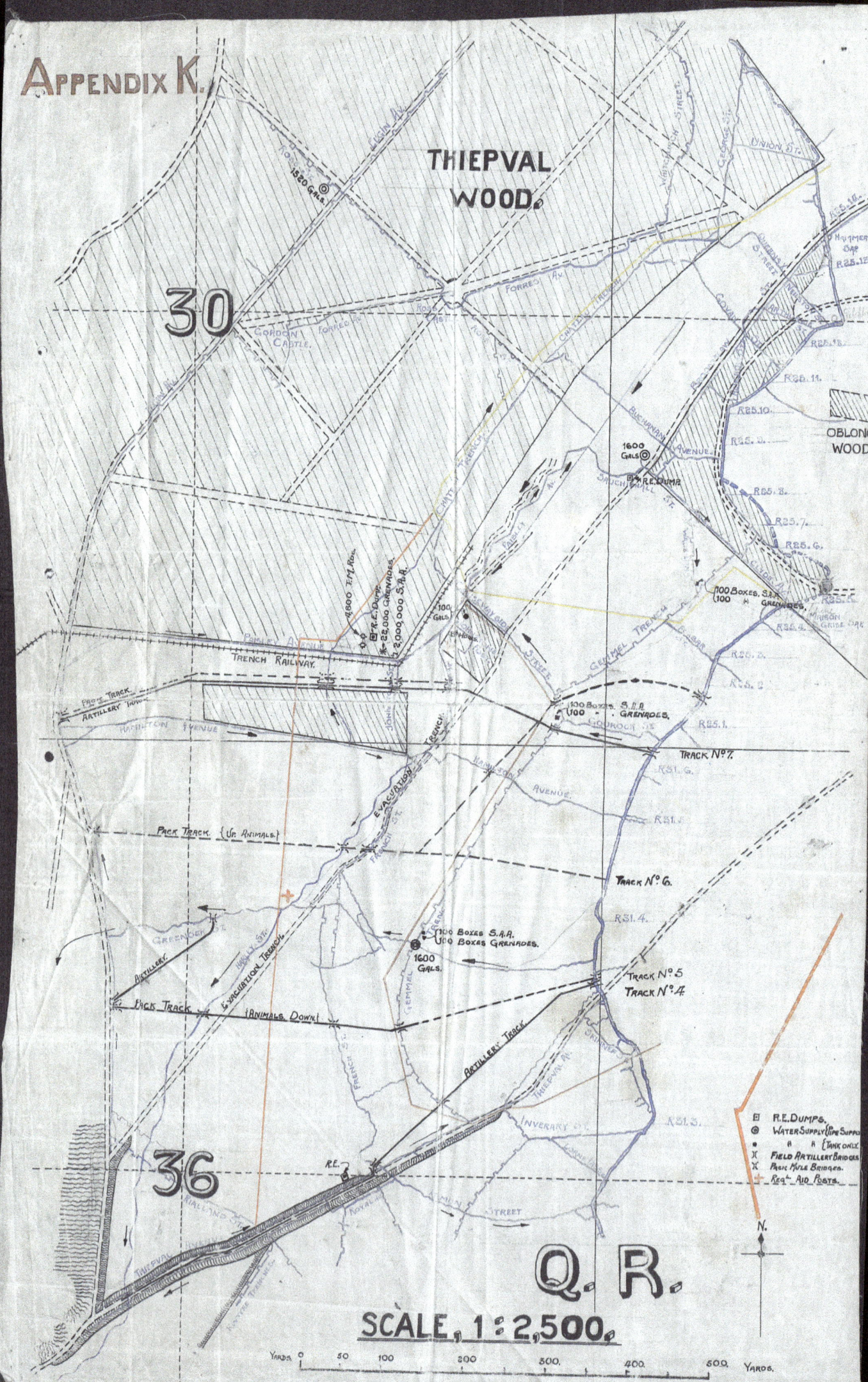

96th Brigade.
32nd Division.

15th BATTALION

LANCASHIRE FUSILIERS

AUGUST 1 9 1 6

Vol 9

9.T.
6mark

Confidential

War Diary

15th Lancashire Fusrs

from 1st August 1916 to 31st August 1916

Army Form C. 2118

15th Lancashire Fus. WAR DIARY or INTELLIGENCE SUMMARY

(Erase heading not required.)

Instructions regarding War Diaries and Intelligence Summaries are contained in F. S. Regs., Part II. and the Staff Manual respectively. Title Pages will be prepared in manuscript.

Place	Date	Hour	Summary of Events and Information	Remarks and references to Appendices
Mat HALLU COURT	1-8		In Billets Batt's Holiday to celebrate MINDEN DAY.	
"	2-8		" " Training	
"	3-8		" " "	
"	4-8		" " "	Draft of 125 O.R. from 13th, 17th, 16th & 19th & 2nd Kings Ryl. Rifle Regt
"	5-8		" " at 5:30 pm marched to Billets at BEUVRY	
BEUVRY	6-8		" " at BEUVRY. Training	
"	7-8		" " "	
"	8-8		" " "	
"	9-8		" " "	
"	10-8		" " "	
"	11-8		" " "	
"	12-8		" " "	
"	13-8		" " "	
"	14-8		" " "	
"	15-8		" " "	
"	16-8		" " "	
"	17-8		" " "	
"	18-8		" " "	

Army Form C. 2118

WAR DIARY
or
INTELLIGENCE SUMMARY
(Erase heading not required.)

Instructions regarding War Diaries and Intelligence Summaries are contained in F. S. Regs., Part II. and the Staff Manual respectively. Title Pages will be prepared in manuscript.

Place	Date	Hour	Summary of Events and Information	Remarks and references to Appendices
BEUVRY.	19-6		In Billets Training	
"	20-8		" " "	
"	21-8	12·30 pm	Marched to trenches	
TRENCHES	22-8		In trenches	
	23-8	9·0 pm	Marched to trenches RIGHT SUBSECTOR of CAMBRIN SECTION. relieved 11th BORDER REGT. We successfully blew a mine about the point A25C 20.72 (i.e. on the right of railway crater) The enemy replied with a short bombardment. All was quiet again soon after 11 p.m. Our casualties were 1. O.R. wounded.	
	24-8	11·40 pm	The enemy front line was heavily bombarded by our artillery, T.M.s etc about N and S of MINE POINT in conjunction with an a venture by the Division on our right. The enemy retaliated heavily on our front line blowing in a deep dugout. Our casualties, chiefly due to falling in of above dugout were:- Killed O.R. 10. Wounded O.R. 6.	
	25-8	30 pm	Relieved by 16th Lon Fus:- Marched to Reserve billets ANNEQUIN NORTH	
ANNEQUIN NORTH	26-8		In Billets, In Brigade Reserve.	
	27-8		" " " "	

WAR DIARY
or
INTELLIGENCE SUMMARY
(Erase heading not required.)

Army Form C. 2118

Place	Date	Hour	Summary of Events and Information	Remarks and references to Appendices
ANNEQUIN NORTH	28-8		In Billets, in Brigade Reserve.	
"	29-8		" " " " "	
TRENCHES	29-8	1·0pm	Marched to trenches RIGHT SUBSECTION of CAMBRIN SECTION. Relieved 16th LAN FUS	
"	30-8		In trenches	
"	31-8	6·0am	Enemy blew a mine on left of MINE CRATERS. This did not alter the situation to any appreciable extent. Our casualties resulting from this were Killed O.R. 2 Wounded O.R. 3. Weather since 29/8/16 has been very wet and has had bad effects on the trenches which, however, dry up wonderfully quickly here. Work on trenches has been difficult and owing to the weather has made little progress.

The strength of the Battn by Coys at present is as follows.
    A Coy   195   Off O.R.
    B "   175   28 — 630
    C "   94
    D "   162
    Not on Coy Rolls.   4
                  630

A Stone
Major Commdg
15th (S) Battn Lan Fus. | |

96th Brigade.

32nd Division.

15th BATTALION

LANCASHIRE FUSILIERS

SEPTEMBER 1 9 1 6

Vol 10

CONFIDENTIAL.

original WAR DIARY.

OF

15th (Service) Battalion The LANCASHIRE FUSILIERS.

from 1st September 1916 to 30th September 1916

(Volume 10)

Army Form C. 2118

WAR DIARY
or
INTELLIGENCE SUMMARY

(Erase heading not required.)

Instructions regarding War Diaries and Intelligence Summaries are contained in F. S. Regs., Part II. and the Staff Manual respectively. Title Pages will be prepared in manuscript.

Place	Date	Hour	Summary of Events and Information	Remarks and references to Appendices
TRENCHES	1/9/16		In trenches RIGHT SUBSECTION of CAMBRIN SECTION.	
"	2-9-16.		" "	
"	2-9-16	2.0pm	Relieved by 16th Can Inf. marched to VILLAGE LINE (SUPPORT TRENCHES).	
"	3-9-16		In VILLAGE LINE (SUPPORT TRENCHES)	
"	4-9-16		" " " "	
"	4-9-16	2.0pm	Marched to trenches RIGHT SUBSECTION of CAMBRIN SECTION in relief of 16th Can Inf.	
"	5-9-16		In trenches " "	
"	6-9-16		" "	
"	7-9-16		" "	
"	8-9-16		" "	
"	9-9-16		" "	
"	10-9-16		" "	
"	10-9-16	2.0pm	Relieved by 16th Can Inf.: Marched to Reserve Billets ANNEQUIN NORTH.	
ANNEQUIN	11-9-16		In Reserve Billets, ANNEQUIN NORTH.	
"	12-9-16		" "	
"	13-9-16		" "	
"	14-9-16		" "	
"	15-9-16		" "	
"	16-9-16		" "	
"	17-9-16		" "	

1875 Wt. W593/826 1,000,000 4/15 J.B.C. & A. A.D.S.S./Forms/C. 2118.

Army Form C. 2118

WAR DIARY
or
INTELLIGENCE SUMMARY
(Erase heading not required.)

Instructions regarding War Diaries and Intelligence Summaries are contained in F. S. Regs., Part II. and the Staff Manual respectively. Title Pages will be prepared in manuscript.

Place	Date	Hour	Summary of Events and Information	Remarks and references to Appendices
ANNEQUIN	18-9-16		In Reserve Billets ANNEQUIN NORTH.	
"	19-9-16		"	
"	20-9-16	4-0pm	Relieved by 1st Dorset Regt & marched to Rest Billets ANNEZIN	
ANNEZIN	20-9-16		Arrived Rest Billets ANNEZIN. In Divisional Reserve	
"	21-9-16		" " " "	
"	22-9-16		" " " "	
"	23-9-16		" " " "	
"	24-9-16		" " " "	
"	25-9-16		" " " "	
"	26-9-16	9-0am	Marched to Trenches LEFT SUBSECTION, GUINCHY SECTION, in relief of 17th H.L.I.	
TRENCHES	27-9-16		In Trenches	
"	28-9-16		" "	
"	29-9-16		" "	
"	30-9-16	12-0 noon	"Relieved" by 16th Can Inf & marched to VILLAGE LINE to SUPPORT TRENCHES in relief of 16th NORTHUMBERLAND Fus in Brigade Support.	
"	30-9-16		The strength of Battn by Coys is as follows:— A Coy. 184 B. " 196 C. " 116 D. " 154 Total. 650	

A Stone
Major Commanding
15th (S) Batt. Can Inf.

WAR DIARY
or
INTELLIGENCE SUMMARY

Diary
- of -
15th Lancashire
Fusiliers

Sept:- 1916

96th Brigade.

32nd Division.

15th BATTALION

LANCASHIRE FUSILIERS

OCTOBER 1 9 1 6

Vol II

Confidential
War Diary
of
15th (S) Batt. Lancashire Fusiliers

from October 1st 1916 to October 31st 1916

Vol II

11.T.
3 sheets

WAR DIARY or INTELLIGENCE SUMMARY

Army Form C. 2118

(Erase heading not required.)

Instructions regarding War Diaries and Intelligence Summaries are contained in F.S. Regs., Part II. and the Staff Manual respectively. Title Pages will be prepared in manuscript.

Place	Date	Hour	Summary of Events and Information	Remarks and references to Appendices
SUPPORT TRENCHES	1-10-16		In Support Trenches (VILLAGE LINE) in Brigade Support.	
CUINCHY	2-10-16		"	
"	3-10-16		"	
TRENCHES	4-10-16		Marched to LEFT SUBSECTION of the CUINCHY SECTION relieved 16th Can Inf.	
"	5-10-16		In trenches	
"	6-10-16		"	
"	7-10-16		"	
"	8-10-16		Relieved by 16th Can Inf. marched to Billets at LE QUESNOY in Bde Reserve.	
LE QUESNOY	9-10-16		In Billets at LE QUESNOY in Bde reserve.	
"	10-10-16		"	
BETHUNE	10-10-16 2-30pm		Marched to Billets at MONTMORENCY BARRACKS. BETHUNE. Relieved by 1st D.C.L.I.	
"	11-10-16		In Billets	
"	12-10-16		"	
"	13-10-16		"	
"	14-10-16		"	Received Reinforcement 150 O.R.
OURTON	15-10 to 9-0am 16-10-16		Marched to Billets at OURTON	
MAGNICOURT-EN-CONTE	16-10-16 8-0am		" " " " MAGNICOURT-EN-CONTÉ	
MAIZIÈRES	17-10-16 9-0am		" " " " MAIZIÈRES	
ORVILLE	18-10-16 6-30am		" " " " ORVILLE	
"	19-10-16 -		In Billets at "	

INTELLIGENCE SUMMARY

(Erase heading not required.)

Summaries are contained in F.S. Regs., Part II. and the Staff Manual respectively. Title Pages will be prepared in manuscript.

Place	Date	Hour	Summary of Events and Information	Remarks and references to Appendices
ORVILLE	20-10-16		In Billets at ORVILLE.	
"	21-10-16		Draft of 50 O.R. arrived from Base.	
"	21-10-16	11-10am	Marched to VADENCOURT WOOD.	
VADENCOURT WOOD	22-10-16		In Billets Huts	
"	23-10-16	12-45pm	Marched to Bivouacs in BRICKFIELDS AREA. BOUZINCOURT – ALBERT ROAD	
BRICKFIELDS	24-10-16		In " " " "	
"	25-10-16		" " " " "	
"	26-10-16		" " " " "	
"	26-10-16	12-20pm	Marched to Billets at WARLOY.	
WARLOY	27-10-16		In " " "	
"	28-10-16		" " " "	
"	29-10-16		" " " "	
"	30-10-16		" " " "	
"	31-10-16		Marched to Billets at HERISSART.	
"	31-10-16		Strength of Battn on 31st inst was as follows:-	

```
        A  213.
        B  195
        C  227
        D  200
     Total 835.
```

R. Stone
Major Commdg
15th (S) Battn Lan Fus.

96th Brigade.

32nd Division.

15th BATTALION

LANCASHIRE FUSILIERS

NOVEMBER 1916

W A R   D I A R Y.

15th LANCASHIRE FUSILIERS.

From November 1st to 30th. 1916.

WAR DIARY
or
INTELLIGENCE SUMMARY

(Erase heading not required.)

Army Form C. 2118

Instructions regarding War Diaries and Intelligence Summaries are contained in F. S. Regs., Part II. and the Staff Manual respectively. Title Pages will be prepared in manuscript.

Place	Date	Hour	Summary of Events and Information	Remarks and references to Appendices
HERISSART	12th–15th		In billets at HERISSART.	
	13th		Marched to Billets at WARLOY.	
	14th		Marched to THIEPVAL AREA, Dugouts in PAISLEY AVENUE in support to the 19th Division.	
THIEPVAL AREA.	14th & 17th		Remained at PAISLEY AVENUE in support to 19th Division	
	17th		Marched to billets at MAILLY-MAILLET.	
BEAUMONT HAMEL	18th		Marched to BEAUMONT HAMEL took over NEW MUNICH TRENCH & part of WAGON Rd. (Q.5C.9d) from 17th H.L.I. (Attached 97th Inf. Bde)	
	19th–23rd		Remained in trenches consolidating. (Rejoined 96th Inf. Bde.)	
	24th		Relieved by 1st South Staffordshire Regt. marched to billets at MAILLY-	
	25th		MAILLET. Went to AMPLIERS by Motor bus.	
	26th		Marched to billets at MONTRELET.	
	26th–30th		In Billets at MONTRELET.	

The strength of Batt. on 30th inst. was

Officers O.R.
26. - 812.

A	198	
B	194	
C	221	
D	199	
	Total 812	

A. Stone
Lieut Col Commdg
13th (S) Batth Lancashire Fusiliers

96th Brigade.

32nd Division.

15th BATTALION

LANCASHIRE FUSILIERS

DECEMBER 1916

Vol 13

War Diary
of
15th (S) Battn Lancashire Fusiliers.

From 1-12-16. to 31-12-16.

WAR DIARY
or
INTELLIGENCE SUMMARY
(Erase heading not required.)

Army Form C. 2118

Place	Date	Hour	Summary of Events and Information	Remarks and references to Appendices
MONTRELET	1/12/16.		In Billets at MONTRELET. Training	
	2nd			
	3rd			
	4th			
	5th			
	6th			
	7th			
	8th			
	9th			
	10th			
	11th			
	12th			
	13th			
	14th			
	15th			
	16th			
	17th			
	18th			
	19th			
	20th			
	21st			
	22nd		Lieut Colonel H.G. Harrison, assumed Command of Battn on 23/12/16.	
	23rd			
	24th			
	25th			
	26th			
	27th			
	28th		The strength of Battn by Coys is as follows:- A 238 B 230 C 244 D 236 30 Officers — 948 O.R.	
	29th			
	30th			
	31st		H.G. Harrison Lieut Col Commdg 15th (S) Batt Hampshires	

Vol 14

WAR DIARY
of
15th (S) Battn Lancashire Fusiliers
1-1-17 to 31-1-17.

Army Form C. 2118

WAR DIARY
or
INTELLIGENCE SUMMARY
(Erase heading not required.)

Instructions regarding War Diaries and Intelligence Summaries are contained in F.S. Regs., Part II. and the Staff Manual respectively. Title Pages will be prepared in manuscript.

Place	Date	Hour	Summary of Events and Information	Remarks and references to Appendices
MONTRELET	1-1-17		In Billets at MONTRELET. Training	
"	2-1-17		" " " " "	
"	3-1-17		" " " " "	
"	4-1-17		" " " " "	
"	5-1-17		" " " " "	
"	6-1-17		Marched to Billets at BEAUQUESNE	
BEAUQUESNE	7-1-17		Bus to Atois in relief of 4th Battn. Royal Fusiliers	
BUS	8-1-17		In Billets at Bus, in Divisional Reserve.	
"	9-1-17		" " " " "	
"	10-1-17		" " " " "	
"	11-1-17		" " " " "	
"	12-1-17		" " " " "	
"	13-1-17		" " " " "	
COURCELLES	14-1-17		Marched to Billets at COURCELLES in relief of 11th Border Regt. in Brigade Reserve	
"	15-1-17		In Billets at COURCELLES	
"	16-1-17		Marched to Trenches in RIGHT SUBSECTOR (C3) in relief of 16th Ham Fus.	
Trenches	17-1-17		In Trenches "	
"	18-1-17		Relieved by 16th Ham Fus & marched to Billets at COURCELLES.	
COURCELLES	19-1-17		In Billets at COURCELLES	
"	20-1-17		Marched to Trenches in RIGHT SUBSECTOR (C3) in relief of 16th Ham Fus	
Trenches	21-1-17		In trenches "	
MAILLY-MAILLET	22-1-17		Relieved by 2nd Royal Innis Fus & marched to Billets at MAILLY-MAILLET	

1875 Wt. W593/826 1,000,000 4/15 J.B.C. & A. A.D.S.S./Forms/C. 2118.

Army Form C. 2118

WAR DIARY
or
INTELLIGENCE SUMMARY
(Erase heading not required.)

Place	Date	Hour	Summary of Events and Information	Remarks and references to Appendices
MAILLY-MAILLET	23-1-17		In billets at MAILLY-MAILLET.	
	24-1-17		Marched to trenches. RIGHT SUBSECTOR (C3) in relief of 2nd Royal Irish Fus.	
TRENCHES	25-1-17		In trenches.	
MAILLY-MAILLY	26-1-17		Relieved by 10th Northumberland Fus marched to Billets at MAILLY-MAILLET.	
	27-1-17		In Billets at MAILLY-MAILLET.	
	28-1-17		Marched to trenches RIGHT SUBSECTOR (C3) in relief of 10th Northumberland Fus.	
TRENCHES	29-1-17		In trenches "	
	30-1-17		Relieved by 16th Ham & Fus marched to Billets at BERTRANCOURT.	
BERTRAN- COURT	31-1-17		In Billets at BERTRANCOURT.	

A. Stone
Major Commdg.
15th (S) Battn Royal Fus.

Army Form C. 2118.

WAR DIARY
or
INTELLIGENCE SUMMARY
(Erase heading not required.)

Vol 15

Originals
War Diary
of
15th Bn. Kings Foresters

1st of February 1917
Do. 28th of February 1917

WAR DIARY or INTELLIGENCE SUMMARY

(Erase heading not required.)

Army Form C. 2118

Instructions regarding War Diaries and Intelligence Summaries are contained in F.S. Regs., Part II. and the Staff Manual respectively. Title Pages will be prepared in manuscript.

Place	Date	Hour	Summary of Events and Information	Remarks and references to Appendices
BERTRANCOURT	1/2/17		In Billets at BERTRANCOURT	
MAILLY MAILLET	2/2/17		Marched to Billets at MAILLY MAILLET.	
"	3/2/17		In Billets at MAILLY MAILLET	
"	4/2/17		" " "	
Trenches	5-2-17		Marched to Trenches, Rt Subsector BEAUMONT HAMEL in relief of 17th H.L.I.	
"	6-2-17		In trenches	
"	7-2-17		" "	
"	8-2-17		" "	
MAILLY-MAILLET	9-2-17		Relieved by 16th Ran Regt & Marched to Billets MAILLY-MAILLET. (2 companies in reserve at AUCHONVILLERS)	
"	10-2-17		In Billets at MAILLY MAILLET.	
"	11-2-17		" " "	
LOUVENCOURT	12-2-17		Marched to Billets at LOUVENCOURT.	
"	13-2-17		In Billets at LOUVENCOURT	
HERRISART	14-2-17		Marched to Billets at HERRISART.	
"	15-2-17		In Billets at "	
PIERREGOT	16-2-17		Marched to Billets at PIERREGOT	
VILLERS BOCAGE	17-2-17		" " " VILLERS-BOCAGE	
"	18-2-17		" " " "	
"	19-2-17		" " " "	
RIVERY	20-2-17		" " " RIVERY	
THENNES	21-3-17		" " " THENNES.	
"	22-2-17		In Billets at "	
LE QUESNEL	23-2-17		Marched to Billets at LE QUESNEL.	

Army Form C. 2118

WAR DIARY
or
INTELLIGENCE SUMMARY
(Erase heading not required.)

Instructions regarding War Diaries and Intelligence Summaries are contained in F.S. Regs., Part II. and the Staff Manual respectively. Title Pages will be prepared in manuscript.

Place	Date	Hour	Summary of Events and Information	Remarks and references to Appendices
LE QUESNEL Trenches.	24-2-17		Marched to Trenches JENA Sub Sector. S. of KUROPATKIN (2 Coys in support at WARVILLERS).	
"	25-2-17		In Trenches. " " " "	
"	26-2-17		" " " " "	
"	27-2-17		" " " " "	
"	28-2-17		Relieved 2nd R. Innis Fus. in Trenches. WAGRAM Sub Sector.	

H.G. Hanson Lieut Col.
Commdg. 15th (S) Bn. Lancashire Fusiliers.

1875 Wt. W593/826 1,000,000 4/15 J.B.C. & A. A.D.S.S./Forms/C. 2118.

Vol 16

16.T
5 sheets

W A R   D I A R Y.

of

15 th (s) Bn. Lancashire Fusiliers.

From 1st March 1917.   To 31st March 1917.

WAR DIARY

of

105th (S) Battalion Two

from 1/8/17 to 31/8/17

WAR DIARY
or
INTELLIGENCE SUMMARY
(Erase heading not required.)

Army Form C. 2118

Instructions regarding War Diaries and Intelligence Summaries are contained in F.S. Regs., Part II. and the Staff Manual respectively. Title Pages will be prepared in manuscript.

Place	Date	Hour	Summary of Events and Information	Remarks and references to Appendices
In Trenches	1/3/17		In trenches WAGRAM SUBSECTOR	
"	2/3/17		Relieved by 16th H.L.I. & Marched to billets at LE QUESNEL	
LE QUESNEL	3/3/17		In Billets at LE QUESNEL	
"	4/3/17		" " " "	
"	5/3/17		" " " "	
"	6/3/17		" " " "	
"	7/3/17		" " " "	
"	8/3/17		Marched to BOUCHOIR in Brigade Reserve	
BOUCHOIR	9/3/17		In Brigade Reserve at BOUCHOIR	
"	10/3/17		" " " "	
"	11/3/17		Marched to trenches in relief of 2nd R INNIS. FUS.	
Trenches	12/3/17		In Trenches	
"	13/3/17		"	
"	14/3/17		Relieved by 16th Lan Fus in	
"	15/3/17		a THE QUESNOY	
LE QUESNOY	16/3/17		Marched to LE QUESNOY	
"	17/3/17		Batn relieved French troops 62nd Division in BOIS-ENZ. WOOD at about 11-30am. 16th Northumberland Fus on our left. Batn moved back to S.A.P. 7 in AUSTERLITZ Subsector at about 8-30pm. being relieved by 2nd R Innis Fus.	

1875 Wt. W593/826 1,000,000 4/15 J.B.C. & A. A.D.S.S./Forms/C. 2118.

WAR DIARY
or
INTELLIGENCE SUMMARY

(Erase heading not required.)

Army Form C. 2118

Place	Date	Hour	Summary of Events and Information	Remarks and references to Appendices
	18/3/17		Battn will advance on right with 16th R.F on the left relieving 2nd R. Innis. Two of the Southern edge of DAMERY. This was completed by 11.0 a.m. Battn continued to advance at 5.0 p.m. to SEPT-FOURS & took up a position there relieving the 140th French Regt. Pushed our a patrol to RETHONVILLE.	
	19/3/17		Battn continued advance to the line BREUIL exclusive to QUIQUERY BRIDGE inclusive. Battn in position by 12-0 noon. Battn ordered at 4-30 pm to take up line WEST side of the SOMME CANAL – OFFOY BRIDGE inclusive to CANIZY inclusive, Battn HQ. Dugouts near OFFOY BRIDGE.	
	20/3/17		Battn (again) ordered to cross River SOMME & take up line OFFOY – TOULLE Road inclusive to junction of the OFFOY-BUNY Railway – OFFOY-MATIGNY Road inclusive. Battn crossed River at 5-30 a.m. B Coys (C & D) on outpost duties (B Coy ordered to join up with 14th Suffolks on the BUNY-MATIGNY Road) A Coy in support.	
	21/3/17		Battn relieved by 16th Lancs. two marched to CANIZY where they were billetted.	
	22/3/17		Battn worked on trenches for main line of defence.	
	23/3/17		" " " " " " " "	
	24/3/17		" " " " " " " "	

WAR DIARY
or
INTELLIGENCE SUMMARY
(Erase heading not required.)

Army Form C. 2118

Place	Date	Hour	Summary of Events and Information	Remarks and references to Appendices
	25/3/17		Battn. marched on Denoeux for Main line of Defence	
	26/3/17		" " " " " " "	
	27/3/17		" " " " " " "	
	28/3/17		" " " " " " "	
	29/3/17		Marched to Billets at MATIGNY.	
	30/3/17		In Billets	
	31/3/17		Taken over Billets of 17th K.L.I. in GERMAINE.	

J.C. Harrison
Lieut Colonel Comndg
15th (S) Battn Lancashire Fusiliers

CONFIDENTIAL.

WAR DIARY.

OF

15th (S) BATTN. LANCASHIRE FUSILIERS.

From 1st April 1917.

To 30th April 1917.

Confidential
War Diary
of
15th (S) Battalion Lancashire Fusiliers

from 1st/17 to 30th/17

Army Form C. 2118

WAR DIARY
or
INTELLIGENCE SUMMARY
(Erase heading not required.)

Instructions regarding War Diaries and Intelligence Summaries are contained in F.S. Regs., Part II. and the Staff Manual respectively. Title Pages will be prepared in manuscript.

Place	Date	Hour	Summary of Events and Information	Remarks and references to Appendices
	1/7/17		Battalion ordered to hold itself in readiness at short notice any time after 6 am & proceed to Le CHATEAU de POMMERY. Battalion proceeded at 7.30 am from GERMAINE, at 12.0 noon Battalion got orders to attack SAVY WOOD in conjunction with 2nd R. Innis Fus who were to take Small wood on the S.E of SAVY WOOD. Battalion attacked SAVY WOOD at 3-30 pm. Casualties approximately 7 Officers & 100 O.R. Battalion entrenched & consolidated along Railway line running through SAVY WOOD where it remained until morning of 15th. during which time the weather was very changeable chiefly Rain, snow & hail. About 20 Casualties were suffered during this time from enemy shelling.	
	15/7/17		The Battalion was relieved by 15th H.L.I. in the Railway Cutting & proceeded to Billets at GERMAINE. Remained here until 9.30 am 14th instant during which time the Battalion was bathed & had a clean change of clothing.	
	14/7/17		Received orders to proceed to HOMMON WOOD & be in Reserve to 97th Inf Bde & act with their orders.	

A/Lt Faurier Lt Colonel

WAR DIARY
or
INTELLIGENCE SUMMARY
(Erase heading not required.)

Army Form C. 2118

Place	Date	Hour	Summary of Events and Information	Remarks and references to Appendices
	14/7/17		The Battalion (Greacles) to HORNON.	
	15/7/17		The Battalion took over the line extending from BEPY FARM exclusive to the FAYET-OMISSY Road inclusive from the 16th to H.L.I. where it remained until night 16th/17th when it was relieved by 16th Lancs Fus. During the time it came under heavy shelling. On relief marched back to ATILLY	
	18/7/17		ATILLY. Battalion chiefly on Working parties between HORNON & FAYET.	
	19/7/17		Batt relieved by 4th R. Berks Reg? & marched to Billets at GERMAINE	
	20/7/17 21/7/17		In billets GERMAINE. The Battalion proceeded to FLEZ where it has been since (2nd). Weather much improved.	

Jeff. Harrison
Lieut Col Commg
15th (S) Batt. Lancs Fus.

Vol 18

War Diary
of
15th S. Batt. Lancashire Fusiliers
from May 1st 1917 to May 31st 1917.

18.T.
2 sheets

Army Form C. 2118

WAR DIARY
or
INTELLIGENCE SUMMARY
(Erase heading not required.)

Place	Date	Hour	Summary of Events and Information	Remarks and references to Appendices
FLEZ	1/5/17 – 16/5/17		In Billets at FLEZ. Training.	
	16/5/17		On 15/5/17 The Battalion was inspected by G.O.C. 32nd Division. 3/5/17, 11/5/17, 15/5/17 took part in Brigade Field day. IV th Corps.	
	16/5/17 – 17/5/17		Marched to Billets at LICOURT, ROSIERES.	
	18/5/17 – 30/5/17		In Billets at ROSIERES. Training. Brigade Sports were held on 26/5/17.	
	30/5/17	7.30 a.m.	Marched to Billets at GUILLAUCOURT.	
	31/5/17		In Billets at GUILLAUCOURT.	

J.H. Harrison
Lieut Colonel
Commdg 15th (S) Battn Lancs Fus.

Vol 19

Confidential
War Diary
of
15th (S) Battn Lancashire Fusiliers
from 1/5/17 to 30/6/17

WAR DIARY
or
INTELLIGENCE SUMMARY
(Erase heading not required.)

Army Form C. 2118

Instructions regarding War Diaries and Intelligence Summaries are contained in F. S. Regs., Part II. and the Staff Manual respectively. Title Pages will be prepared in manuscript.

Place	Date	Hour	Summary of Events and Information	Remarks and references to Appendices
GUILLAUCOURT	1/6/17		Marched to GUILLAUCOURT STATION & entrained for CAESTRE.	
CAESTRE	2/6/17		Detrained at CAESTRE & marched to billets at NOOTE-BOOM-STEENT-JE.	
NOOTE-BOOM	3/6/17	10½	In Billets at NOOTE BOOM.	
	11/6/17		Marched to fields at ST. SYLVESTRE-CAPEL.	
	12/6/17		Marched to fields at WORMHOUDT.	
	13/6/17		In Billets at WORMHOUDT.	
	14/6/17		Marched to Billets ZUYDCOOTE.	
	15/6/17		In Billets at ZUYDCOOTE. Battalion bathed in the Sea	
	16/6/17	1·00pm	Marched to LEFFRINCKHOUCKE and entrained for COXYDE. Detrained at COXYDE & marched to CHAMPERMONT CAMP.	
		4·30pm	Marched to Support line "A" Subsector, Left Sector. Relieved 165th French Inf. Regt.	
	17/6/17		In Support line "A" Subsector Left Sector	
	18/6/17		Relieved 165th French Inf. Regt. in front line "A" Subsector, Left Sector. "A" Co. became first Battalion to be on extreme left of British Front covered on this day.	

WAR DIARY
or
INTELLIGENCE SUMMARY

(Erase heading not required.)

Army Form C. 2118

Place	Date	Hour	Summary of Events and Information	Remarks and references to Appendices
	19/6/17		In trenches "A" Subsector, Reft Sector.	
	20/6/17		" " " " "	
	21/6/17		" " " " "	
	22/6/17		" " " " "	
	23/6/17	10-0p	Relieved by 1st Batth. Black Watch & marched to huts at JEAN BART Camp COXYDE-BAINS. 16 casualties during the tour of the trenches viz. 1 Officer wounded & 30 O.R. killed - 13 O.R. Wounded.	
	24/6/17		In huts at JEAN BART Camp.	
	25/6/17		Marched to Camp (under Canvas) at GHYVELDE.	
	26/6/17-30/6/17		In Camp at GHYVELDE. Training.	

J.G. Jamieson
Lieut. Colonel
15th (S) Batth. Lanco Fus.

Vol 20

War Diary
of
15th (S) Battalion Lancashire Fusiliers

from 1/7/17 to 31/7/17

20 T
3 sheets

WAR DIARY
or
INTELLIGENCE SUMMARY
(Erase heading not required.)

Army Form C. 2118

Place	Date	Hour	Summary of Events and Information	Remarks and references to Appendices
GHYVELDE	12-6-17		In Camp GHYVELDE Training (Under Canvas)	
RIBAILLET	6/7/17	6.0am	Marched to Camp RIBAILLET (60x40E) in Dunkerque Reserve. Relieved 15th C.I.	
	7/17		In Huts at RIBAILLET CAMP	
	8/17		" "	
	9/17		" "	
	10/17	10.45pm	Battalion proceeded to Support line in NIEUPORT. Relieves 16th Northd Fus	
	11/17		Battalion in Support line NIEUPORT	
	12/17	7.0am	Relieved by 16th Northd Fus. Proceeds to RIBAILLET CAMP Major G.T. Hunter-Gray (Black Watch) took over Command of Batt. from Lieut Col. H.G. HARRISON (2nd Manchester Regt)	
	13/17		In Huts at RIBAILLET CAMP.	
	14/17	11.45pm	Marches to Support line — NIEUPORT Relieves 5/6 Royal Scots	
	15/17		In Support line	
	16/17		Relieved 2nd Manchester Regt in Right Sub Sector	
	17/17		Relieved by 11th Yorks & Lancs Reg. 9.1 marches to RIBAILLET Camp	
	18/17		Marches to JEAN BART. Camp	Grey

Army Form C. 2118

WAR DIARY
or
INTELLIGENCE SUMMARY
(Erase heading not required.)

Place	Date	Hour	Summary of Events and Information	Remarks and references to Appendices
Jean-Bart Camp.	18-27/7		In Huts at Jean-Bart Camp.	
Bray-Dunes	27/7	3-0pm	Marched to Camp at Bray-Dunes.	
	28/7		In Camp (Canvas) at Bray-Dunes	
	29/7			
	30/7			
	31/7	6-0am	Marched to Coxyde (Bivouacs).	
			Casualties during the month were as follow	
			Officers Wounded Capt. Moody	
			Capt. R. Morton 11/7	
			2nd Lieut. Smith Ryder 11/7	
			2nd Lieut. Hudson 11/7	
			Bennyson (since returned) 11/7	
			Other Ranks. 114. 91. 11	
			Total Casualties 1 off 125 O.R.	
			G.Y. Hunter Orr Major Comdg	
			15th (S) Batt. Royal Scots Fus.	

War Diary

15th (S) Battalion Lancashire Fusiliers

From 1/8/17 to 31/8/17

Army Form C. 2118

WAR DIARY
or
INTELLIGENCE SUMMARY
(Erase heading not required.)

Instructions regarding War Diaries and Intelligence Summaries are contained in F.S. Regs., Part II. and the Staff Manual respectively. Title Pages will be prepared in manuscript.

Place	Date	Hour	Summary of Events and Information	Remarks and references to Appendices
COXYDE	1/7	6·0pm	The Battalion marched to Huts at RIBAILLET CAMP in Brigade Reserve	
	2/7		In Brigade Reserve at RIBAILLET CAMP	
	3/7		—	
	4/7	8·15pm	Two Companies marched to Trenches in ST GEORGES SECTOR (S.E. NIEUPORT) and Relieved 2nd R. Innis. Fus.	
			The remaining two Companies in Huts at REBAILLET CAMP.	
	5/7		In Trenches in ST GEORGES SECTOR.	
	6/7		—	
	14/7			
	15/7	1·0am	The two Companies in the line relieved by the two Companies in Reserve at RIBAILLET CAMP. The relieved proceeded to RIBAILLET CAMP.	
	16/7		In Trenches ST GEORGES SECTOR.	
	17/7	10·0pm	Relieved by 4th Battn. Kings Liverpool Regt & marched to Billets at COXYDE	
	18/7	3·30pm	Marched to BRAY DUNES (Under Canvas)	
	19/7		Under Canvas at BRAY DUNES (Training).	
	28/7			
	29/7	6·0am	Marched to COXYDE (AUSTRALIA CAMP) in Divisional Reserve.	

G.4.E.G

WAR DIARY
or
INTELLIGENCE SUMMARY
(Erase heading not required.)

Army Form C. 2118

Place	Date	Hour	Summary of Events and Information	Remarks and references to Appendices
COXYDE	30/5/17 31/7		In Huts at AUSTRALIA CAMP in Divisional Reserve " " " " " " " " " " " " Casualties during the month were as follows. Killed Wounded Missing Gassed Officers — — — — O.R. — 4 36 2 1 Total Casualties 43 G.Y. Hunter Gray Lieut Col. Commdg 15th (S) Battn Lancashire Fusiliers	

22.T
3 sheets

Vol 22

Confidential

War Diary

of

15th (S) Battn Lancashire Fusiliers

From 1-9-17 to 30-9-17

WAR DIARY
or
INTELLIGENCE SUMMARY
(Erase heading not required.)

Army Form C. 2118

Place	Date	Hour	Summary of Events and Information	Remarks and references to Appendices
COXYDE	1/7		In huts at AUSTRALIA Camp in Divisional Reserve	
	6/7		"	
	12/7		"	
NIEUPORT	12/7	8.0pm	Relieved 1st DORSET REGT in Left Subsector of LEFT SECTOR.	
	13/7		In trenches in Left Subsector	
	14/7		"	
	15/7		"	
	16/7		Battalion relieved 16th LAN FUS in Support line REDAN	
	17/7		In Support line REDAN (Dragon's)	
	18/7		"	
	19/7		"	
	20/7		Battalion relieved 16th LAN FUS in Left Sub-Sector.	
	21/7		In trenches in Left Sub-Sector	
	22/7		"	
	23/7		Battalion relieved 16th LAN FUS in Support line. REDAN	
	24/7		In Support line REDAN (Dragon's)	
	25/7		"	
	26/7		"	
	27/7		Relieved by 11th BORDER REGT in Support line REDAN,	
	28/7		marched to Billets at AUSTRALIA CAMP.	
	29/7		In huts at AUSTRALIA CAMP	
	30/7		"	

C.Y.A.G.

Army Form C. 2118

WAR DIARY
or
INTELLIGENCE SUMMARY
(Erase heading not required.)

Place	Date	Hour	Summary of Events and Information	Remarks and references to Appendices
			Casualties during the month were as follows	
			Killed Wounded	
			Officers 1 3	
			O.R. 11 46	
			Total Casualties 61	
			C.H. Amster Gray, Lieut-Col.	
			Commdg 15th (S) Batln Lancashire Fusiliers	

Instructions regarding War Diaries and Intelligence Summaries are contained in F. S. Regs., Part II. and the Staff Manual respectively. Title Pages will be prepared in manuscript.

Confidential.

War Diary

of

15th (S) Batt. Lancashire Fusiliers

from October 1st 1917.   October 31st 1917.

Army Form C. 2118.

WAR DIARY
or
INTELLIGENCE SUMMARY.
(Erase heading not required.)

Instructions regarding War Diaries and Intelligence Summaries are contained in F. S. Regs., Part II. and the Staff Manual respectively. Title pages will be prepared in manuscript.

Place	Date	Hour	Summary of Events and Information	Remarks and references to Appendices
COXYDE.	1/5/17		In Divisional Reserve. In Huts at AUSTRALIA CAMP.	
	2/5/17	5:0p	Marched to Billets at LA-PANNE.	
LA-PANNE	3/5/17 4/5/17		In Billets at LA-PANNE. " " "	
ZUYDCOOTE	5/5/17	6.0am	Marched to ZUYDCOOTE & took over Coast Defence System & Billets from 20th D.L.I.	
	16		On Coast Defence & Training at ZUYDCOOTE.	
	24th		" " " "	
	25th	11:0am	Marched to Billets at UXEM.	
	26th	7:0am	" " " " ERINGHEM.	
	16		" " " "	
	31st		In Billets at ERINGHEM (Training).	

H K Watson Major Lieut Col
Commdg 15th (S) Battn Lancashire Fusiliers

Vol 24

Confidential

War Diary
of
15th Batt. Lancashire Fusiliers

November 1st 1917
to
November 30th 1917

24.T
8 mls

WAR DIARY
or
INTELLIGENCE SUMMARY.

(Erase heading not required.)

Army Form C. 2118.

Place	Date	Hour	Summary of Events and Information	Remarks and references to Appendices
ERINGHEM	1/4/17		In Billets at ERINGHEM Training	
	6/4/17		" " " "	
	10/4/17		Battalion marches to billets at H.b.t.9.3. (Ref Sheet 27) near ARNEKE	
ARNEKE	11/4/17		" " " " "	
WINNEZEELE	12/4/17		" " " WINNEZEELE Area.	
SCHOOL CAMP	13/4/17		" " " School Camp (h.3.d.) Ref Sheet 27 near POPERINGHE.	
"	16/4/17		" " " " " "	
"	22/4/17		In Huts at School Camp (h.3.d) Ref Sheet 27. Training	
HOSPITAL FARM	23/4/17	8-10am	Battalion marched to Camp at HOSPITAL FARM (B.19a.3.2) Sheet 28.	
"	26/4/17		Battalion in Huts at HOSPITAL FARM. Training	
"	27/4/17		" " " " "	
IRISH FARM	28/4/17	9.15am	Battalion proceed by rail to IRISH FARM near YPRES	
"	29/4/17		Battalion in tents at IRISH FARM Camp	
"	30/4/17	6.30pm	Marched to trenches, left sector of 32 Divn front in relief of 16th Bav Inf	

HK Ottum
Major Commdg
15th (S) Batto Lancashire Fusiliers

Confidential

War Diary of

15th Bn. Canadian Infantry

From December 1st 1917

To December 31st 1917

WAR DIARY
or
INTELLIGENCE SUMMARY.
(Erase heading not required.)

Army Form C. 2118.

Place	Date	Hour	Summary of Events and Information	Remarks and references to Appendices
In Flanders	1/12/17		Holding front line, Left sector (32nd Div Front) preparatory to attack.	
	2/12/17		The Battalion was attached to the 97th Inf Bde for operations near WEST ROOSEBEKE. On the night of the 1/2nd the Battalion was formed up on a tape line ready to move by 1.30AM and moved forward at 3.40. 1.55AM on a three company frontage of 450 yards. The forming up line was reconnoitred & tape successfully laid by 2nd Lieut J.G. SCRIVENER, who was afterwards killed when leaving the objective.	
			Dispositions were	
			A Coy on the RIGHT under 2nd LIEUT W.J. BROCKMAN	
			B. in the CENTRE " CAPT R.F. GREENHILL	
			C. on the LEFT " 2nd LIEUT C.H. SMITH	
			D. in Support }	
			behind A Coy } LIEUT H.G. HUGHES.	
			A Coy advanced, keeping touch with the 17th H.L.I. on their RIGHT, but came under heavy machine gun fire. All the Officers & the senior	R.S

Army Form C. 2118.

WAR DIARY
or
INTELLIGENCE SUMMARY.

(Erase heading not required.)

Place	Date	Hour	Summary of Events and Information	Remarks and references to Appendices
In Trenches	2/10/17		N.C.Os. became casualties. They advanced quite near to their objective, but their casualties were heavy & the Company became very scattered. "B" Coy advanced without much opposition, reached their objective & commenced consolidating. "C" Coy joined up from the original line at TOURNANT FARM on the LEFT, to "B" Coy on the objective forming a defensive flank of about 250 yards. After "A" Coy had suffered so many casualties, two platoons of "D" Coy under 2ND LIEUT. J HURST & 2ND LIEUT J PLITT were pushed forward & the gap which had been caused was filled in & the line held intact. The Battalion dug in and consolidated on its objective, which was held & the new line was handed over intact to the 2ND MANCHESTER REGT. on the night of the 3rd/4th. Casualties were. Killed Wounded Missing Died of wounds	as.
			Officers 1 1 1 - 5 -	
			Other Ranks 12 3 62 17	
			Total 102	

A5834 Wt.W4973/M687 750,000 8/16 D.D.& L. Ltd. Forms/C.2113/13.

Army Form C. 2118.

WAR DIARY
or
INTELLIGENCE SUMMARY.
(Erase heading not required.)

Instructions regarding War Diaries and Intelligence Summaries are contained in F. S. Regs., Part II. and the Staff Manual respectively. Title pages will be prepared in manuscript.

Place	Date	Hour	Summary of Events and Information	Remarks and references to Appendices
In Trenches	9/12/17		Relieved by 2nd Manchester Regt at midnight & marched to Irish Farm Camp.	
Irish Farm	10/12/17		In Huts at Irish Farm Camp.	
Nurst Farm	12/12/17	6.30 pm	Marched to Bivouacs at Nurst Farm & relieved 2nd R. Innis. Fus.	
" "	11/12/17 13/12/17		In Bivouacs at Nurst Farm.	
In Trenches	13/12/17	9.0 pm	Marched to trenches in relief of 16th Lancs. Fus.	
" "	14/12/17 17/12/17		In Trenches (Right Sector 32nd Div Front)	
" "	17/12/17	9.0 pm	Relieved by 17th H.L.I., marched to Corner Cot & entrained for Hospital Farm.	
Hospital Farm	18/12/17 23/12/17		In Huts at Hospital Farm (Training)	
	23/12/17		The battalion entrained at Trois Tours at 7.30 am & detrained at Corner Cot for working parties in trenches, afterwards returning to Irish Farm Camp 3.0 pm	
Irish Farm	24/12/17 29/12/17		Battalion in Huts at Irish Farm Camp & found working parties daily.	A.S.

WAR DIARY
or
INTELLIGENCE SUMMARY.

(Erase heading not required.)

Army Form C. 2118.

Place	Date	Hour	Summary of Events and Information	Remarks and references to Appendices
	29/12/17		Relieved by 16 NOTTS & DERBY REGT, marched to ST JEAN STATION, entrained for AUDRUICQ and marched to AUDENFORTE.	
AUDENFORT	30/12/17		In Billets at AUDENFORTE (training)	
"	31/12/17		" "	

A. Stone
Major,
Commdg. 15th (S) Battn Lancashire Fusiliers.

26.T.
2 sheets

Confidential

War Diary of

15th S. Batt. Lancashire Fusiliers

From 1st January 1915   To 31st January 1915

Army Form C. 2118.

WAR DIARY
or
INTELLIGENCE SUMMARY.
(Erase heading not required.)

Place	Date	Hour	Summary of Events and Information	Remarks and references to Appendices
AUDENFORT	1/7/18 to 17/7/18		The Battalion in Billets at AUDENFORT (training).	
	18/7/18	8·0am	Battalion marched to Billets at NORTKERQUE.	
	19/7/18	5·30am	Battalion marched to AUDRUICQ & entrained for 7·0am for ELVERDINGHE, afterwards marching to Hospital Farm Camp.	
HOSPITAL FARM.	20/7/18		In Huts at Hospital Farm Camp.	
	21/7/18			
	22/7/18	9·0am	Battalion marched to HUDDLESTON CAMP (Houtkerque).	
	23/7/18		In Huts at HUDDLESTON CAMP.	
	24/7/18			
	25/7/18	10·0am	Battalion marched to EMILE CAMP (Houtkerque) near ELVERDINGHE.	
	26/7/18		In Huts at EMILE CAMP	
	27/7/18		Dugouts Elektrix	
	28/7/18	9·0am	Battalion marched to ABRI WOOD CAMP (Elverdinghe) in Bde Support.	
	29/7/18 to 31/7/18		In Camp at ABRI WOOD in Brigade Reserve.	
			Casualties during month 1 O.R. wounded.	

H.K. Watson Lieut Col
Commd'g 15th Bn. Can. Inf.

Vol 27

27.T.
3 sheets

War diary
of

15th (S) Bn Lancashire Fusiliers

From 1-2-18. To 28-2-18

Army Form C. 2118.

WAR DIARY
or
INTELLIGENCE SUMMARY.
(Erase heading not required.)

Instructions regarding War Diaries and Intelligence Summaries are contained in F. S. Regs., Part II. and the Staff Manual respectively. Title pages will be prepared in manuscript.

Place	Date	Hour	Summary of Events and Information	Remarks and references to Appendices
	1st		In tents in ABRI WOOD in Brigade Reserve	
	2nd	5.0 pm	Marched to trenches in HOULTHURST FOREST (centre) relieved 16th Bar. Two (Right Centre)	
	3rd	7.0 pm	Relieved by 2nd Manchester Regt & proceeded to BOESINGHE CAMP.	
	4th to 9th		In tents at BOESINGHE CAMP.	
	10th		"	
	11th		Relieved 16th Bar. Two in Support System of the Forward Zone	
	12th		In Shelters in Support Line.	
	13th	6.0 pm	Marched to trenches in left Subsector of HOULTHURST FOREST Sector relieved 16th Bar. Two	
	14th		In trenches	
	15th		"	
	16th		"	
	17th		"	
	18th		Raid on RENARD FARM. now marked (BIXSCHOOTE map U 5 a 9 9) carried out by A Coy in conjunction with operations by 97th Bde & 16th Bar. Two at 11.0 pm. 14 prisoners captured Casualties 3 Officers + 6 O. R. wounded	
	19th		In trenches in Left Subsector.	
	"	7.0 pm	Relieved by 2nd Manchester Regt and proceeded to ABRI WOOD in Bde Reserve.	
	20th to 22nd		In Tents & Shelters in ABRI WOOD	
	23rd	5.0 pm	Relieved 16th Bar. Two in Support System of the Forward Zone.	

A 5834 Wt. W4973/M687 750,000 8/16 D. D. & L. Ltd. Forms/C.2118/13.

WAR DIARY
or
INTELLIGENCE SUMMARY.
(Erase heading not required.)

Army Form C. 2118.

Place	Date	Hour	Summary of Events and Information	Remarks and references to Appendices
	24/7/18 to 27th		In Shelters in Support System of Leonard Zone.	
	"	7.05pm	Marched to trenches in Regt Subsector HOULTHURST FOREST Sector relieved 16th & two (?) Coys in conjunction with a raid carried out by the 2nd Manchester Regiment on MARECHAL FARM & neighbourhood, between 7.52pm & 9.12pm. One platoon of D Coy endeavoured to exploit the success by a second entry after a 15 minutes barrage at 11.22pm. The area previously raided was found to be devastated & no enemy could be found. The party returned at 11.44pm without loss.	
	28th		In trenches in Regt Subsector.	

A. Stone
Major
Commandg. 15(S) Batt. Lancashire Fusiliers

32nd Division.

96th Infantry Brigade.

15th BATTALION

LANCASHIRE FUSILIERS.

MARCH 1918

Vol 28

War Diary

of

15th (S) Battalion Lancashire Fusiliers

from 1-3-18. to 31-3-18.

28.T.
3 sheets

Army Form C. 2118.

WAR DIARY
or
INTELLIGENCE SUMMARY.
(Erase heading not required.)

Instructions regarding War Diaries and Intelligence Summaries are contained in F.S. Regs., Part II and the Staff Manual respectively. Title pages will be prepared in manuscript.

Place	Date	Hour	Summary of Events and Information	Remarks and references to Appendices
	1/5/18 2/5/18		In trenches in left Subsector HOULTHULST FOREST Sector.	
	3rd	10 pm	Batt. relieved by 11th Border Regt. & proceeded by rail to VANDAMME CAMP. In Hutts at VANDAMME CAMP. Training.	
	4th 5th 6th 7th 8th 9th			
	10th	3.0 pm	Marched to CANAL BANK (Shelters) in Brigade Reserve.	
	11th 12th			
	13th	2.30 pm	Battalion marched to Support line MONDOVI FARM (relieving 10th Dorset Regt.) Battalion in	
	14th 15th 16th			
	17th	7.30 pm	Battalion marched to Trenches in Left Subsector Hour System 6 the Battn. 2nd Battn. The Manchester Regt. In Trenches in Left Subsector. Front System, forward zone.	
	18th 19th 20th			
	21st	8.0 pm	Battalion carried out a Raid on Enemy Posts N. of POTTE DREEF. Captured 1 Garrison (an officer). Our casualties were 3. O.R. killed & 16 O.R. wounded. In trenches.	
	22nd	8.0 pm	Relieved by 2nd Battn. The Manchester Regt. & proceeded to Support line at VANDOORM FM. In Support line in MONDOVI FARM	
	23rd	3.0 am	"B" Coy. 15th Bn. carried out a Raid on Enemy Posts N. of POTTE DREEF & captured 3 prisoners. Our casualties were 1 Officer wounded. 1. O.R. killed 1. O.R. wounded.	

WAR DIARY
or
INTELLIGENCE SUMMARY.
(Erase heading not required.)

Army Form C. 2118.

Instructions regarding War Diaries and Intelligence Summaries are contained in F. S. Regs., Part II. and the Staff Manual respectively. Title pages will be prepared in manuscript.

Place	Date	Hour	Summary of Events and Information	Remarks and references to Appendices
	23rd		Battalion in Support line at MONDOVI FARM.	
	24th			
	25th	7.30pm	Battalion (proceeded) to trenches in Support Sector, front System of the forward zone, relieving 2nd Batt. The Manchester Regt.	
	26th		In Trenches	
	27th		"	
	28th	8.0pm	Battalion was relieved by the 10th Belgian Inf Regt, & proceeded by LARRY CAMP nr ELVERDINGHE.	
		3.0am	" Entrained at ELVERDINGHE for PROVEN.	
		4.0am	" Entrained at PROVEN for SAVY.	
	29th	1.30am	" Detrained at SAVY & marched to HAUTEVILLE. (In Billets).	
	30th	3.0pm	" Marched to Support line at QUESNOY WOOD, in Support to 2nd Guards Brigade	
	31st	9.0pm	" Trenches in HAYETTE Subsector. relieving 3rd Coldstream Guards.	

C.O. Patch Capt & Qm.
for Lieut Col Comdg
10th (S) Batt. Kennear Rifle Fusiliers

96th Inf.Bde.
32nd Div.

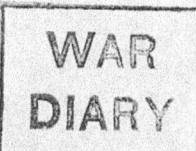

15th BATTN. THE LANCASHIRE FUSILIERS.

A P R I L

1 9 1 8

Confidential

War Diary
of
15th Lancashire Fusiliers

April 1st 1915
to
April 30th 1915.

Army Form C. 2118.

WAR DIARY
or
INTELLIGENCE SUMMARY.
(Erase heading not required.)

Instructions regarding War Diaries and Intelligence Summaries are contained in F.S. Regs, Part II. and the Staff Manual respectively. Title pages will be prepared in manuscript.

Place	Date	Hour	Summary of Events and Information	Remarks and references to Appendices
In trenches AYETTE Subsector.	1/4/18 to 7/4/18			
		9.0 pm	On the night of April 4th about 9.0 pm, "D" Coy 15th Lan Fus carried out an attack on enemy front line trench & forced an entry but failed to consolidate. Casualties were Officers Killed 1, Wounded 1, Other Ranks Killed 11, Wounded 7, Missing 1	
	8/4/18 to 10/4/18		Battalion relieved the 16th Lan Fus & proceeded to the PURPLE LINE in Support.	
			In Support trenches PURPLE LINE	
	10/4/18 11/4/18 to 16/4/18	9.0 pm	Battalion marched to trenches in left Subsector & relieved the 2nd MANCHESTER REGT. Major G.N. Burleigh D.S.O. took command of the Battalion on 11th inst from Lt Col G.K. Ultersen D.S.O. Gassed (wf) 13-4-18 In trenches left Subsector	
	16/4/18	8.0 pm	Battn relieved by 16th Lan Fus & proceeded to the PURPLE LINE in Support	
	17/4/18 to 19/4/18		In support trenches PURPLE LINE	
	19/20/4/18	8.0 pm	The Battalion relieved the 2nd MANCHESTER REGT. in the Right Subsector	

Army Form C. 2118.

WAR DIARY
or
INTELLIGENCE SUMMARY.

(Erase heading not required.)

Place	Date.	Hour	Summary of Events and Information	Remarks and references to Appendices
	20/4 to 25/4		In trenches. Right Subsector. {Major D Lindsay M.C took Command of the Battalion on the 20th from Major E.N Evelegh D.S.O M.C (To 32nd Div. HQ 20-4-18)	
	26th	9.0 PM	Battalion relieved by the 1st WELSH GUARDS & marched to billets at BIENVILLERS.	
	26th	10.0 AM	Marched to billets at BARLY	
	27th to 30th		In billets at BARLY (Training)	

J. Lindsay
Major
Comdg. 15th Lancashire Fusiliers.

Nov 30

Confidential

15TH (S) BATTN LANCASHIRE FUSILIERS

War Diary for Month

Ending 31-5-1918

Army Form C. 2118.

WAR DIARY
or
INTELLIGENCE SUMMARY.
(Erase heading not required.)

Instructions regarding War Diaries and Intelligence Summaries are contained in F. S. Regs., Part II. and the Staff Manual respectively. Title pages will be prepared in manuscript.

Place	Date	Hour	Summary of Events and Information	Remarks and references to Appendices
	1-5-16 to 12-5-16		In billets at BARLY (Training)	
	12-5-16	6 pm	Left BARLY by bus for BLAIREVILLE & relieved the 1st KINGS in Reserve	
	13-5-16 to 15-5-16		In Reserve at BLAIREVILLE	
	15-5-16		Left BLAIREVILLE & relieved the 2nd BATTN the MANCHESTER REGT in the Left Sub-sector Front Line Trenches	
	16-5-16		In Trenches. About 9-0 am enemy raided two of our Posts held by B Coy. 6 of our men are missing. We captured 1 prisoner.	
	17-5-16 to 20-5-16		In Trenches	
	21-5-16		About 3-0 am we raided the enemy's trenches successfully & captured 3 prisoners + 1 Machine Gun. Several of the enemy were killed. Our casualties were 10 O.R. Wounded (most of them very slight).	
	22-5-16		In Trenches	
	23-5-16		In Trenches. Relieved about 11-0 pm by 16th LAN FUS & returned to BLAIREVILLE in Reserve.	

Army Form C. 2118.

WAR DIARY
or
INTELLIGENCE SUMMARY.
(Erase heading not required.)

Place	Date	Hour	Summary of Events and Information	Remarks and references to Appendices
	24-5-16 to 27-5-16		In Reserve BLAIREVILLE	
	27-5-16	9.45p	Left BLAIREVILLE & relieved 2nd Batt. the MANCHESTER REGT in the Right Sub-sector front line trenches	
	28-5-16 to 31-5-16		Lieut Col A.R. Watevson DSO took Command of the Battn on the 31-5-16 from Lieut Col. D. Lindsay. M.C. In Trenches.	

JK Wateron
Lieut Col
Commdg 15th (S) Batt. Lancashire Fusiliers

Confidential

Vol 31

War Diary

of

15th (S) Bn Lancashire Fusiliers

From 1st June 1918.   To 30th June 1918.

31.T.
3 sheets

Army Form C. 2118.

WAR DIARY
or
INTELLIGENCE SUMMARY.
(Erase heading not required.)

Instructions regarding War Diaries and Intelligence Summaries are contained in F.S. Regs., Part II. and the Staff Manual respectively. Title pages will be prepared in manuscript.

Place	Date	Hour	Summary of Events and Information	Remarks and references to Appendices
	1-6-19		In Front line trenches. Right Subsector.	
	4-6-19	11 PM	Relieved by the 16th Lancashire Fusiliers and marched to trenches in Reserve.	
	5-6-19		In Reserve Trenches.	
	8-6-19		Marched to Front line trenches and relieved the 2nd Batt. Manchester Regt. in left Subsector.	
	9-6-19	10 PM	In trenches.	
	10-6-19		" "	
	11-6-19		" " — On night 11th/12th "C" Coy carried out a successful raid on enemy post. We captured 3 prisoners and killed several of the enemy. Our casualties were Officers Wounded 2. Other Ranks Wounded 15 Killed 2	

Army Form C. 2118.

WAR DIARY
or
INTELLIGENCE SUMMARY.

(Erase heading not required.)

Instructions regarding War Diaries and Intelligence Summaries are contained in F. S. Regs., Part II. and the Staff Manual respectively. Title pages will be prepared in manuscript.

Place	Date	Hour	Summary of Events and Information	Remarks and references to Appendices
	12-6-15 to 15-6-15		In Front Line Trenches Left Subsector	
	16-6-15	11 p.m	" " " " " - Relieved by the 16th Lancashire Fusiliers and marched to Reserve Trenches.	
	17-6-15 to 20-6-15		In Reserve Trenches.	
	20-6-15	10 PM	Marched to Front Line Trenches and relieved 2nd Battn The Manchester Regt. in Right Subsector.	
	21-6-15 to 25-6-15		In Front Line Trenches.	
	25-6-15	11 PM	Relieved by 2nd Bn. The Manchester Regt. and marched to Reserve Trenches.	
	26-6-15 to 30-6-15		In Reserve Trenches.	

H.R. Watson Lieut. Col.
Comdg. 15th K.S. Bn Lancashire Fusiliers

Army Form C. 2118.

15-L.F

Vol 32

WAR DIARY
or
INTELLIGENCE SUMMARY.
(Erase heading not required.)

Instructions regarding War Diaries and Intelligence Summaries are contained in F.S. Regs., Part II and the Staff Manual respectively. Title pages will be prepared in manuscript.

Place	Date	Hour	Summary of Events and Information	Remarks and references to Appendices
	1-7-19		In Reserve Trenches BLAIREVILLE	
	2-7-19		Marched to Front Line Trenches and relieved 2nd Batn the Manchester Regt.	
	3-7-19 to 6-7-19		In Front Line Trenches. Command of Lieut Col W.K. Ufferan D.S.O. took over, temporary command of 96th Inf. Brigade 3-7-19. Major D. Lindsay M.C. took over command of Battalion 3/6	
	6-7-19	11 PM	Relieved by 3rd Welsh Guards, marched to BLAIREVILLE, then proceeded in buses to LACOUCHIE.	SHEET 51 S.E V.18 a
	7-7-19 to 14-7-19		In billets at LACOUCHIE (Training)	
	15-7-19	3-0 PM	Left LACOUCHIE in buses to DOULLENS, where Battalion entrained and detrained at HEIDBEEK on the morning of 19th, afterwards marched to PEKIN CAMP.	
	19-7-19 to 31-7-19		In huts Pekin Camp (Training) PROVEN.	SHEET P.7 F2 c & neighborhood

B. Lindsay
Major
Comdg 15th (S) Bath Lancashire Fusiliers

Confidential.

War Diary

of

15th Bn. Lancashire Fusiliers

1st August 1918 to 31st August 1918.

Army Form C. 2118.

WAR DIARY
or
INTELLIGENCE SUMMARY.
(Erase heading not required.)

Instructions regarding War Diaries and Intelligence Summaries are contained in F. S. Regs., Part II. and the Staff Manual respectively. Title pages will be prepared in manuscript.

Place	Date	Hour	Summary of Events and Information	Remarks and references to Appendices
PEKIN CAMP. PROVEN	1/8 2nd Bn		Minden Day The Battalion held Sports. (Training)	Sheet 27 F 2 c, Central
"	7/8		" "	
"	7/8	2.0 pm	Battalion entrained at HEIDBEEK	
	8/8	11.0 am	Detrained at HANGAST	
		2.0 pm	Proceeded to DOMART in busses and stayed the night in bivouacs	
	9/8	2.0 pm	Marched to BEAUCOURT (In bivouacs)	
	10/8	11.0 am	Left bivouacs behind at BEAUCOURT.	
			Marched along AMIENS - ROYE Road to LE QUESNEL WOOD	
		7.15 am	Broke off into Artillery formation on left of road.	
		7.45 am	In position between BOUVENOIR and LA FOLIE.	
		8.0 am	The advance began. Order of Battle 'A' Coy on RIGHT	
			'B' " in CENTRE	
			'C' " on LEFT	
			'D' " in SUPPORT	
			behind 'A' & 'B' Coys.	
		12.30 pm	'D' Coy & part of 'A' Coy holding old German third line West of BOIS EN EQUERRE. 'B' & 'C' Coys holding old British front line & part of old German front line, West of DANERY and PARVILLERS Sports. Battalion Headquarters at BOIS 101.	

Army Form C. 2118.

WAR DIARY
or
INTELLIGENCE SUMMARY.
(Erase heading not required.)

Instructions regarding War Diaries and Intelligence Summaries are contained in F. S. Regs., Part II. and the Staff Manual respectively. Title pages will be prepared in manuscript.

Place	Date	Hour	Summary of Events and Information	Remarks and references to Appendices
				G41
Bois de la Futaie	10th	3.15 PM	Lieut-Col H.K. Uttrim. D.S.O was instantaneously killed while entering the Bois de la Futaie.	
		9.0 PM	2nd Battn the Manchester Regt & 15th Lancashire Fusiliers holding outpost line running approx. 400 yards W. of Bois de la Futaie - 400 yards W. of Damery. 16th Lancashire Fusiliers in support in old British front line E of Bois. 101	
		10.0 PM	16th Lancashire Fusiliers relieve 2nd Battn The Manchester Regt. who go into support in front of Bois. 101 15th & 16th Lancashire Fusiliers are amalgamated for tactical purposes.	
	11th		Line advanced. On Right E of Bois en Equerre. L/5 to the time Le Quesnoy was reached, the ground was open and easy. From Le Quesnoy onwards there were many old trenches covered with grass and affording cover for enemy machine guns. The old wire was still intact and extremely thick and difficult to negotiate. Enemy machine gun was very heavy. Tanks co-operated but were soon knocked out.	

A5834 Wt. W4973/M687 750,000 8/16 D. D. & L. Ltd. Forms/C.2118/13.

Army Form C. 2118.

WAR DIARY
or
INTELLIGENCE SUMMARY.
(Erase heading not required.)

Instructions regarding War Diaries and Intelligence Summaries are contained in F. S. Regs., Part II. and the Staff Manual respectively. Title pages will be prepared in manuscript.

Place	Date	Hour	Summary of Events and Information	Remarks and references to Appendices
	12th	3·0 AM	Relieved by 3rd Canadian Division and proceeded to LE QUESNEL (In bivouacs)	
		12·30 PM	Marched to IGNACOURT (bivouacs)	
	13th	1·0 PM	Marched to COTTENCHY.	
	14th to 17th		Battalion in bivouacs (Re-organising)	
	17th	5·0 PM	Entrained to HARBONNIERES (In Reserve Trench System)	
	18th to 23rd		In Reserve. Lieut·Col· C. E. R. G. Allan D.S.O. assumed command of Battalion 21·8·18	
	23rd		Battalion proceeded to front line trenches and relieved the 13th & 16th Batts Australian Imperial force. The French were on our RIGHT and the 16th Lancashire Fusiliers on the left. From S.14.C.15.50 to LIHU FARM at S. 20 central	62 C. S.W
	24th to 26th		In front line trenches	
	26th	11·0 PM	Relieved by the 2nd Manchester Regt & proceeded to Support trenches.	
	27th	5·0 PM	Battalion took over the outpost line held by the Border Regt. E of STARRY WOOD	62° S.W.
	29th	5·0 AM	The Border Regt passed through our outpost line, the Battalion following in support. The advance through VERMANDOVILLERS on to A BLAINCOURT	Opt.

Army Form C. 2118.

WAR DIARY
or
INTELLIGENCE SUMMARY.
(Erase heading not required.)

Instructions regarding War Diaries and Intelligence Summaries are contained in F. S. Regs., Part II. and the Staff Manual respectively. Title pages will be prepared in manuscript.

Place	Date	Hour	Summary of Events and Information	Remarks and references to Appendices
	28th		The Border Regt not having retained touch with the enemy, the advance was again continued. The Battalion took up its position in support. T.15.b.	62 C.S.W. B.H.Q. T.15.a.5.5.
	29th	5.30AM	continued the advance and formed a defensive flank on left of the Brigade taking up position N.W. of MISERY astride the Valley & Railway.	T.15.b. T.12.a.
		4.30PM	Battalion withdrew into billets at MISERY	
	30th		Billets in MISERY evacuated & battalion moved into bivouacs in the BERNY Area. M.33.a.5.5.	M.33.a.5.5.
	31st		In bivouacs (BERNY Area)	

CRGAlban Lieut Col.
Comdg 15th Lancashire Fusiliers

Confidential

War Diary

of

15th Batt. Lancashire Fusiliers

from 1st September 1918.   to   30th September 1918.

Army Form C. 2118.

WAR DIARY
or
INTELLIGENCE SUMMARY.
(Erase heading not required.)

Place	Date	Hour	Summary of Events and Information	Remarks and references to Appendices
	1st to 5th		In Reserve Trenches (BERNY AREA) M 33 a 55	62°SW.
	6th	6.0AM	Marched to ENNEMAIN (In bivouacs)	
	7th	6.50AM	Marched to MONCHY LAGACHE (bivouacs)	
	8th to 10th		In bivouacs (MONCHY LAGACHE)	
	10th	2.40 PM	Marched to GUALAINCOURT - Battalion took up position in rear of VERMAND - (Battn Headquarters in GUAINCOURT WOOD)	
	11th		Companies in OUTPOST LINE near VERMAND	
	12th		Relieved by 1/1 Welsh Borderers and marched to Wood at GUALAINCOURT. In Wood GUALAINCOURT (bivouacs)	
	13th	3.0 PM	Marched to TERTRY and embussed, debussed at FOUILLEY and marched to AUBIGNY.	
	14th		Battalion in billets at AUBIGNY (Training)	
	15th to 21st			

Army Form C. 2118.

WAR DIARY
or
INTELLIGENCE SUMMARY.
(Erase heading not required.)

Instructions regarding War Diaries and Intelligence Summaries are contained in F.S. Regs., Part II. and the Staff Manual respectively. Title pages will be prepared in manuscript.

Place	Date	Hour	Summary of Events and Information	Remarks and references to Appendices
	24th	3.50 PM	Battalion moved to forward area, embussing point O.29.d.5.8 near VILLERS BRETONNEUX and debussed at about P.30.d (Sheet 62c), afterwards marched to bivouacs at Q.31.a.5.5 (Sheet 62c) TERTRY AREA	Sheet 62D
	25th to 28th		In bivouacs (TERTRY AREA) training. Q.31.a.5.5	Sheet 62c
	28th	7.0 PM	Marches to VENDELLES (In trenches)	
	29th	2.0 PM	Battalion moved forward to trenches in front of BELLENGLISE.	
	30th		Crossed ST QUENTIN CANAL and advanced towards JONCOURT.	

A Barclay Lt
Acting Capt
for Lieut Col
Comdg 15th Lancashire Fusiliers

Vol 35

35.T

Confidential.

War Diary
of
15th Lancashire Fusiliers

From October 1st 1918.   To 31st October 1918

Army Form C. 2118.

WAR DIARY
or
INTELLIGENCE SUMMARY.
(Erase heading not required.)

Instructions regarding War Diaries and Intelligence Summaries are contained in F. S. Regs., Part II. and the Staff Manual respectively. Title pages will be prepared in manuscript.

Place	Date	Hour	Summary of Events and Information	Remarks and references to Appendices
	Oct 1st	3.0 AM	Entered village of JONCOURT, capturing some prisoners and gun (approx 77 M.M) and established a line E of JONCOURT.	
	2nd		Relieved by Staffordshire Regt and proceeded to trenches near LEHAUCOURT.	
	3rd		In trenches (Resting) near LEHAUCOURT	
	4th	2.30 PM	Marched to VENDELLES and stayed the night in trenches.	
	5th	9.0 AM	Marched to HANCOURT	
	6th to 18th		In bivouacs at HANCOURT. (Training)	
	18th	9.0 AM	Marched to LEHAUCOURT and bivouacked for the night	
	19th		Rested and cleaned up generally	
	20th	9.30 AM	Marched to BOHAIN, in billets	
	21st		In billets BOHAIN.	
	22nd	2.0 PM	Marched to BUSIGNY, in billets.	
	23rd to 27th		In billets at BUSIGNY (Training)	
	27th	9.30 AM	Marched to BIGUIGNY, in billets.	

Army Form C. 2118.

WAR DIARY
or
INTELLIGENCE SUMMARY.
(Erase heading not required.)

Place	Date	Hour	Summary of Events and Information	Remarks and references to Appendices
	Oct 28th		In billets at BICAVIGNY (training)	
	29th		Marched to St SOUPLET in billets	
	30th	2.0 PM	Battalion moved to front line and relieved 1st Buffs 6th Division on the night 30th/31st October.	
	31		Battalion holding front line.	

Through for Lieut Col
Comdg 15th Lancashire Fusiliers

Vol 36

Confidential

War Diary
of
15th S. Batt. Lancashire Fusiliers

From November 1st 1915
To November 30th 1915

Place	Date	Hour	Summary of Events and Information	Remarks and references to Appendices
	Nov 1st		The Battalion holding line in front of HAPPEGARBE.	
	2nd		At 06.00 the battalion attacked the HAPPEGARBE SPUR. The objectives were all taken and 62 prisoners taken, a very large number of the enemy were killed. Three tanks assisted but only one reached its objective. At 09.00 the enemy counter-attacked but was driven off. At 14.00 under fire of a heavy barrage he again attacked and working through gaps in the line got in behind the centre and part of the right off the line. Casualties had been heavy and the line being in a sharp salient on the right, the reserve company was thrown in to fill the gap and the line re-adjusted on the right and stretched. The enemy fought strongly and were heavily reinforced with M.G.s One strong front in the village alone yielding 15 heavy & light M.G.s but casualties again caused long gaps in the line, the enemy again filtered in behind and between the centre & right companies.	
	3rd		At 06.15 the attack was launched again. All objectives were taken. The Reserve Coy was again put in, but was only able to gain touch with companies in the flanks, and was not able to force the enemy back.	

WAR DIARY
or
INTELLIGENCE SUMMARY.

Army Form C. 2118.

Place	Date	Hour	Summary of Events and Information	Remarks and references to Appendices
	11th		Later after heavily bombarding the line of the Railway he attacked against the right flank. His fire had been heavy and the M.G. & infantry posts were met with no exception blown in. The enemy came round and attempted to attack across the ground between Battn. H Qrs. and the Farm on the high ground immediately in front. He was finally driven off and retired to the lines of the Railway and later neither E along the cutting after we had launched a local counter attack against that flank. The enemy barrage on that day was extremely heavy and the heavy casualties combined with the very close country was of great assistance to the gunnery. At 06.45 the battalion and 2 Coys K.O.Y.L.I. again attacked with the Canal as objective. All objectives were taken, but casualties were again very heavy. His defensive barrage was very heavy and accurate. The line of the Canal was held until orders were received to cross Canal W. of LANDRECIES and came up on the right of the 25th Division. This was carried out and the Battalion working round, with the left fronted on the 25th Division right during the night, making for the line	

Army Form C. 2118.

WAR DIARY
or
INTELLIGENCE SUMMARY.

(Erase heading not required.)

Instructions regarding War Diaries and Intelligence Summaries are contained in F. S. Regs., Part II. and the Staff Manual respectively. Title pages will be prepared in manuscript.

Place	Date	Hour	Summary of Events and Information	Remarks and references to Appendices
	5/11		of the LANDRECIES-OISY ROAD. Touch was gained with the 2ND MANCHESTER REGT on this road in early morning of the 5th	
	6th to 11th		In billets at SAMBRETON (training)	
	11th	10 a.m.	Marched to PETITT FAYT.	
	12th		Battalion in billets at PETITT FAYT (training)	
	13th	10.30am	Marched to AVESNES (billets for one night)	
	14th	1.15pm	Marched to FELLERIES	
	15th to 18th		In billets at FELLERIES. MAJOR L.C. MANDLEBERG D.S.O. M.C took over command of battalion on 17/11/18 from LIEUT COL. C.E.R.G ALBAN D.S.O (Hospital 17·11·18)	
	19th	10.30am	Marched to LEISSIES and stayed the night in billets. MAJOR R.C WYNTER. M.C (2ND BN THE MANCHESTER REGT) took over command of battalion 19/11/18 from MAJOR L.C. MANDLEBERG. D.S.O. M.C (Hospital 19.11.18)	
	20th	9.30am	Marched to MONTBLIART.	
	21st to 23rd		In billets at MONTBLIART. (Resting + cleaning up generally)	
	24th	9.30 am	Marched to FROIDCHAPELLE.	

Army Form C. 2118.

WAR DIARY
or
INTELLIGENCE SUMMARY.
(Erase heading not required.)

Place	Date	Hour	Summary of Events and Information	Remarks and references to Appendices
	25th to 30th		In billets at FROIDCHAPELLE. MAJOR L.C. MANDLEBERG D.S.O. M.C returned from hospital & assumed command of battalion.	Returned from hospital 25-11-19
	1-11-19			

L.C.Mastens Major.
Cmdg 15th Lancashire Fusiliers

WAR DIARY or INTELLIGENCE SUMMARY

Army Form C. 2118.

15 Bath N?37

Place	Date	Hour	Summary of Events and Information	Remarks and references to Appendices
	Dec 1st to 12th		In billets at FROIDCHAPELLE (Training)	
	12th	08.30	The battalion marched to PHILLIPEVILLE and was inspected by the Army Commander en route.	
	13th	08.30	Battalion marched to ORET and was inspected by the Divisional Commander en route.	
	14th	08.45	Battalion marched to YVOIR	
	15th	09.30	" " " ASSESSE	
	16th	10.30	" " " NATOYE and was inspected by the Brigadier-General en route.	
	17th to 31st		In billets at NATOYE (Training)	

WWandsby Major
Cmdg. 15th S. Bn. Lancashire Fusiliers

LANCASHIRE DIVISION
(LATE 32ND DIVN)

96TH INFY BDE (2ND LANCS. INFY BDE)

15TH BN LANCS FUS.
JAN-OCT 1919

WO 38 A.O.

CONFIDENTIAL

War Diary of 15th Lancashire Fusiliers

from 1-1-1919 to 31-1-1919

Army Form C. 2118.

WAR DIARY
or
INTELLIGENCE SUMMARY.
(Erase heading not required.)

Place	Date	Hour	Summary of Events and Information	Remarks and references to Appendices
	Jan 1st		In billets at NATOYE (Training)	
	2nd		37721 A/R.S.M. CLARKE. J. was awarded the Victoria Cross (extract D.R.O. dated 3-12-1918	
	3rd		In billets at NATOYE (Training)	
	4th		-	
	5		-	
	6th		- & was inspected by the Corps & Divisional Generals.	
	7th		In billets at NATOYE (Training)	
	8th		-	
	9th		-	
	10th		- LIEUT COL C.F.R.G. HEBAH. D.S.O. returned from leave & resumed Command of the Battalion	
	11th to 31st		In billets at NATOYE (Training)	

C.F.R.G.H[signature]
Lieut Col
Commdg 15th Lancashire Fusiliers

CONFIDENTIAL

War Diary of

15ᵗʰ (S) Battn Lancashire Fusiliers

From 1-2-1919   To 28-2-1919

Army Form C. 2118.

WAR DIARY
or
INTELLIGENCE SUMMARY.
(Erase heading not required.)

Instructions regarding War Diaries and Intelligence Summaries are contained in F. S. Regs., Part II. and the Staff Manual respectively. Title pages will be prepared in manuscript.

Place	Date	Hour	Summary of Events and Information	Remarks and references to Appendices
In Billets at NATOYE	1st to 5th		Training	
	6th		Left NATOYE at 09.30 hrs & marched to NAMUR arriving there about 15-30 hrs. Battalion billeted in Cavalry Barracks	
	7th & 8th		Left NAMUR at 14-30 hrs 7th & proceeded by train to BEUEL arriving there about 12.15 hrs on the 8th & marched to BONN where the Battalion was billeted in Huts.	
	9th		Rested & cleaned up generally.	
	10th & 11th		Training	
	12th		Training	
	13th & 14th		Training	
	15th		Took over duties of BONN-BEUEL Bridge Guard from 2nd MANCHESTER REGIMENT	
	16th & 17th		Training	
	18th		Took over all duties of Guards & Picquets in the Town of BONN.	
	19th		Battalion moved to billets in the Museum. BONN.	

Army Form C. 2118.

WAR DIARY
or
INTELLIGENCE SUMMARY.

(Erase heading not required.)

Place	Date	Hour	Summary of Events and Information	Remarks and references to Appendices
	20th		Training	
	21st		Relieved from BONN-BEUEL Bridge Guard by 16th LANCASHIRE FUSILIERS	AREA
	22nd		Training	
	23rd		"	AREA
	24th		"	
	25th		Relieved Piquets & Guards in the town by 16th LANCASHIRE FUSILIERS	
	26th		Training	
	27th			
	28th			

CRMcAWare Lieut Col
Commdg 15th Lancashire Fusiliers

Appx 40

H.O.T.
2 sheets

Confidential

War Diary

of

16th (S) Battalion The Lancashire Fusiliers.

From 1st March 1919 To 31st March 1919.

Army Form C. 2118.

WAR DIARY
or
INTELLIGENCE SUMMARY.
(Erase heading not required.)

Instructions regarding War Diaries and Intelligence Summaries are contained in F. S. Regs., Part II. and the Staff Manual respectively. Title pages will be prepared in manuscript.

Place	Date	Hour	Summary of Events and Information	Remarks and references to Appendices
BONN GERMANY.	1st		Presentation of Colours to the Battalion on the Hofgarten by General Sir Herbert C.O. Plumer. C.C.B. G.C.M.G. C.C.V.O. A.D.C.	
	2nd to 8th		Training. Battalion billeted in Koblenzerstrasse Bonn	Nil.
	9th		Took over duties of BONN-BEUEL Bridge Guard from the 2nd Manchester Regiment.	Nil.
	10th-11th		Training	Nil.
	12th		Took over all duties of Guards and Picquets in the Town of Bonn	Nil.
	13th to 15th		Training	Nil.
	16th		Relieved from BONN-BEUEL Bridge Guard by the 16th Lancashire Fusiliers	Nil.
	17th 18th		Training	Nil.
	"		Relieved from Guards and Picquets in the Town by 16th Lancashire Fusiliers	Nil.
	21st 22nd		Training	Nil.
	23rd		Took over duties of BONN-BEUEL Bridge Guard from 16th Lancashire Fusiliers	Nil.
	24th 25th		Training	Nil.
	26th		Took over all duties of Guards and Picquets in the Town of Bonn	Nil.
	27th 28th 29th		Training	Nil.
	30th		Relieved from BONN-BEUEL Bridge Guard by the 16th Lancashire Fusiliers	Nil.
	31st		Training	Nil.

CRR Ulan Lieut. Colonel
Commanding 15th (S) Battalion Lancashire Fusiliers

Confidential

War Diary

15th (S) Battalion Lancashire Fusiliers

From 1st April 1919 To 30th April 1919

WAR DIARY
or
INTELLIGENCE SUMMARY.

Army Form C. 2118.

Place	Date	Hour	Summary of Events and Information	Remarks and references to Appendices
Bonn Germany.	1st		Two Companies finding Guards & Picquets in Town of Bonn.	
	2nd		Two Companies Training	
	3rd to 12th		Relieved from Guard and Picquets in the Town by 16th Lancashire Fusiliers.	
	13th		Training	
	14th		Took over duties of Bonn-Beuel Bridge Guard from 1/5th Border Regiment.	
	15th		Training	
	16th		Took over all duties of Guards & Picquets in the Town of Bonn.	
	17th to 26th		Training	
	27th		Relieved from Bonn-Beuel Bridge Guard by 16th Lancashire Fusiliers	
	28th		Two Companies M.O. inspected by Divisional Commander on Brigade Parade on Venusburg	
	29th		Training	
	30th		Relieved from Guards & Picquets in the Town by 16th Lancashire Fusiliers.	

J.W. Kirby Lieut Colonel.
Commanding 15th (S) Batt Lancashire Fusiliers

Original.

CONFIDENTIAL.

WAR DIARY.

15th (S) Bn. Lancashire Fusiliers.

From May 1st 1919. to May 31st 1919.

Army Form C. 2118.

WAR DIARY
or
INTELLIGENCE SUMMARY.

(Erase heading not required.)

Instructions regarding War Diaries and Intelligence Summaries are contained in F. S. Regs., Part II. and the Staff Manual respectively. Title pages will be prepared in manuscript.

Place	Date	Hour	Summary of Events and Information	Remarks and references to Appendices

Army Form C. 2118.

WAR DIARY
~~INTELLIGENCE SUMMARY~~

(Erase heading not required.)

Instructions regarding War Diaries and Intelligence Summaries are contained in F.S. Regs., Part II. and the Staff Manual respectively. Title pages will be prepared in manuscript.

Place	Date 1919	Hour	Summary of Events and Information	Remarks and references to Appendices
BONN. Germany	1-6th		Training. Battalion billeted in the Museum, COBLENZERSTRASSE, BONN.	
"	7th		Lieut. Col. A.H. SPOONER. C.M.G. D.S.O. joined Battalion from 52nd Kings Liverpool Regt. and assumed command of the Battalion vice Major. H.B. KIRKBY. D.S.O.	
"	8th		Training.	
"	9th		Training in morning. Museum inspected by H.R.H. Duke of Connaught at 14.30 hrs.	
"	10th & 11th		Training	
"	12th		The 2nd Lancs. Inf. Bde. was inspected at 10.15 hrs. on the VENUSBERG, BONN, by the Commander-in-Chief. Army of the Rhine.	
"	13th		Training in morning. Museum inspected by Commander-in-Chief at 15.20 hrs.	
"	14th.15th		Training.	
"	16th		Marshal FOCH visited the Army coming by river from COBLENZ accompanied by the French flotilla. The Battalion lined the bank of the Rhine opposite ZWEITE FAHRGASSE and cheered the Marshal as he passed.	
"	17th-20th		Lt. Col. A.H. SPOONER. C.M.G. D.S.O. assumed temporary command of the 2nd Lancs. Inf. Bde. during the absence of the Brigadier, Capt. R.A.V. WHITE. assuming temp. command of Battn. Training.	
"	21st		The Battalion proceeded on a trip up the Rhine by steamer leaving Bonn Bridge at 09.30 hrs. & arriving at COBLENZ at 14.30 hrs. One hour was spent in COBLENZ the Battalion returning to BONN by 19.00 hrs	
"	22nd		Training.	
"	23rd		Training. Lt. Col. A.H. SPOONER. C.M.G. D.S.O. returned from Brigade & re-assumed command of the Battalion. Major. R.F. BESWICK. M.C. joined from the 11th. Lan. Fus.	
"	24th-27th		Training.	

Army Form C. 2118.

WAR DIARY

~~INTELLIGENCE SUMMARY.~~

(Erase heading not required.)

Instructions regarding War Diaries and Intelligence Summaries are contained in F. S. Regs., Part II. and the Staff Manual respectively. Title pages will be prepared in manuscript.

Place	Date	Hour	Summary of Events and Information	Remarks and references to Appendices
BONN Germany.	1918 Nov 28		The Battalion took over duties of Guards & Piquets in the town of BONN from 1/5th Border Regt.	
	29th-31st		Training.	

A.R.Hooson
Lieut-Colonel.
Commanding 15th (S) Bn. Lancashire Fusiliers.

Confidential

War Diary

15th (S) Battalion The Lancashire Fusiliers

From June 1st 1919

To June 30th 1919

Army Form C. 2118.

WAR DIARY
or
INTELLIGENCE SUMMARY.
(Erase heading not required.)

Instructions regarding War Diaries and Intelligence Summaries are contained in F. S. Regs., Part II. and the Staff Manual respectively. Title pages will be prepared in manuscript.

Place	Date 1919	Hour	Summary of Events and Information	Remarks and references to Appendices
BONN GERMANY	June 1-10th		Two Companies on Town Duties in Bonn. Battalion billeted in Mauserin Cothengerstrasse. Bonn. Remainder of Battalion Training	
	11th		Relieved from Guards and Picquets in the Town by 16th Lancashire Fusiliers	
	12th to		Training	
	18th			
	19th		Battalion marched to SIEGBURG and took up positions in readiness to advance	
	20th to		Training	
	29th			
	30th		Major R. K. Beurich M.C. assumed temporary command of the Battalion in the absence of Lieut. Colonel A. H. Spooner C.M.G., D.S.O., who proceeded on Leave	
	30th		Advance Party proceeded to BONN to take over Billets preparatory to return of Battalion. Demob.° during month 10 off. 10 OR. Strength of Battalion 30-6-19	

With Unit   29   594
Detached   17   339
             ──   ───
             46   933

R. Beurich
Major
Cmdg 15th (S) Bn. Lan. Fusiliers

= Confidential =

= War Diary =

15th (s) Batt. The Lancashire Fusiliers

From July 1st 1919

To July 31st 1919

Army Form C. 2118.

WAR DIARY
or
INTELLIGENCE SUMMARY.
(Erase heading not required.)

Instructions regarding War Diaries and Intelligence Summaries are contained in F. S. Regs., Part II. and the Staff Manual respectively. Title pages will be prepared in manuscript.

Place	Date	Hour	Summary of Events and Information	Remarks and references to Appendices
Bonn Germany	July 1st		Battalion moved back to Bonn from Siegburg. Billeted in Moltran Coblenzerstrable	
	2nd		Training	
	3rd		General Holiday	
	4th to 15th		Battalion held Sports - Sports Platz Coln Strable	
	16th		Training	
	16th		Took over duties of Guards & Piquets in Bonn from 5th Border Regiment	
	17th to 21st		Training	
	22nd to 24th		Training and Practicing Trooping of Colour and Ceremonial Parade for Minden Day.	
	25th to 26th		Divisional Sports held on Sports Platz Coln Strable. The Battalion carried off Silver Cups for Relay Race; together with the Divisional Commanders Cup for highest number of points gained on the days events.	
	27th to 31st		Training & Practicing Trooping of Colour	

R. Reid
Major
Cmdg 1st Bn Lan Fus

CONFIDENTIAL.

WAR DIARY.

15TH (S) BATTALION THE LANCASHIRE FUSILIERS.

From 1st August, 1919 To 31st, August, 1919.

Army Form C. 2118.

WAR DIARY
or
INTELLIGENCE SUMMARY.

(Erase heading not required.)

Place	Date	Hour	Summary of Events and Information	Remarks and references to Appendices
BONN.	1st.		Battalion billetted in Museum, Coblenzerstrasse.	
	1st.		MINDEN DAY. Ceremonial Parade and Trooping of Colours on Hofgarten by amalgamated Companies of 15th & 16th Bn.Lancashire Fusiliers before Major.Gen. H.S.Jeudwine.,K.C.B.	
	2nd		Battalion moved into Camp on VENUSBURG.	
	3rd.		Lt.Col.A.H.Spooner.C.M.G.,D.S.O assumed temporary command of 2nd.Lancs.Inf.Brigade.	
	3rd.		Major R.K.Beswick. M.C.; assumed temporary command of the Battalion vice Lt.Col. A.H.Spooner. C.M.G.,D.S.O.	
	4th.		Training.	
	5th to 9th.		Training.	
	9th.		Capt.R.A.V.White M.C.; assumed duties of Adjutant vice Capt.G.H.Smith M.C.,D.C.M.	
	10th to 24th.		Firing General Musketry Course - Dottendorf Range.	
			Capt. P.C.Brierley assumed temporary Command of the Battalion vice Major R.K.Beswick M.C. on leave	
	25th.		Battalion moved back into Museum, Coblenzerstrasse, BONN.	
	26th to 30th.		Training.	
EUSKIRCHEN.	31st.		Battalion moved to EUSKIRCHEN. In barracks at Euskirchen.	

P.C.Brierley
Captain.
Comdg. 15th (S) Batt. Lancs. Fus.

46.T.
2 sheets

= Confidential =

= War Diary =

15th (S) Battalion The Lancashire Fusiliers

From 1st September 1919 to 30th September 1919

Army Form C. 2118.

WAR DIARY
or
INTELLIGENCE SUMMARY.
(Erase heading not required.)

Instructions regarding War Diaries and Intelligence Summaries are contained in F.S. Regs., Part II. and the Staff Manual respectively. Title pages will be prepared in manuscript.

Place	Date	Hour	Summary of Events and Information	Remarks and references to Appendices
Euskirchen Germany	Sept 1st		Battalion billeted in Barracks in Euskirchen	
	1st		" in Training.	
	16 M 30 M		The strength of Unit is low owing to Demobilization	

A. H. Horne. Lieut. Colonel.
Comdg 16th (s) Bn Lancashire Fusiliers

47.T.
Oakes

CONFIDENTIAL.

WAR DIARY.

15th.(S)Bn.THE LANCASHIRE FUSILIERS.

From October 1st.1919.   To October 24th.1919.

Army Form C. 2118.

WAR DIARY
or
INTELLIGENCE SUMMARY.
(Erase heading not required.)

Instructions regarding War Diaries and Intelligence Summaries are contained in F. S. Regs., Part II. and the Staff Manual respectively. Title pages will be prepared in manuscript.

Place	Date	Hour	Summary of Events and Information	Remarks and references to Appendices

Army Form C. 2118.

WAR DIARY
or
INTELLIGENCE SUMMARY.
(Erase heading not required.)

Instructions regarding War Diaries and Intelligence Summaries are contained in F. S. Regs., Part II. and the Staff Manual respectively. Title pages will be prepared in manuscript.

Place	Date	Hour	Summary of Events and Information	Remarks and references to Appendices
Euskirchen.	Oct. 1	1919.	Battalion billeted in Euskirchen Barracks. Battalion re-organised into 2 Companies. A.Coy. Retairable men. B.Coy. Releasable men. A.Coy. under the command of Capt. P.B.Brierley. B.Coy. under the command of Capt. H.W.J.Lermit.	
	2.		Completion of re-organisation, and training.	
	3-8		Training. Lt.Col.A.H.Spooner CMG. DSO. took over temporary command of 2nd. Lancashire Infantry Bde. Major R.K.Beswick MC. took over temporary command of the Battalion.	
	9.		Training.	
	10-23.		Under instructions from G.H.Q. Rhine Army 15th(S)Bn. disbanded and all personnel posted to 16th(S)Bn. The Lancashire Fusiliers as from 24-10-1919.	
	24.		All Battalion stores, Transport & etc. handed in. Lt.Col. A.H.Spooner CMG.DSO posted to command 52nd L'pool Regt. as from 18-10-1919. Major. R.K.Beswick MC posted to 52nd. Manchester Regt. as from 24-10-1919.	

Officers demobilized during October 1919.
```
    Lt. E.Riley        12-10-1919.   Lt. L.A.Wilson MC,   24-10-1919.   151 O.R.'s demobilized
    2/Lt.H.A.Goodman        "        2/Lt. J.Acton              "       during month of October
    2/Lt.T.H.Clarkson       "        2/Lt. A.Ruston             "       1919.
    2/Lt.S.D.Irlam          "        2/Lt. D.R.Jobson.
```

R. Beard.
Major.
Commanding 15th.(S)Bn. The Lancashire Fusiliers.

W295/2397(4)

D205/2397(4)

32ND DIVISION
96TH INFY BDE

16TH BN. LANCS FUS.
NOV 1915-DEC 1918
1919 OCT

32ND DIVISION
96TH INFY BDE

Confidential

WAR DIARY
of
16 LANCASHIRE FUSRS.

from Nov 21 to November 30th 1915

Turdenhunde LVM
16 LF

1. U.
5 sheets

96/32

16th Lauer: Pro:
Vol I
Nov '15

32

16th Lancashire Fusiliers
Nov. 17th

Army Form C. 2118.

WAR DIARY
or
INTELLIGENCE SUMMARY.
(Erase heading not required.)

Place	Date	Hour	Summary of Events and Information	Remarks and references to Appendices
TERING HEM	1-10th		Training. 9 m. Bn. inter Coy football competition.	A4.
	11th		Bn. marched to ROUBROUCK & took over billets from 15th H.L.I.	A4.
	12th		Bn. marched to WORMHOUDT area & took over billets from 19th H.L.I	A4.
	13th		" School Camp near POPERINGHE & took over Camp from Naval Brigade.	A4.
	14th to 22nd		Remained in School Camp, & carried out Sports Programme & Training.	A4.
	23rd		Bn. marched to DAMBRE Camp & took over Camp from Gloucesters (1st Division)	A4.
	24th 25th			A4.
	26th		Bn. moved by Train to Hill Top Camp & look over Camp from 19th H.L.I.	A4.
	27th		Bn. relieved XI Borders in the left section of the right sector of the II Corps Front. The 2nd R. Innis Fus were on our right and the 35th Division on our left. 2Lt. BAMPTON was wounded. Casualties O.R. 3 W. 17 Sniper located also M.G. position.	A4.
	28th		In the line. 2Lt. BELL was killed. Patrol went out from 'B' Coy under 2Lt. Baron & 2Lt. Riley. They were fired on from direction of VAT COTTAGE by M.Gun. They returned after being out nearly 3 hours.	A3.

WO 95/
Box 2397

WAR DIARY or INTELLIGENCE SUMMARY

Army Form C. 2118

16 Lancs F[us?] 13
96 I Inf B'de

Place	Date	Hour	Summary of Events and Information	Remarks and references to Appendices
Codford Salisbury	Nov 21		Advance party & Transport left CODFORD for SOUTHAMPTON - HAVRE	
	Nov 23		Batt" (un abons) left CODFORD 7.10 a.m arrived FOLKESTONE 2.15. p.m. BOULOGNE 4.30 p.m	Weather poor
Boulogne	24		Left BOULOGNE 2 a.m arrived LONGRE 10 a.m, COULONVILLIERS 4 p.m. when Advance party & Transport arrived —	
Coulonvilliers	27		Marched to FLIXÉCOURT, arriving 1.30 p.m. left w/p COULONVILLIERS 7.15 a.m	Thaw
Flixécourt	28		Left at 6 a.m. marched to COISY arrived 3.0 p.m	
Coisy	30		Left at 10 a.m marched to ALBERT arrived 6.30 p.m	
			Marching hard whole, one man W/V behind on march to ALBERT, rejoined 2days later. One mule W/V behind at FLIXÉCOURT, received 3 weeks later.	
			Zawalancourt Lt Col Comdg 16 L.F.	

16 Lancs Fus ?.
96 I Inf B'de

WAR DIARY
or
INTELLIGENCE SUMMARY
(Erase heading not required.)

Army Form C. 2118

Copy

Place	Date	Hour	Summary of Events and Information	Remarks and references to Appendices
Camp CODFORD SALISBURY	Nov 21.		Advance party & Transport left CODFORD for SOUTHAMPTON - HAVRE.	
	Nov 22		Batt". (less above) left CODFORD 7·10 a.m. arrived FOLKESTONE 2·15. p.m. BOULOGNE 4·20. p.m.	Weather rough
BOULOGNE	24		Left BOULOGNE 2 a.m. arrived LONGPRÉ 10 a.m., COULONVILLERS 4·p.m. where Advance party & Transport arrived ws-	
COULONVILLERS	27		Marched to FLIXECOURT, arriving 1·30 p.m. held COULONVILLERS 7·15 a.m	Thaw
FLIXECOURT	28		Left at 8. a.m. marched to St COISY arrived 3·0. p.m.	
COISY	30		Left at 10 a.m. marched to ALBERT arrived 6·30. p.m.	
			Marching good on the whole, one man left behind on march to ALBERT, rejoined 2 days later. one made left behind at FLIXECOURT, rejoined 3 weeks later.	

Mackworth Lt Col
Comdr. 16 L.F.

16th Lancers: War
Vol: 2

CONFIDENTIAL

WAR DIARY
of
16 LANCS. FUSRS
from Dec 1. to Dec 30th. 1915

Macewen? Lt.Col.
Commdg 16 L.F.

Dec 30. 1915

WAR DIARY or INTELLIGENCE SUMMARY

Army Form C. 2118

16 LANCS. FUSRS
DEC. 1915.

Place	Date	Hour	Summary of Events and Information	Remarks and references to Appendices
Albert. La Somme.	Dec 1	6 p.m.	Trench Training begins. B'de attached to 1st Div? 16 Lan Fus. attached to 53 & 55 Brigade. Individual Training	nil
"	Dec 2	6 p.m.	Individual Training – nil.	
"	Dec 3	6 p.m.	Platoon Training nil.	
"	Dec 4	6 p.m.	Platoon Training nil. One casualty. Pte. Murphy (B Co.) wounded	Casualty 1 wounded
"	5	6 p.m.	? Platoon Training	
"	6	6 p.m.	Zam-Coy Training nil.	
"	7	6 p.m.	Company Training nil.	
"	8, 9, 10	6 p.m.	Company Training nil.	
"	12	6 p.m.	Albert bombarded. 9.20 p.m. Dec 11th about 30. 6" + 40 12lbr shells.	
E 3 Sector	15		Took over E3 sector between ALBERT and LA BOISELLE (SOMME). 51st Div on left. 53rd Brigade between very hot + Difficult situation at I not Superior enemy overlooking sap heads, all available men required for mining fatigues, no possibility of repairing trenches. Enemy blew two mines – 11.30 and 1.35 – Same damage done to Galleries + one trench. Five mines buried (killed), one man 16 L.F. killed (crushed) & two wounded – futile by Trench Mortars	Casualty 1 killed, 4 snipers 1 killed " 4 killed, 2 wounded
"	19		Our guns bombarded La Boiselle – Enemy blew mine at 3.15 – Blew in DUNDALO St. and 3 H.q.prob. killing 2 men. At trench Sap.ms underground lost 5 miners buried.	7 3
"	20		Wounded Rice canal (Marshall (2) sniper (1)	2
"	21		Very quiet. Two men wounded	
"	22		Very quiet.	
"			Very quiet. G.O.C. 96 B'de took over command of ALBERT	
				13 – 8

Army Form C. 2118

WAR DIARY
or
INTELLIGENCE SUMMARY
(Erase heading not required.)

16 LANCS FUSRS
Dec 1915

Place	Date	Hour	Summary of Events and Information	Remarks and references to Appendices
ALBERT E 3 Section	23		We blew small mine at 12.25 p.m. R.E. satisfied with result. Enemy blew mine at 3.10 p.m. No damage either surface of below. One man killed / wifer, one by shrapnel	Casualties K. 3. W. 8 2nd Lt Page 13 2
	24		Handed over E 3 section to 2/4 Col Lloyd. 15 Lanes Fusrs.	
ALBERT	25		a few shells into ALBERT during afternoon.	
	27		Billeting party sent to MARTINSART.	Casualty (shrapnel, fatigue party in trenches) 1
	28		Batt'n moved to billets in MARTINSART	
MARTINSART	29		Nothing to report.	
	30		Note. During our time in the trenches 61 men were sent out with trenchfeet. Of these 37 were evacuated, the remainder (24) rejoining after 48 hours in billets.	1 Wounded man died in hospital, Dec 27. 15 9 1/16 ˣ ˣ Of these 8 were sappers, 179 Co R.E.

E Malenvida Ll Col
Comd. 16 L.F.
Dec 30 1915 —

96th Brigade.

32nd Division.

16th BATTALION

LANCASHIRE FUSILIERS

JANUARY 1 9 1 6

16th Lanc. Fusiliers

Vol. 3.

Confidential

WAR DIARY
of
16th LANCASHIRE FUSRS.
from Jan 1st to Jan 31st 1916.

[signature]
Comdr 16th Bn Two.

Original

Army Form C. 2118

WAR DIARY
or
INTELLIGENCE SUMMARY
(Erase heading not required.)

16 Lancs Fus^rs
96 Inf B'de, 32nd Div^n

Place	Date 1916	Hour	Summary of Events and Information	Remarks and references to Appendices
MARTINSART G1 Sector	Jan. 1		Billets in MARTINSART.	
	2		Took over G1 Sector (new delimitation) opposite AUTHUILLE. On right, 16th H.L.I. (97th Brigade). On left, 2nd R. Innis Fus^rs (96 Brigade) — Note, the trenches I took over form new G1 Sector were: — 1 company frontage of F2 Sector (from 16 H.L.I.) G1 A Sector (old map) (from 1/4 K.O. Lancs.) } 154th Brigade G1 B Sector (old map) (from 1/4 L.N. Lancs.) 200 yards frontage of old G2 Sector (from 2 R Innis Fus^rs) The Sector on new front runs from BOGGART HOLE on Right to HAMILTON AVENUE on left.	
	4		Enemy bombarded HAMIEL (left of G2 Sector) — at 4 p.m. opened heavy rifle fire & barrages front & communn. trenches — Enemy very active, shrapnel, slight — No movement.	Casualties K.— W.— 4.
	5		Casualties by rifle grenades	
AUTHUILLE	6		Handed over G1 Sector to Lt. Col. Lloyd 15 L.F. and took over AUTHUILLE (Billets) Brigade reserve.	
BOUZINCOURT	10		Went into Corps Reserve at BOUZINCOURT (huts & billets).	
	12		Major C. Wallace to 32nd Div. H.Q. to act as G.S.O. 3. for 1 month.	
	18		Moved to MARTINSART, as Div^n Reserve.	

3

WAR DIARY
or
INTELLIGENCE SUMMARY

(Erase heading not required.)

Army Form C. 2118

16 LAN FUS
96 Inf B'de 32 Div C

Place	Date 1916	Hour	Summary of Events and Information	Casualties K. W.	Remarks and references to Appendices
MARTINSART	Jan 21		Took over G.1 Subsector from Lt.Col. Lloyd. 15 Lan. Fus. Yorks. L.I. on right. 2 Innisk. Fus. on left.	Nums that S.Reet. 5	self inflicted
G.1 Subsect.	22		Our Arty. bombarded THIEPVAL. Enemy replied on AUTHUILLE. No casualties. Roughly no much damage.	2	self inflicted
	23		I went to BEAUVAL to attend Senior Officers Artillery Course leaving Major Mumford in command. Entries by Major E.M. Mumford.	1	self inflicted
	24		A number of oil cans on our left. We replied with Trench Mortars. Enemy's mortars, oil cans, Rifle Grenades and 77mm guns were active. We replied with Trench Mortars, Rifle Grenades and 18 Pdr guns.	1 2 3	
	25		Our Artillery fired on THIEPVAL cemetery Trench. and at 11.30 PM on Enemy's Sap from Gun pour 4.11		
	26		Enemy very active all day with oil cans (60) 77mm guns & 5.9 guns. We replied with guns 18 pdr. We called from BEAUCOURT direction 4.5", 6", & 8" Handed over to O.C. 2nd Dorset Regt. and returned to Billets in BOUZINCOURT.	1	

E. Moore Mumford
Major 16 L.F.

3 13

Army Form C. 2118

WAR DIARY
or
INTELLIGENCE SUMMARY
(Erase heading not required.)

16 L^{AN} FUS 3/
96 Inf B'de 32 Div

Place	Date 1916	Hour	Summary of Events and Information	Remarks and references to Appendices
BOUZINCOURT	Jan 27			Casualties K. W. from last list 3. 13
			No 11202 Pte DERBYSHIRE accidentally shot 2 men in billets. EMM	2
	28		2 returned from BEAUVAL. EMM	3 . 15
			Amalgamated with 16 Lan Fus. on 30th.	

96th Brigade.
32nd Division.

16th BATTALION

LANCASHIRE FUSILIERS

FEBRUARY 1916

32   16th Lancs: Fus:
        Vol: 4

                              H. V.
                              Barker

Army Form C. 2118

WAR DIARY
or
INTELLIGENCE SUMMARY
(Erase heading not required.)

16 hours Aug 15.
96 Inf Bde.

Place	Date	Hour	Summary of Events and Information	Remarks and references to Appendices
				Killed / Wd.
BOUZINCOURT	Jan 31.		Billets.	
		Feb 2	Sent patrols to take part in wiring & digging new trench opposite F1 subsector. One man killed or missing fatigue. Other casualt. 1 man wounded.	1 / 1
			in E3 subsector.	
		Feb 6	Took over G2 subsector from 19 Lanc. Fus. On right, 2 Inniskilling Fus. on left (E of river ANCRE) 7 R.I. Fusiliers. Line runs opposite THIEPVAL to river ANCRE. Trenches in bad condition except for parts of front line — destroyed recent bombardment.	
		7	Some artillery & Trench mortar activity. Otherwise quiet. Casualt. rifle-shot, one absent.	1
		8	As on 7th. Capt. J. Tattersall, A.C. wounded by rifle grenade.	1. officer
		9	Enemy bombarded "THE NAB" F3 subsector with H.E. & gas shells. Gas alarm passed down line — no effect.	
		10	Sky reported to have visited our lines disguised a Staff officer — spoke to our sentry but cleared our trenches. He knew. occurred between 1-2 am.	
		11	Very quiet. One man shot (killed) our sentry. Enemy shelled GORDON CASTLE & wood, killing 1 wounding 1 7/15 Lanc. Fus.	1
		12	Artillery (enemy) very active in afternoon, no reply — Handed over G2 to Col. Alexander 8. W. Yorks and Major Scott 6. W. Yorks and returned to billets in SENLIS.	

Army Form C. 2118

16 Lane Fus'
2
96 Inf Bde

WAR DIARY
or
INTELLIGENCE SUMMARY
(Erase heading not required.)

Instructions regarding War Diaries and Intelligence Summaries are contained in F.S. Regs., Part II. and the Staff Manual respectively. Title Pages will be prepared in manuscript.

Place	Date 1916	Hour	Summary of Events and Information	Remarks and references to Appendices
SENLIS	Feb.13		Marched to huts camp 3/4 mile E. of HENENCOURT	
	17		Marched to AVELUY. Brigade reserve to J. Sector. 4 divis[ions] sent to J 2 instructor	Killed wounded 2 3
	18		Carried in two from Ortrecht	1
	19		" Aprés bat, shrapnel	1
	22		Accident in Grenadier class, 2 (1 officer) very slightly wounded	2 accidentally
	24		Took over J1. from 15 Lanc. Fus. (L.W.L. Lloyd) 6th Norfolks on right (E 3) & 2nd Inniskill. Fus. on left (F2) — Sector lies E. of AVELUY.	
	25		Frost + fall of snow.	
	26		Frost.	
	27		Thaw set in about mid-day. Trenches in bad condition, especially new parts	1
	28			1
	29		Hostile enemy's trenches than from some soft parts. later we cut some wire enemy's light we fell. Nights were very cold + thaw made matters much worse; two men were evacuated with trench feet (both had some frostbite) one with trench hands.	Total Casualties 2 . 9

Malcolm
Lt Col.
16 L.F.

96th Brigade.
32nd Division.

16th BATTALION

LANCASHIRE FUSILIERS

MARCH 1916

16th Jan Jus
32nd Dec 3
Vol. 5

5-V.
5 sheet

WAR DIARY
or
INTELLIGENCE SUMMARY

(Erase heading not required.)

Army Form C. 2118

16 R.N. Fus.
96. Inf. Bde. 32 Div.

Place	Date 1916	Hour	Summary of Events and Information	Remarks and references to Appendices
31. Sub-sector	Jan. 1		Dug new comm'n Trench parallel to ARGYLL ST. 3.50 cards, 4ft deep.	Killed men 1.
	2		Handed over to B to 10th K.L.L.D. 15 Lance Spy'g marched to Billets in Mailly Maillet. Enfd'd on Rumeln & Ramay to front & subsequent Thaw. During 7 days in Trenches, 6 men evacuated with Trench feet and 2 with French hands.	
ALBERT	7		Marched to Billets in BOUZINCOURT	
	8		Took over S.I. Subsector from 17th K.L. Lloyd. 13th L.F. having 2.3 L.N.L. F. in ? m'n right + 1st Borderers Reg't (109.Bde) on our left. There had been a good deal of shelling in this sector before we got in but all quiet during relief which was effected between 8 p.m. and 11 p.m. Some damage done to trenches but nothing further.	
	9		Our battalion's enemy trenches putting over about 200 shells + 40 ? M. ?	2
	10		Day + early part of night very quiet. We had large working parties, this was driven in by fire just before 11 soon after a very heavy bombardment began along whole sub-sector front and ? Trenches, Vimont ? etc. Most of the shelling fell on our front line, one salient amo'st at man in shelters but in left centre, parapet & front line was much beaten flat, and many of shelters were killed + wounded. It was found afterwards that a raid had been effected at a point in the French + 1 officer + ? men are missing. Most remain is before our front, removed from German Line to a crater which formed by a mortar German hand grenades, and that the front had answered this before entering the French. There were signs of a struggle in + near the C.S. M's store which was a shelter in front line, the hands of a Mills grenade. Wristwatch cap of one of the enemy	

1875 Wt. W593/826 1,000,000 4/15 J.B.C. & A. A.D.S.S./Forms/C.2118.

Army Form C. 2118

WAR DIARY
or
INTELLIGENCE SUMMARY

16 R.N.Fus.
96 Inf. Bde. 32 Div.

(Erase heading not required.)

Place	Date	Hour	Summary of Events and Information	Remarks and references to Appendices
	Jan 10th		Men who H.gun cape & two men had blood stains at left entrance to the shelter. No other traces of our men could be found. A lewis gun post on the left of C.S.M.'s shelter and a rearly post on right had left been post not taken (the bombardment caused no response and damage was rather more than two posts buried or wounded) of the killed & one wounded on a dig out in reserve line	Casualties
				K W M Shock
			Enemy extremely shelly, couldn't make out all	Bombers 3
				Lewis gunners 1 4 1
				Snipers & riflemen 1
				Other ranks 12 31 7 16
				Draftsmen 1 1
Givenchy	11		Quiet Day	
	12		Handed over G.1 to 16 North Fus? Moved to billets in AUTHUILLE	
AUTHUILLE	13		Enemy shelled village throughout night - no damage	
	14		Some shelling during day, no damage	
	15		Enemy shelled village throughout night - very little damage	
	16		Took over 3.2 subsector (now called 3.Q.1.) from 2nd Manch 15 L.F. having 15 H.L.I. in our right & 2nd R. Scottish Fus in our left	
	17		Very quiet - a few salvos of (Shrapnel) on camalets, slight wounds	17 41 8 16

Army Form C. 2118

WAR DIARY
INTELLIGENCE SUMMARY
(Erase heading not required.)

16 J.A.N. Fus.
96 I. B'de. 32 Div.

Place	Date 1916 March	Hour	Summary of Events and Information	Remarks and references to Appendices
	19		Some shrapnel at night	
	20		Enemy shelled severe point with 4.2. shell, signallers dug out near centre Co. H.Q. Casualties counted. Handed J.G.1 to Lt. Col. Lloyd 15. L.F. & marched to billets in BOUZINCOURT	
	24		Took over J.G.1 from Lt. Col. Lloyd, 15.L.F. having 19 Jan. Fus. on night to 2 R. Inniskn. Fus. and left. Enemy very quiet	
	26		Garrison ready for counter attack to an action at LA BOISSELLE. There was a raid on enemy's trenches at Y Sap. About E.3 Schwaben. No action taken by the enemy against this subsector.	
	28		Handed over J.G.1 to Major Archer, 16 North'd Fus. & proceeded to AUTHUILLE in Brigade Reserve. Casualties slight, wounded by rifle grenade.	1
	29		I go home on leave handing over Batt. to Capt. O. Smith.	

Casualties for four days: K. 14 W. 41 M. 8 Shock 16

                                                    15 . 44 . 8 16

J. McClintock Lt. Col.
16 L.F.
16th J.N. Fus. 29.

K. W. M. Shock
Casualties/four/per. pers.   14   41   8   16
                               1   1
                                    1
                                         1
                              _____
                              15   44   8   16

96th Brigade.

32nd Division.

16th BATTALION

LANCASHIRE FUSILIERS

APRIL 1 9 1 6

Army Form C. 2118

Original

WAR DIARY
or
INTELLIGENCE SUMMARY
(Erase heading not required.)

16 L'ary. Fus
96 I. B. de 32 Div.

April 1916 Vol 6

6.V.
1 sheet

Place	Date 1916	Hour	Summary of Events and Information	Remarks and references to Appendices
	April 1.		marched to WARLOY. Divisional reserve training	K. W.
Warloy	4		Marched to CONTAY. Major E.M. Mumfrie struck off having accepted appointment under India office	
	7		Marched to CONTAY. Divisional reserve training.	
	23		Major C.C. Stallan, 2nd Manchester Regt. attached appointed 2nd in command.	
	24		marched to BOUZINCOURT	
			Took over THIEPVAL subsector from Col Laidlaw, 16 H.L.I. having 2nd R. Innisk. Fus. on right + 11th R. Innisk. Fus. (36th Div.) on left.	
	26		Quiet Day. At night (9.55) enemy shelled our wiring parties and made very bad shooting; he is probably alarmed by sound (a digging party in rear of wire) connection	K. W. 2. 12. 1
	27		the night being very still.	2.13.
	28		Handed over to Lt Col Lloyd 1st L.F. + went into Brigade Reserve at AVELUY.	

Mualcourd Lt Col
16 L.F.

96th Brigade
32nd Division.

16th BATTALION

LANCASHIRE FUSILIERS

M A Y 1 9 1 6

WAR DIARY or INTELLIGENCE SUMMARY

Army Form C. 2118

MAY. 1916.
16 LAN FUS
96. B'de. 32 Div'n.

Original

Place	Date May 1916	Hour	Summary of Events and Information	Remarks and references to Appendices
AVELUY.	2.		Took over THIEPVAL Subsector from Lt.Col. Lloyd, 15 L.F. having 2nd R. Inniskg. on right and 14th R. Irish Rifles (36th Div'n) on left.	Casualties K. W.
	3.			1. 2.
	4.		Man killed, 1 sniper & 2 wounded by shells.	1
	5.		Enemy shelled a good shot a crossbeam, killing 2 & wounding 3. 4 men wounded by trimmies near front line. At 12 midnight we put up a bombardment & a raid was successfully made by 15 L.F. from Subsector on our right. he tried to make enemy think raid was coming from our Subsector & drew a good deal of retaliation — we had 1 killed & 14 wounded. Trenches a good deal knocked about and I think an casualties light considering the weight of bombardment, this was owing to the skilful my Coy officers dis pored of their men.	3. 21.
	6.		Handed over to Major SHUTE, 2nd Dorset Regt. Marched to SENLIS, in Div'l reserve.	4. 24.
	13.		Marched to BOUZINCOURT, in Div'l Reserve.	
	17.		Marched to MIRVAUX, in Corps Reserve	
	25.		Batt'n inoculated against typhoid & paratyphoid.	
	29.		Marched to WARLOY, taking billets vacated by 1st DORSET Regt.	
	30.		Marched to AVELUY (CRUCIFIX CORNER) relieving 17. H.L.I. Brigade reserve support to the NAB subsector.	

Tmalcundulhill
16 LanFus.

96th Brigade.
32nd Division.

1/16th BATTALION

LANCASHIRE FUSILIERS

JUNE 1916:

O c/o D.A.G's Office
3 Echelon, Base

Herewith War Diary of
16 Lan Fusiliers for month
of June 1916. Duplicate
has been sent to Records

 Cmdg [illegible] Lt Col
 16 L.F.

June 30th

Original free

WAR DIARY or INTELLIGENCE SUMMARY

Army Form C. 2118

16 Lanc. Fus.
96. Inf Bde   32. Divn
June 1916.

Vol 8

Place	Date June	Hour	Summary of Events and Information	Remarks and references to Appendices
AVELUY	3		Took over AUTHUILLE subsector from 2/Lt Lloyd 15. Lan Fus, having 2. W. Yorks on right and 2. R. Innis. Fus on left. One officer (2/Lt Kiel) slightly wounded at H.Q. by H.G. 3 men on working party Wounded	Casualties K. W. Sshell 3. Other 1. Other
	5		Raid carried out by 11 Border Regt. from our sector. Raid successful. 11 prisoners being taken, Casualties 11 Border Regt. 1 officer 5 men killed, wounded not known. Enemy put up Paul barrage, our casualties in trenches near slight most of the rounds being in rear little hurt, 9 that 5 minutes 9 rejoined within 6 days. after the Borders had come in a patrol of 1/6 L.F. under 2 Lieut Roth went out strong ft in following B.now casualties. 1 officer three men killed 1 man wounded shelling in crater. This patrol did very good work searching the ground till about 90 yards. Other names mentioned for good work that night. 11478 Sgt A. Smith, 11752 Pte T. Wigston 12452 Pte W. Davis. Sgt Cawdrey 11452 Pte W. Lloyd 15 L.F. aid and news unit support at Crucifix Corner	1 15 1 Died 1. named
	7		Handed sector to 2/Lt Lloyd 15 L.F. and marched to SENLIS AVELUY	
	13		Relieved by Major A. Smith 19 L.F. (14 Inf Bde) + marched to SENLIS	
	15		Renewed practice for attack on Enemy's trenches	
	19		ditto	
	21		ditto	
	22		Practice	
	22		Practice	
	23		Marched to AVELUY Wood. Took on THIEPVAL sector from Major Grant 11th H.L.I. Casualties from shrapnel machine in. Enemy very (paid) active shrapnel + machine in the brackets about.	2 self inflicted 4

J.C. 3 shock

J.C. 3 shock

WAR DIARY or INTELLIGENCE SUMMARY

Army Form C. 2118

Place: 16 LANTUS
Date: June 1916

Date	Hour	Summary of Events and Information	K.	W.	S.Shel	Remarks and references to Appendices
June 24		Our guns began wire cutting along whole front – Enemy's rifle [and] sniper's fire but local – he evidently has not enough guns to make a good show under concentration.	1	25		1 wounded-shock
25		Still wire cutting our heavy guns registering, some heavy bombardment – also our heavy T.M. fired two rounds registering. Capt Bradshaw very slightly wounded		4		self inflicted
				2		1 officer
26		Our Arty stood out in am bombarded to distract enemy rifle wire 77:10 H's can's. In aftn. our gas was the to let off from our lines, to right + left of us, enemy concentrated his heavy fire on us, shewing a good deal of GEMMEL TRENCH. Our casualties much less than I expected. Gas prepared in our line but not used, one very slight [serious] from leaky cylinder. Handed over to Lt Col Crawford. 2 R. Inniske. Dns. + mins to BLACK HORSE Dug outs. AUTHUILE.	2	5		1 gassed (slight)
27		Bombardment continues, enemy shelling village roads, casualties on road parties.		7		
28		As yesterday, casualties in working party + patrine.	2	4		2 self inflicted
29		As yesterday but every much shorter.		2		1 shell shock
30		As yesterday. Enemy shell our road in rear of ships but without effect. The enemy have a limited number of (4.2 – 0.9 – nly stone the [guns])		1		
			5	48		1 Gas
				1 off	2 shellshock
					4 self inflicted
			5	53	3	

Awlemande LtCol
16 Lanfus

96th Inf.Bde.
32nd Div.

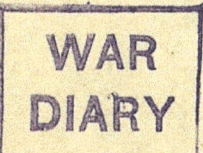

16th BATTN. THE LANCASHIRE FUSILIERS.

J U L Y

1 9 1 6

5.

WAR DIARY
or
INTELLIGENCE SUMMARY
(Erase heading not required.)

Army Form C. 2118.

CONFIDENTIAL
WAR DIARY
16th Lancashire Fusiliers

1st July 1916 — 31st July 1916

ORIGINAL

Original

WAR DIARY
INTELLIGENCE SUMMARY

16 Lan Fus
July 1916

Army Form C. 2118

Place	Date	Hour	Summary of Events and Information	Remarks and references to Appendices
AUTHUILE	July 1		The frontage of the 96 Bde in the attack ran from SHAVER ST to QUEENS X ST trench R.31.3 to R.25.14 inclusive. On the enemy lines the attack of the Brigade (THIEPVAL - ILEAVING position South of the village) included the 97 Bde on our right and the 36th Divn on our left. She assaulting Batts. 2 96 Bde were the 16 N.F. + 15 L.F. — Both Batts were indeed to attack the asserting Batts + from two strong points in rear of THIEPVAL. My Coys were about equal in strength, 120 each including 2 L temns + I had 40 men with Batt H.Q. including memgm, bomb: carriers + salvage party + bombers. Bn Coys Batt left BLACKHORSE dugouts about 11 p.m. (June 30) + moved into places of assembly as under: FRENCH TRENCH A + C Coys toulshot Right Assaulty Bn. — QUEENS X BANK B. — D. — Left — C + D Coys went to construct strong points + carried RE materials (in the platoon —) They each sent assault party with leading platoon of A + B Coys (detached to make out strong points + trench for construction party. Lieut Grant 208 Co RE. + party found there Coys in assembly for this work B Co lost 4 men killed, 1 off + 6 men wounded (getting into position but no casualties were suffered whilst in assembly trenches. Zero hour was 7.30 a.m. Lieut A N ALLEN commanding ACoy. received no message from his advance officer sent forward who was badly wounded close to the bombardment, 20 to at 7.55 he moved forward to KENNELL TRENCH where he met the reserve Coy of the 16 N.F. moving to the front line just E of KENNELL TRENCH when he had no platoon in the parapet under 2/Lieut M.E FOSS The N.F attack was making no progress head. ALLEN kept the rest of his Co in the front line. C Coy was now in GEMMELL Stop + Lieut KNOTT seeing that himself he decided to adopt the attack ahead.	

Original — **16 LAN Fus** — Army Form C. 2118

WAR DIARY or INTELLIGENCE SUMMARY

his men to deposit R.E. material went to see Col. W.H. RITSON CMG Cmdg 16 N.F. in front line. Later he brought his Coy into the front line. A/C. kept that part of the line until relieved at 11 p.m. by 2/R. Inniks Sergt. who held on to a GREENOCK line running to the right on a line on SKINNER ST. The casualties suffered by my C Coy were much from shells which however the front line which was much battered about were little infantry.

Our left B Coy meet better places for observation & the 15/L.F. new seen to advance in front under the 36 Divn. now left to machine (wood) fragm. at 8 o'clock its first line V.B. advanced between heavy enemy M.G. fire which came from QUEEN'S X BANK, the trench in O Coy followed. The first line reached the own trench beyond HAMMERHEAD SAP had suffered severely from M.G. fire from direction STHEORAL, Capt TWEED reckoning that his Coy was only about 40 strong at this point. Word was sent to Capt TWEED that the three officers of O Co had all be launched out & hence lack & instruct 2/Lieut TOWES but to bring the rest of D on out if B Co cmdr made letter-pigeons. Capt TWEED then went back to the front line & tried to get men forward by various means. He advanced another trench forward to a tank that remains inspection. but all were heaved down; a few men crawling met the same fate. Further officers of B Co were wounded as advance as informed. Capt TWEED signalled to the remainder of the men to lie under the banks of HAMMERHEAD SAP while he awaited word to see if it mixed informed to get though to more that way. This was equally inform as nothing could be seen 9/KO/15 L.F. advance Indeed Capt TWEED & withdraw

WAR DIARY or INTELLIGENCE SUMMARY

16 LAN. FUS (Jul/1916)

Army Form C. 2118

Place	Date	Hour	Summary of Events and Information	Remarks and references to Appendices
	2		his men never came in QUEENS X ST. This was one out of a few further casualties & the remainder (B) D Co were ready to meet again an attack. Two further attacks were attempted during the afternoon by the 2 R. SAXNS. FUS. Later, the 8. W. YORKS. but it was found that beyond our wire- The 2 R. IRISH. & 7 US took over the front line & B Co crept never withdrawn after nightfall. It is evident that the bombardment had failed to destroy the pillboxes M.G.s in the THIEPVAL defences and it is heard that some of them were in advanced pos'ns near town line/that were suffered; there must also have been some M.G.s with a high command for men crawling were instantly detected. Fire was directed. During Jan bombt. went before the attack enemy M.G.s could be heard firing funnel pos'ns in... Enemy continued shelling front line & comm'n trenches with 77c + 4.2 m's spent the day clearing casualties & equipment etc from front line & retain in where we arrived. he new which about 3 a.m. (July 3rd) to 2 S. LANCS + with drew to AVELUY WOOD. Casualties During July 1 + 2. Officers, wounded 2Lt Ingles. Anstell's hut. A Co 1 B Co 3 { 2Lt Hart Waton. W. wounded 2Lt. Powell. S.L. 2" 2Lt. Brennan. E.J. 2" C Co 1. 2Lt Aiken. N.C. 2" D Co 3. { 2Lt Hough 3.3. B" 2Lt Ellison J.B.R. 2" 2Lt Milligan H.W. 2" Capt. Stourton. G.3. 2" attached (R.A.M.C.) Other ranks:- K. W. Died/wounds Shell sh. Missing A Co 2 42 1 3 1 B Co 20 47 2 1 18 C Co 6 28 - 6 - D Co 11 30 1 4 - 39 147 4 14 19	

Original

WAR DIARY
or
INTELLIGENCE SUMMARY
(Erase heading not required.)

Army Form C. 2118

16 Lanc Fus
July 1916.

Place	Date July	Hour	Summary of Events and Information	Remarks and references to Appendices
	3		Left AVELUY WOOD about 5:30 p.m. & marched to WARLOY. I proceeded on special leave England. Major C.C. Stapleton took command & continues the diary.	
	5			
	8		Bn marched to VARENNES at about 6 p.m. Bn formed into two fighting Coys No.1 Co under Lieut A.N. Allen No.2 Co under Capt W.O. Smith. At 8 p.m. the Bn marched to billets in BOUZINCOURT.	
	9th		At 8 p.m. the Bn moved into bivouacs on football ground east of BOUZINCOURT	
	11th		Bn took over part of trenches in OVILLERS from 1st Bn Dorset Regt. having 19th L.F. on right & 2nd R. Innis Fus in support by 16th NF on left. This trench had recently been captured so the night & following day were spent in clearing & consolidating. Casualties caused by shell fire.	Casualties K W M O 3 1 55 O.R.
	12th		No action on either side until night. At 11 p.m. patrols were sent forward to try & advance our line to join with the advanced position of 19th L.F. on the right. No suitable position could be found & patrols were compelled to withdraw at daylight.	Casualties — 2 1
	13th		Orders were received that an attack would be made by the 25th Divn to the east of us the Bn was to join in & take 3 points of our front	— 4 2
	14th		Enemy up night the 19th L.F. This attack did not take place The Bn was relieved by the 1st Dorsets & withdrew to the vicinity of DONNET Post	— 6 23
	15th		Bn found carrying parties to troops in OVILLERS. At 11 p.m. the Bn left the trenches their place being taken by the 6th Gloucs. we marched to Bivouacs at SENLIS	3 13 4

Original

WAR DIARY
or
INTELLIGENCE SUMMARY
(Erase heading not required.)

16 LAN FUS.
July 1916.

Army Form C. 2118

Place	Date	Hour	Summary of Events and Information	Remarks and references to Appendices
	17ᵗʰ		At 11 a.m. the Bn. marched with the 14ᵗʰ Bde to HALLOY where we were accommodated in huts. at 6.30 p.m. Lt Col C. Abercrombie rejoined from special leave & took over command of the Bn. E.C. Stapledon Major	
	18		Marched to BOUQUEMAISON. arriving 5.30 p.m. rejoined 96ᵗʰ Bde.	
	19		Marched to CROISETTE. left 7.30 a.m. arrived 12 noon.	
	20		Marched to HEUCHIN left 9.0 a.m. 1 p.m.	
	21		Marched to AUCHY AU BOIS left 9.15 a.m. arrived 12.30 p.m.	
	26		Marched to MARLES LES MINES left 7.25 a.m. arrived 11.20 a.m.	
	29		Marched to HALLICOURT left 10 a.m. arrived 11.30 a.m.	

T. Abercrombie Lt Col

96th Brigade.

32nd Division.

16th BATTALION

LANCASHIRE FUSILIERS

AUGUST 1 9 1 6

Vol 10

Confidential

War Diary
of
16th Lancashire Fusiliers

from 1st August 1916 to 31st August 1916

Original

16 Lan Fus

WAR DIARY or INTELLIGENCE SUMMARY
(Erase heading not required.)

Army Form C. 2118

Aug. 1916.

Place	Date	Hour	Summary of Events and Information	Remarks and references to Appendices
HAILLICOURT	5		Left HAILLICOURT at 5.30 p.m. and marched to ANNEZIN	K. W. J.
	8		Draft arrived of 100 men from 2/6 Lancs Fus, (rest from England) - good men	
	9		Draft arrived of 39 men. About half new of E Lancs Regt, remainder various L.F. Batts. all men who have been in the country before.	
	21		Left at 1 p.m. marched to ANNEQUIN - Sank. Brigade Reserve to CAMBRIN Section.	
	22		Villar killed - one wounded	K. 1
	24		He blew mine at RAILWAY POINT towards right of rang of craters	
	25		Took over CAMBRIN Right Subsection from Major Stores. 15 L.F. having 1st Worcesters on right + 2 R Innisk on left. Rather noisy night with T.M.s with grenade + Stokes - we firing always for one.	
	26		A good deal of T.M. etc activity on both sides	
	27		Enemy blew mine at 5 30 a.m. at RAILWAY POINT - new crater at extreme right of range of craters - one man killed by falling debris in front line. Enemy took no action in mine (air) up. I stayed quiet all day.	1 2
	28		Enemy quiet - we threw a few bombs which we have gyllin safe to his crater. Major Stopfred on left to take command of 10 East Lancs a few casualties.	2
	29		Hurricane canon about 3 pm. Trench Guards (Fr in trabstadt. Handed over Subsection to Major Stone 15 L.F. + turned to MAISON ROUGE in Brigade support. Casualty officer	1/4 · 3

Malcolm. Ltd Col
16 L.F.

Army Form C. 2118.

WAR DIARY
or
INTELLIGENCE SUMMARY.
(Erase heading not required.)

Instructions regarding War Diaries and Intelligence Summaries are contained in F.S. Regs., Part II. and the Staff Manual respectively. Title pages will be prepared in manuscript.

Place	Date	Hour	Summary of Events and Information	Remarks and references to Appendices
Cambrin	August 30th.		Copied from Diary for Septembr 1916. Special patrol sent out to examine enemy's wire preparatory to a proposed raid Lieut C.W.Smith, 2/lt C.S.Marriott and 2 N.C.Os went out, both N.C.Os were wounded close to enemy's wire. the officers dragged them about 40 yards under fire, the 2/Lt Marriott stayed with the wounded men while Lieut Smith went back for help. Both N.C.Os were brought in but both died	Casualties K. W. 1 self inf 2.
	31st		Enemy blew a mine at Railway Point at 6.15 a.m.	

96th Brigade.

32nd Division.

16th BATTALION

LANCASHIRE FUSILIERS

SEPTEMBER 1 9 1 6

Vol 11

11.U.
3 sheets

original

Confidential.

War Diary
of
16 Lancashire Fusiliers

from August 30th to September 29th 1916.

Volume II. 11

Original

WAR DIARY or INTELLIGENCE SUMMARY
(Erase heading not required.)

Army Form C. 2118

16 Lan Fus
September 1916.

Instructions regarding War Diaries and Intelligence Summaries are contained in F.S. Regs., Part II and the Staff Manual respectively. Title Pages will be prepared in manuscript.

Place	Date	Hour	Summary of Events and Information	Remarks and references to Appendices
CAMBRIN	Aug 30.		Special patrol sent out to examine enemy's wire preparatory to attempted raid. Lieut C.N. Smith, 2Lt C.S. Marriott + 2 N.C.O.s went out, both N.C.O.s were wounded close to enemy's wire. The officers dragged them along 20 yards under fire, then 2Lt Marriott stayed with the wounded men while Lieut Smith went back for help. Both N.C.O.'s were brought in but W.E.D. died.	casualties K. W. 1 self inflicted 2
	31		Enemy flew a mine at RAILWAY POINT at 6.15. a.m. Zone	
	Sept 2.		Took over CAMBRIN RIGHT SUB SECTION from 15 Lan Fus - 1st Worcesters on right Zone. 2 R. Irish Fus on left. Lieut Hick. Wounded	1
	3.		Casualties from shell + mine safo Zone	
	4.		Handed over to 15 L.F. Moved to MAISON ROUGE in Brigade sullying rm	1 3
	6		Moved to ANNEQUIN in Brigade Reserve Zone	
	7		We attempted a raid on enemy's lines about A.28.a.10. Enemy's wire was found to be stronger than reported & gapo not cut by Artillery, not masticated. Somewhere was silent trying to cut by hand but a this little, too long had been cut, it decided to withdraw. Casualties caused by flints furled from our own shells.	3
	8		Took over Rt Subsection from 15 L.F. 2 Rifle Brigade on Right. 2 R. Irish Fus on Left.	1
	10		R. carried out the Raid that failed on Sept 7th - Two Bangalore Torpedoes were carried to left hand to be used to get through enemy's wire. 4 Arise were new broken the minutes (one six) + two other Germans were seen. Enemy's trenches in bad condition, 3 Comm't Trenches were unseen was broken up + front line much battered. Enemy brought heavy M.G. fire to bear two signal was sent up. The raid was preparatory to the capture of TP TW.E.D. and the other officer were Lieut C.N. Smith, 2 Lts Marriott and W.E. Foss. Raiders part 71. 2 R.A.I.B. Fus. Syke attacked Railway Crater, occupied crater all but. 4 7 + 6 men	

Original

Army Form C. 2118

WAR DIARY
or
INTELLIGENCE SUMMARY
(Erase heading not required.)

2/16 LAN FUS
September 1916.

Instructions regarding War Diaries and Intelligence Summaries are contained in F.S. Regs., Part II. and the Staff Manual respectively. Title Pages will be prepared in manuscript.

Place	Date	Hour	Summary of Events and Information	Remarks and references to Appendices
Cambrin Right Subsection.	Sep 13		March to main front. Left Maud. was made by Lewis gun. The Artillery bombarded enemy front line for 15 seconds only then lifted to the barrage. Zero hour 2:30 am. Men were made hold but infact climb. Our casualts mostly slight shrapnel & splinter from our own shells.	Casualti. K. W. 5pm 4. 8. [?/page 4.] 7
	14		Draft of 28 men arrived - all L.F. men various Batts, all 2 men had been in this country before. Qualifi poor, not up to standard of 2 previous drafts.	
	15-18		Handed over to 2 Manchester Regt - (Capt. Erskine in command) and moved to Willots in Bethune, Divisional Reserve.	2
	19		2 Lt Milligan (wounded inf 1.24) rejoined.	1.
	24		Lt. Kerr joined.	
	26		Moved to LEQUESNOY - Brigade Reserve.	
	27		Casual att? T.M. Batty. 2 Lt L.H. Macdonough joined	1
	30th		Took over Cuinchy Left Sub Section from Lt.Col Girdwood 11th Border Regt.	

Smalecombe Lt Col
16 L.F. 4.19

Raid night of 10th/11th Septr.1916, carried
out by 16th (S) Bn., Lancashire Fusiliers.

Object.

To kill the enemy, obtain identifications.

Arrangements worked smoothly and the Artillery support was very good.

Communication was maintained by telephone from front line where Commander of Operations and F.O.O. were situated and by messengers from the raiding parties out in front.

Pt. of entry A.28.a.1.0.

Zero. 2.30 a.m.

Artillery fired intense from O to 10" on front line and box barrage from O. to 0.50'.

Raiding party in position near enemy's wire at - 10'. As soon as Artillery had fired for 10" party moved forward.

Wire was blown by two 10 ft. Bangalore Torpedoes brought up and fired successively (tandem wise).

2nd.Lt. C.S. Marriott examined front line as far as the right boyau and found no one. 2 dug outs in this area and these found empty.

2nd.Lt. Foss, and a party examined front line as far as the left boyau and found a dug out from which a man came out with a pistol. He did not hands up when ordered so 2nd.Lt. Foss shot him. The pistol turned out to be a Very Pistol with a red cartridge.

2nd.Lt. W.E. Foss called down the dug out and 1 wounded and 1 unwounded man came out and were made prisoners. A little further on a man was found in the trench and made prisoner.

There were only 4 dug outs and these were all searched. Lt. C.W. Smith led and commanded the party which entered the trenches.

The entrances to these Boyaux were properly located but the Boyaux themselves were much knocked about by our fire, muddy, neglected and apparently not used. One boyau was used as a mud and debris dump.

The recall signal was given at 0.35' and Lt.Smith and 2nd.Lt.Marriott came out 0.50' having first seen that everyone had left the enemy trenches.

No difficulty was found in getting back to our trenches where three avenues of return had been prepared through our wire.

2nd.Lt. W.J. Sydes and a party advanced through the craters about A.28.c.2.7. and found the sap leading from the crater had had a great deal of fresh wire put up since they bombed it on night 7th/8th.

The blew the wire with a 10 ft. Bangalore Torpedo and cut a good deal of wire as well, but owing to the tremendous tangle of wire put out by the enemy they could not enter the sap.

No one was seen in the sap but observation was difficult so they might have been there, as on 7th/8th there were three men in this sap who bombed back.

Enemy's retaliation weak. Only a few H.E. and shrapnel. A Machine Gun fired in the direction of the party which attacked the sap behind the craters.

We had 7 wounded, all brought in.

Recommended for special leave owing to good work
in raid on night 10th/11th Septr.1916.

    Tempy.2nd.Lt.C. Marriott.
    Tempy. Lt. C.W. Smith.
    Serjt. Wilkinson...............12431.
    Cpl. Smith....................11993.
    Cpl. Rothwell.................15188.
    Pte. Marchmont................11639.
     "   Towers...................11590.
     "   Croden...................12135.
     "   Williamson...............12414.

Septr.11th.1916.   Brigadier General.
                                          96th Infantry Brigade.

Equipment.

Body snatching and fighting parties carried knobkerries and the commander of each of these parties carried a revolver.

Everyone carried 4 bombs each.
Bomb Carriers 24 bombs.
Bombers had their aprons full. 15 bombs.

Electric Torches with a ring of blue painted inside the lens were easily identified.

Handcuffs were used for the unwounded prisoners.

Rope nooses were taken but were not used owing to the small number of prisoners.

It was found that two 10 ft. of Bangalore Torpedoes were more useful owing to the complicated ground and wire, than one of 20 ft.

Lt. Smith who fired the Torpedoes was only 10x away when the Torpedoes went off and was perfectly safe.

Dayfield Shields were worn.

For recall purposes a whistle was tried but did not carry far, but a code word, viz. "MARMALADE" was used and was easily heard.

Several 8 ft. ladders were taken. These were most useful as enemy trenches were deep.

Septr.11th.1916.
Brigadier General.
96th Infantry Brigade.

Raiding Party.

Captain T. F. Tweed. a. Command of Operation.

Commander of Raiding parties...Lt.C.W.Smith. b.

Officers i/c. Detachments......2nd.Lt.Foss. c.
                                      2nd.Lt.Marriott. c.
                                      2nd.Lt.Sydes. d.

Detail of Parties.

	Offr.	O.R.
Commanding Operation.	1 a.	
Tape, Bangalore & wire cutters.	1 b.	10
5 Blocking Parties, 5 each.		25
9 Fighting and body snatching parties, 4 each.	2 c.	36
1 Lewis Gun Detmt. on left flank.		4
Crater party with Bangalore Torpedo.	1 d.	18
1 Lewis Gun Detmt. on right flank.		7
Spare Bangalore Torpedo and reserve party.	1	10
Messengers.		4
Signallers.		2
Escort for prisoners, at pt. of exit from our trenches.		3
Stretcher Bearers.		12
	6.	131.

"C" Form (Duplicate)
MESSAGES AND SIGNALS.

Army Form C. 2123.
(In books of 50's in duplicate.)
No. of Message....

~~WAR DIARY~~

Service Instructions. Mallwood MS

Charges to Pay. Office Stamp. [ARMY -Z 11.IX.16 1F]

Handed in at........ Office..... 2.1.... Received.......

TO: 96th Inf Bde

Sender's Number	Day of Month	In reply to Number	AAA
G 50	11/9		

Following from First Army Begins AAA The Army Commander desires his congratulations to be conveyed to all concerned for their good and useful work in carrying out the raids last night AAA The identifications are of great importance not only to the First Army but to all allied armies fighting

FROM PLACE & TIME: on Western Front 1.55 PM

32nd Division 2.45

(1)

G. O. C., I st. Corps.

I should be glad if you will direct the G.O.C., 32nd. Division to convey to Brig. Gen. YATMAN, Commanding 96th. Brigade, my thanks and appreciation of the action of 16th. Bn. The Lancashire Fusiliers under the Command of Lt. Col. ABERCROMBIE, last night, in carrying out their successful raid into the German trenches.

The identifications they obtained by the capture of prisoners are of exceptional value at the present time, and this information will be of the greatest service not only to the British Army, but to those of all the Allies fighting in all theatres of war.

      (sd) R. HAKING,
            General,
11..9..16.   Cmdg. Ist. Army.

(2)

I Corps.

The Army Commander would like the contents of this letter to reach the Brigade and Battalion concerned to-day.

      (sd) A. WOOD,
            Capt., G.S.,
11th. September, 1916.   First Army.

(3)

         11...9...16.

Dear General,

   The Corps Commander in sending you the enclosed wishes to add his own congratulations on the efficient manner in which the raid was planned and carried out.

        Yours sincerely,

       (sd) G. V. HORDEN.

96th Brigade.

32nd Division.

16th BATTALION

LANCASHIRE FUSILIERS

OCTOBER 1 9 1 6

Confidential

WAR DIARY
of
16 LANCASHIRE FUSILIERS
for
Oct–Dec 1916.

Vol II

Original

Army Form C. 2118

WAR DIARY
or
INTELLIGENCE SUMMARY
(Erase heading not required.)

16 LANC. FUSRS.
October 1916.

Instructions regarding War Diaries and Intelligence Summaries are contained in F.S. Regs., Part II. and the Staff Manual respectively. Title Pages will be prepared in manuscript.

Place	Date 1916	Hour	Summary of Events and Information	Remarks and references to Appendices
LE QUESNOY	Sept 30		Took over CUINCHY LEFT SUBSECTION from Lt Col. Girdwood 11 BORDER Regt.	
	Oct 1.		16 N.F. on right – 10 E. Yorks on left – our left boundary in LA BASSÉE canal. Zzzz	
	3		Casualty at relief: rifle shot wound 2 Lt. L.C. Price wounded. Zzzz	1
	4		Handed over to 15 LAN. FUS. + moved to HARLEY ST. in Bde Support Zzzz	1
	7		Casualties in workpath in Feunchegna	
	8			3
	9		Took over from CUINCHY LEFT SUBSECT from 15. L Fus	
	10.		I went on leave handing over command to Major T. F. TWEED Queens Regt & went in Billets at ANNE QUIN. Zzzz	1
	14		Handed over to 12th East Surrey Regt. Zzzz Relieved Billets in 97 Inf Bde.	
	15		In Bde Reserve in BETHUNE + rejoined 96? Bde. Zzzz	
	16		Marched to Billets at OURTON. Zzzz	
	17		Marched to BETHONSART. Zzzz	
	18		Marched to BERLINCOURT. Zzzz	
	19		Marched to AUTHIEULE. Zzzz	
	21		Huttements at VADENCOURT. Zzzz	
			Thomas F. Tweed Major	
	23		I rejoined & resumed command. Zzzz	
	25		Marched to BRICKFIELDS area (bivouacs) ALBERT – BOUZINCOURT Rd Zzzz	
	26		Partie went to POZIERES and (ward area)	
	28		Marched to Billets in HARLEY ave Parties razor proof area Zzzz	Mal Casualties 1 5
	31		Marched to billets at RUBEMPRÉ Zzzz	

Emmerwerde Lt Col
16 L.F.

96th Brigade.

32nd Division.

~~16th~~ BATTALION

LANCASHIRE FUSILIERS

NOVEMBER 1 9 1 6

W A R   D I A R Y.

16th LANCASHIRE FUSILIERS.

November 1st to 30th.1916.

WAR DIARY
INTELLIGENCE SUMMARY

Army Form C. 2118

16 LANC. FUSRS.
November 1916.

Place	Date 1916	Hour	Summary of Events and Information	Remarks and references to Appendices
RUBEMPRE	Nov. 13		Marched to billets in WARLOY.	
	14		Marched to THIEPVAL, Dug outs & shelters, relieving 16 Rifle Brig. Support to 56 Inf Bde (19 Div) who were holding front line zone.	Map HEBUTERNE 1/10,000
	17		Marched to billets in MAILLY MAILLET.	
	18		To ELLIS SQUARE (K 33 & 49) - Relief to 14 Inf. Bde. (in instructions — 2 Coys attached 14 Bde for carrying. Did one journey, and shewn very bad and muddy way there hopes. Remaining 2 Coys at H.Q. in support of 97 Inf Bde. No shelters — news entrances very much	Map BEAUMONT 1/10,000
	19		Relieved by 16 N.F. & marched via MAILLY MAILLET, AUCHONVILLERS, BEAUMONT HAMEL to WAGGON ROAD (Q 5.6-65) relieving 2 ROYLI. (H.AC Brig) W.M. 3. K. 1. Enemy shelling WAGGON RD intermittently with 5.9 & 4.2. BEAUMONT HAMEL also heavily. BEAUMONT HAL & 5.9m & shelled WAGGON ROAD	Map BEAUMONT 1/10,000
	20		Enemy barrage — no attempt at attack	8 20
	21		Occasional shelling	
	22		Heattacked MUNCH TRENCH between WALKER ALLEY and CRATER TRENCH but arrived too early & part of 11 BORDER & 16 HLI who were isolated in FRANKFORT TRENCH at Q 6.6.16. The attack was made of 2.40 new 16 LF & 80 new 2 R. Innis. 5 Pr. 5 formed in 4 waves, a platoon of Innis 91 on the right of each wave. Withdrawn the whole was under command of Capt CW MERRY WEATHER. 16 LF. The troops much indessed of RIGCROFT ALLEY the new front, the 1st, 2nd, 3rd & 4th waves, of 16 LF were to capture MUNCH there it while its 2 nd waves under Lieut G.N. HIGGINSON went on to FRANKFURT, effect the rescue & return.	4 10
	23			13 35

Original

WAR DIARY or INTELLIGENCE SUMMARY

Army Form C. 2118

Place: 16 LANC FUSRS 2
Date: November 1916

Date	Hour	Summary of Events and Information	Remarks and references to Appendices
Nov 23		Zero was 3:30 p.m. and the advance was made under cover of an intense Arty. barrage. MUNICH TRENCH was occupied without much opposition but on attacking parties (N advanced) allowed the enemy who were in considerable force to keep ours in small parts of our objective so prevented in from sending back the prisoners extracted from dug outs - about 20 enemy in charge of one officer were reported. Some of the 2nd Bn CW past MUNICH to the 3rd barrage line but Lieut HIGGINSON took the N.C.O.'s name and when the barrage lifted there seem to have been only about 10 men left & they did not go forward. The remainder then withdrew. The officers 16 L.F. who went forward were 1st wave Lieut D. ROBERTSON, 2Lt C.S. TOMES, 2nd wave Lieut G.N. HIGGINSON. 3rd wave 2Lt W.N. WATTS, 4th wave Capt C.W. MERRYWEATHER (in command) 2Lt H.B. RYLANDS. All the officers did extremely well - Capt MERRYWEATHER was seen to fall whilst standing in the edge of MUNICH directing operations, Lieut HIGGINSON, having along the few men he had left under the barrage, pressed on beyond MUNICH, 2Lt RYLANDS was apparently sent forward to take on the advanced party after Lt HIGGINSON fell + was not seen. These three officers did not return. Lieut ROBERTSON was able helped by 2Lts WATTS and TOMES in MUNICH TRENCH. Block were established on the left and dug out bombed + prisoners taken, then had he rejected to fight other parties of the enemy who emerged from dug outs that were overlooked in entering the trench. He names the three officers have all been sent forward for whose and the following N.C.O.'s have also rendered for doing excellent work —	Casualties K. W. M. S.S. (from previous sheet) 13 35

WAR DIARY or **INTELLIGENCE SUMMARY**
(Erase heading not required.)

Army Form C. 2118

16 LANCS FUSRS
November 1916.

Place	Date 1916	Hour	Summary of Events and Information	Remarks and references to Appendices
	Nov 23		A Co. 11348 L.Cpl. G. HUGHES, 22686 Segt A. FAULKNER, 15765 L.Cpl. J. CUNLIFFE, 15016 Pte P. CHAPMAN. B Co. 11349 Segt J. TIMPERLEY 39439 Pte R. ATKINSON. C Co. 39422 Pte D. TONES, 11500 Pte E. LAKING, 11454 Pte C. WILLIAMS, 11375 Pte J. DEWHURST. D Co. 11915 Segt J. HOLLAND, 12095 Pte O. DAVIES, 11878 Segt GIBSON, 11627 Pte J. TONES, 11761 Pte RABY. I have also to call attention to the heavy, desperate and unknown work of Army Chaplain Capt W.H. FAWKES. who fought in many desperate fights beside wounded men at least 3 times the wire in MUNICH TRENCH. The failure to reach the MUNICH & FRANKFORT TRENCHES. to heavy mm. M.G. fire between MUNICH & FRANKFORT TRENCHES. Officer Casualties nil. Capt. C.W. MEREYWEATHER killed. Lt. G.N. HIGGINSON missing, believed killed. 2Lt R.B. RYLANDS wounded & missing. OMA.	Hmkbrunn Sheet. Casualties. K. W. S.S. M. 13 35— Casualties. 2 1. Officers O.R. 10 94 1 56 25·129·1·57

Original

WAR DIARY
or
INTELLIGENCE SUMMARY
(Erase heading not required.)

Army Form C. 2118

16 LANCS FUS(?)
November 1916.

Place	Date 1916	Hour	Summary of Events and Information	Remarks and references to Appendices
	Nov 24		Relieved by 6 DEVONS. Lt.Col. James. Relief complete about 5.30 a.m. marched to MAILLY MAILLET. At 10 a.m. men moved by motor buses to SARTON, transport & details by road.	
	25		marched to billets in ORVILLE Emma	
	26		marched to billets in BONNEVILLE Emma	

Swalenagh Lt.Col
Comdg 16 L.F.

96th Infantry Brigade.

With further reference to the attack on November 23rd, I have examined all the men who came back and can only find one who got any considerable distance past MUNICH Trench. This is an intelligent man, one of the Battalion snipers, and he was in the left of the wave during the advance. He got up to the Barrage, 150 yards beyond MUNICH but states that he could see nobody else with him and retired when the barrage lifted as there was no one to go forward with him. He states that there was some machine gun fire, mostly from his left, whilst he was advancing and that this became very heavy when he turned to go back and on his way back. He saw no signs of anyone in FRANKFORT TRENCH, the line of which he could see quite plainly.

Other reports say that there were about 15 men beyond MUNICH with Lieut. HIGGINSON, but these were on the right of the sniper mentioned above.

I think that the failure of the advance to reach FRANKFORT was owing to:-

(1) M.G. fire from the flanks.
(2) The fact that some of the advanced men ran into) the barrage.
(3) The fact that the Officer & all) the N.C.O.s. became casualties.)

(sd) C. M. ABERCROMBIE. Lt.Col.
Commanding, 16th Lancashire Fusrs.

- 2 -

Headquarters,
  32nd. Division.

96th Infantry Brigade No. 3457/1   29.11.16.

Forwarded.

G.O.C. ....
G.S.O. I. ....
G.S.O. II. ....
G.S.O. III. ....

A.E. Glasgow
Lieut. Colonel.
Commanding, 96th Inf. Bde.

96th Brigade.

32nd Division.

16th BATTALION

LANCASHIRE FUSILIERS

DECEMBER 1916

Vol 14

WAR DIARY
of
16 (S) Batt Lancashire Fusiliers.
for
December 1916.

Amalgamated with
16th

96 Inf Bde

Original

16 Lanc Fusrs Army Form C. 2118

WAR DIARY
or
INTELLIGENCE SUMMARY
(Erase heading not required.)

December 1916.

Place	Date	Hour	Summary of Events and Information	Remarks and references to Appendices
BONNEVILLE	Dec 1		Training & organised sports & games.	
	3		Draft of 38 men received. Daily work material, about 50% "Instruction"	
	6		" 78 " " Very good, mostly old soldiers, many from line Battns	
	7		" 30 " " Prov WO, physical + in training zone	
	10		" 10 " " Prov WO physical + in training zone	
	12		2 Lt H.G. Brinton + 2 Lt P.A. Glascow joined Bn	
	18		Accident in bombing ground. 2 Lts Milligan & Sykes wounded	
	25		@ Le Cornet Malflyn. Received Shelters from Inspector of	
	26		" " " Billet isolated + no further	
			Died	
			Cases. Court of Inquiry on Bombing Accident 18th inst. found accidental, no one to	
			blame. A.O.D reference June	
	29		2 Lt R.Gould joined Bn	

E Maxwell Lt Col
16 L.F.

WAR DIARY
of
16 LANCASHIRE FUSILIERS
for
January 1917.

Maremendu Wood
B.E.F.

Army Form C. 2118.

WAR DIARY
or
INTELLIGENCE SUMMARY

(Erase heading not required.)

Instructions regarding War Diaries and Intelligence Summaries are contained in F. S. Regs., Part II. and the Staff Manual respectively. Title Pages will be prepared in manuscript.

Place	Date	Hour	Summary of Events and Information	Remarks and references to Appendices

2449 Wt. W14957/M90 750,000 1/16 J.B.C. & A. Forms/C.2118/12.

Original

Army Form C. 2118.

16 LAN. FUS.

WAR DIARY
or
INTELLIGENCE SUMMARY
(Erase heading not required.)

January 1917

Place	Date	Hour	Summary of Events and Information	Remarks and references to Appendices
BONNEVILLE	Jan 1/17 6		Left BONNEVILLE and marched to TERRAMESNIL	
	7		To BUS LES ARTOIS.	Casualties W. K.
	11		Officer went into line	1.
	14		Took over C.3 Subsector (Middle SERRE) from 17th. PAUL. 17 HLI having 2 Man't Regt on right, 16 North'ns by on left. Line held by series of isolated posts. Trenches very muddy & wet, many C.T.S impassable - enemy quiet.	
	16		Handed over Middle Hannan 16 North'ns. Returned to billets in COURCELLES	1.
	18		Took over C.3 from 15 LF. Quiet set in line	
	19		Took over post no.14 (in by night) from 2 Man't Regt.	
	20		Handed over to some 15 LF. To billets in COURCELLES	1.
	21		Marched to MAILLY MAILLET	
	22		Took over C.2 from 16 N.F. Line in 15 HLI on right, and 2 R. Irish on our left. Line held by 2 Coys only (A & B) 2 Coys (C & D) in billets in M. MAILLET	
	2 m		No 3 & 4 posts heavily shelled at dawn. C & D Coys relieve A B en	4 1.
	26		Handed over to 2 R. Irish. and 2 Manch Archers. 16 N.F. in command. To billets in BERTRANCOURT	
				7 1.

Original

Army Form C. 2118.

WAR DIARY
or
INTELLIGENCE SUMMARY
(Erase heading not required.)

16 L.N. FUS.
January 1917.

Place	Date	Hour	Summary of Events and Information	Remarks and references to Appendices
	30		Took over R.6 (late C.3) sublocator from 15 L.F. having 2 R. Inniskls on its right and R.W.F. on left.	
	31		Attack on our right advanced posts at 5 a.m. Enemy bombarded our front and flank lines for one hour but nothing was seen of attacking party. One prisoner was taken in our wire & one was taken by R. Innisks on its left post. he and head of the attack though prisoner statement. We had no casualties.	

Malcolm Mc⟨?⟩
16 L.F.

Confidential

War Diary
1/6 Lancashire Fusiliers
for
February 1917
(Volume 2)

Vol 16

Acknowledged J.W.
Amended 16.2.18

Army Form C. 2118.

WAR DIARY
or
INTELLIGENCE SUMMARY

(Erase heading not required.)

Instructions regarding War Diaries and Intelligence Summaries are contained in F. S. Regs., Part II. and the Staff Manual respectively. Title Pages will be prepared in manuscript.

Place	Date	Hour	Summary of Events and Information	Remarks and references to Appendices

2449 Wt. W14957/M90 750,000 1/16 J.B.C. & A. Forms/C.2118/12.

Original

WAR DIARY or INTELLIGENCE SUMMARY

16 Lan. Fus.

February 1917

Army Form C. 2118.

Place	Date 1917	Hour	Summary of Events and Information	Remarks and references to Appendices
	Feb 2		Handed over R.b. Subsector to 10 Worcesters (Wor. Sec.) Moved to Hutts in BERTRANCOURT	
	5		This Campaign sent to ACHONVILLERS for training purposes	
	6		Travel to DOMART to attend C.O's conference under Brig. Genl. Stockwell D.S.O. leaving no command of Batt. to Major Tweed.	
	7		Casualties caused by Whiz Bombs & Shelling K. W. M. – 8 –	T.S.T.
	9		Relieved 15th Lan Fus. in R.I. Sub Sector BEAUMONT - HAMEL	T.S.T.
	10.		Working on Patrol HEN POST	T.S.T.
		8.30 am	Attack on TEN TREE ALLEY & WHITE TRENCH by On Bn. 16th NORTH. FUS. — 2nd K.O.Y.L.I. & 11th BORDER REG. Attack successful on front by 11th BORDER 86 Prisoners passed through our line. Casualties caused by enemy Barrage 3 Killed 4 Wounded	
	12	5.30 A.M.	Relieved by 16th H.L.I. (less 2 Coys) & 11th BORDER (less 2 Coys) T.S.T. & proceeded to Hutments at MAILLY WOOD EAST.	T.S.T.
	14		Marched to HERRISART	T.S.T.
	16		" " MOLLIENS - AU - BOIS	T.S.T.
	17		" " BERTANGLES	T.S.T.
	20		" " CAMON.	T.S.T.
	21		" " HANGARD	T.S.T.
	23		" " BEAUFORT Less 2 Coys at LE QUESNEL T.S.T.	
	24		Relieved in NEW SUBSECTOR the 75th Infantry Battn. (FRENCH) T.S.T.	
	26		Extended Battn. frontage to LEFT Northern 1 Coy 15th LAN FUS. Handed over Command to Lt Col ABERCROMBIE	T.S.T.

Army Form C. 2118.

Original

16 LAN. FUS.
February 1917

WAR DIARY
or
INTELLIGENCE SUMMARY
(Erase heading not required.)

Place	Date	Hour	Summary of Events and Information	Remarks and references to Appendices
	1917 Feb 27		Handed over N.E.4 subsector to 16 Anks Fus ? (Lt.Col. Little) the svg mts in MARVILLERS. Erna.	
			What arneshi	K.W.M. 3.17.1
			Amalewardi Wheh.	R.W.M.

2449 Wt. W14957/M90 750,000 1/16 J.B.C. & A. Forms/C.2118/12.

WAR DIARY.

of

16th Bn. Lancashire Fusiliers.

MARCH 1917½

Vol. 2.

Confidential

War Diary of
16 Lancashire Fusiliers

for

March 1917.
Volume 2

Army Form C. 2118.

WAR DIARY
or
INTELLIGENCE SUMMARY

(Erase heading not required.)

Instructions regarding War Diaries and Intelligence Summaries are contained in F. S. Regs., Part II. and the Staff Manual respectively. Title Pages will be prepared in manuscript.

Place	Date	Hour	Summary of Events and Information	Remarks and references to Appendices

2449 Wt. W14957/M90 750,000 1/16 J.B.C. & A. Forms/C.2118/12.

Original

WAR DIARY or INTELLIGENCE SUMMARY

(Erase heading not required.)

Army Form C. 2118.

16 LAN FUS
March 1917

Place	Date 1917	Hour	Summary of Events and Information	Remarks and references to Appendices
WARVILLERS.	Mar 2		Marched to FRESNOY –	
	5		One recent. Training & workparties	
	9		Took over MARNE POST subsect from 1 Oxfords having 2 R Innis Bn on right & 17 H.L.I. on left	Casualties K W
	10		Casualties; 4 minor &c	
	11		Casualties from 5 minenwerfer	1 4
	14		Handed over to 2 RD Y L I (R A C L Brach) & - To BOUCHOIR, Bde reserve	officers 1
	15		Took over BOUVINES subsect from 15 LF	
	17		Casualties sniper	
			Enemy mg took front line to PARVILLERS – took up positions in FOUQUESCOURT –	
	18		DAMERY and w onwards. Advance 2000 myds.	
			To FRESNOY les ROYE – HATTENCOURT Rd with 2 coys from to SEPT FOURS –	
			ETALON Line – Lets to LIANE WOOD (nr SEPT FOURS) – adv 7500 yds	
	19		En support – marches to NESLE, thence to LANGUEVOISIN – adv 5 6500 yds	
	20		To CANIZY – support in right flank of Bn. C airman 7250 Pigeon	
	21		Took over line OFFOY – BONY from 15 L.F. & covered the line to TOULLE –	
			MATIGNY line – & sent on patrols (at SANCOURT) 14 O.R. (Oxords) in	
			left. Digging during new line. Advance 4500 yards	
	22		Coy guards in reserve at BOIS SAVY	
	23		Handed over to 2 R Innis Bn?. Marched BACQUENCOURT & HOMBLEUX in	
			evening	
	24		Started rigging new line VOYENNES – CANIZY	
	25		had 0 R 000 L.C.L. to fill craters & mend road. Canons 300 o.r.R. (Reyne TOULLE) line	

Lieutenant Col
16 Lan Fus
31.3.17

CONFIDENTIAL.

Vol 18

18-V.
5 sheets

WAR DIARY.

OF

16th BATTN. LANCASHIRE FUSILIERS.

From 1st April 1917.

To 30th April 1917.

96 Inf Bde

Hewitt war diary for April 1917

1 Machine Gun Coy
Coy 16th F

30.4.17

Confidential

War Diary
of
16 S. Batt Lancashire Fusiliers
for
April 1917

Volume 2.

Swallowed up wholly
Cout No 16
30.4.17

Original

Army Form C. 2118.

WAR DIARY or **INTELLIGENCE SUMMARY**
(Erase heading not required.)

16 LAN FUS
April 1917

Place	Date Ap 1917	Hour	Summary of Events and Information	Remarks and references to Appendices
DOUILLY	1.		97. Inf. Bde attacked & captured SAVY. We marched to FORESTE, thence to CHÂTEAU POMMERY where informed up for attack on SAVY WOOD. Order 1st attack on followed. 2 R Inniskillings to capture wood in S.26.b, 1 S.L.F. to capture N.W. SAVY WOOD, as far as Rly running N.W. of toughun & from thro' 1 R.L.F. & capture part of wood N. of Railway. Zero hour 3.0.p.m. Attack successful, in spite of H.E. wood made our advance held between enemy shelled attack with H.E. m.g. + M.G.s active from HOLNON, FRANCILLY & Quarry at in S.21.a. Our casualties were from M.G. Position consolidated - H.Q. established in Railway cutting - anmt. station bought up after dark without difficulty. Casualties: Officers: Killed – 2 Lt E. J. Brownan. Wounded – 2 Lt & J. Brownan. O.R. Killed W. SS. K.W. 1 4 21. 98. Robinson, Chamberlayne. Wounded.	Map 1/20000 62c S.W.
	2.		14 Inf. Bde passed through at dawn & attacked (artillery arm) & captured FRANCILLY + SELENCY. Enemy strong points encountered including from S.27 (joining with French army) S.21 S.14 S.13 nothing substantial for huts advanced. Our left Bde under instructions in S.3.	heavies 1. 2.
	3			
	4		French attack & capture DALLON & LEPINE DALLON	
	5		French left to ROCOURT	
	6			
	8		Moved to SAVY, Bde H.Q.	
			Casualties: shell fire on artillery position. Took over Right sub-sector of Bde front, S.27.c to S.22.c / 2 R. Inniss. L.F. 2nd to Lin ing French army in right + 16 N.F. on left	
	11			
	12		Relieved by 1st Dorsets. Marched to GERMAINE. Bde in Div. Reserve.	
	13		Orders to stand ready to take over to support French attack on St Quentin. Marched at 9.30.p.m. to ATILLY. attached to 97 Bde from midnight.	

Original

Army Form C. 2118.

WAR DIARY
or
INTELLIGENCE SUMMARY

16 Lanr Fus
2
April 1917.

(Erase heading not required.)

Place	Date	Hour	Summary of Events and Information	Remarks and references to Appendices
	Ap 1917 14		97 Inf Bde captured FAYET (Trench beyond from CEPY FARM (S6 & 8.4) to TWIN COPIES (M29C) he marched at 8 am to HOLNON. at 3 pm. to FAYET, supporting 97 Inf Bde who were all in the line. 2 Lt. Laird wounded.	map 62/3. SW 1/20,000 K.W. 6. 7.
	15		Took over line from M36 central to TWIN WOODS (M29C) from 17 H.L.I. 2 KOYLI and 11 Border having 15th on right & 35th Div on left. 96 Bde relieved 97 Bde.	
	16		Quiet. Some casualties from General shelling in	
	17		Regaining front line in an outpost system, taking our posts recaptured by 1/5 LF. estab- on right. CEEPY FARM (redoubt) 14th Bn on right	5
	18		On left posts in contact with 3rd 9th Relieved by 2 R Fusiliers on 7th. marched to HOLNON in support	1 5 1 3
	20		32nd Div relieved by 61st Div. 2/1 Bucks Batt. (Ox & Bks L.I) took over our 96 Bde. march to GERMAINE	
	21 23 26 27		marched to ENNEMAIN. Div in Corps Reserve. Rest & training. I went to PARIS on leave. Capt R.B Knott takes command. Gallier Returned from leave. Lt. B.D. Jackson accidentally wounded. Took over active command 96 Bde. during absence of Brig. Gen. L.W. Ashburn on leave	

Total casualties in month.

Officers Killed 1 OR Killed 30
wounded 6 wounded 118
S. Shock 1

Malumule L.W. 30.4.17 16 L.F.

No 19

Confidential.

War Diary of
16 Lancashire Fusiliers
for
May 1917.

Guademonde Wood
16 L.F.

96 Inf Bde

Herewith original copy of
War Diary for May 1917.
please

[signature]
16 Lt.

31.5.17.

Original

Army Form C. 2118.

WAR DIARY
or
INTELLIGENCE SUMMARY

16 LAN FUS
May 1917

(Erase heading not required.)

Instructions regarding War Diaries and Intelligence Summaries are contained in F. S. Regs., Part II. and the Staff Manual respectively. Title Pages will be prepared in manuscript.

Place	Date 1917	Hour	Summary of Events and Information	Remarks and references to Appendices
ENNEMAIN	May 1. 5.		Training.— On 1/5/17 men arrived, read all belonging to 1/5, 1/6, 1/7 Batts. Lt. from Egypt. Good men on the whole, with 12/18 months service but not trained. Many unfit, fifty ephemera. Zuva	
	16		Marched to MARCHELEPOT. Zuva. Capt. McCann to Hospital zuva	
	17		Marched to CAIX. Training zuva	
	28		Capt R. MacGill, R.A.M.C. rejoined from hospital.	
	31. 5. 17.			

E McMurrough Wilde
Col 16 L.F.
Comd 16 L.F.

Mon Dieu
1
161 avenue des ileus
fr
juin 1917.
Manu 2

Army Form C. 2118.

WAR DIARY
or
INTELLIGENCE SUMMARY
(Erase heading not required.)

Instructions regarding War Diaries and Intelligence Summaries are contained in F. S. Regs., Part II. and the Staff Manual respectively. Title Pages will be prepared in manuscript.

Place	Date	Hour	Summary of Events and Information	Remarks and references to Appendices

2449 Wt. W14957/M90 750,000 1/16 J.B.C. & A. Forms/C.2118/12.

Original

WAR DIARY
or
INTELLIGENCE SUMMARY

(Erase heading not required.)

Army Form C. 2118.

16 LAN. FUS
June 1917

Place	Date 1917	Hour	Summary of Events and Information	Remarks and references to Appendices
CAIX	June 1		Marched to GUILLAUCOURT and entrained at 7 p.m.	
	2		Detrained at CAESTRE 10.20 a.m. Marched to LE VERRIER. 36 Div. handed over XIV Corps as G.H.Q. Reserve.	
	7		Bart standing by in hand notice during operation in MESSINES–WYTSCHAETE.	
	12		Marched to Billets near ECKE.	
	13		Marched to WORMHOUDT.	
	15		Marched to MALO TERMINUS.	
	17		Entrained at LEFFRINCKOUCKE – Detrained at COXYDE, marched to camp near OOST DUNKERQUE.	
	19		Took over NIEUPORT BAINS right support subsector.	
	21		Major T.F. TWEED returned to duty.	
	22		Handed over to 10 Gloucester Regt. (1 Bn. 1 Div.) marched to camp at COXYDE.	
	23		Marched to GHYVELDE.	
	24		G.O.C. went on leave. I took command of 96 Inf Bde, Major TWEED took command of Batt.	
	26		Training & maching at practice trenches.	

Ewallumal LtCol
16 L.F.
30.6.17.

No 21

War Diary
of
16 Lancashire Fusiliers
for
July 1917

M.D.
21.V.
5 sheets

Army Form C. 2118.

WAR DIARY
or
INTELLIGENCE SUMMARY
(Erase heading not required.)

16th Lan Fus.   July 1917.

Place	Date	Hour	Summary of Events and Information	Remarks and references to Appendices
GYVELDE	July 1.		Training + Attack Practice.	
	4.		Marched to JOHNNIOT CAMP. 2 Coys. H.Q. + 2 Coys. RABAILLET CAMP. 1st	
	5.		Relieved 1st Dorset Regiment in 'D' Sub-Sector (St George's) 1st	
	6.		Casualties 2 Wounded 1st	
	7.		do 1 Killed 4 1 Wounded 1st	
	8.		do 2/Lt Preston Wounded. O.R. 2 Killed 1 Died of Wounds 4 1 Wounded 1st	
	9.		do 1 Wounded (at duty) 1st	
	10.		At 2 A.M. the 17th Division on left made enemy trench. Enemy retaliation very heavy.	
			At 4.30 A.M. Enemy commenced to shell front line, support + bridge with heavy calibre H.E.	
			At 10 A.M. Enemy fire increased to great violence. Communication Trenches + Bridges Bad by	
			heavy shells + many houses on fire.	
			damaged. At 1.15 p.m. reconnaissance Heavens concentration on	
			At 1 p.m. Enemy fire slackened. All Coys. of Bn. in battle positions.	
			front of 17th Division + 97th Bde.	
			At 4 p.m. Enemy fire ceased. At 4.15 p.m. reconnaissance which was particularly	
			on front of 1st Div. + 97th Bde. At 6 p.m. enemy commenced drum fire in front of 1st Div. + 97th Bde.	
			At 7 p.m. fire was of great intensity. At 7.15 p.m. many attacks on 1st Div. + 97th Bde.	
			At 8.30 p.m. enemy fire slackened on trench. NIEUPORT still heavy shelled + burning	
			At 11 p.m. fire practically ceased on trenches.	
			Many parts. Wounded. 2/Lt. Morris, Daniel, Joseph. O.R. Killed a	
			Casualties. 2/Lt Barlow Killed.	
			Died of Wounds 9. Wounded 5.5. 1st	
	11		At 1.30 A.M. Capt C.W. Smith + 2 Platoons "B" Co attempted to raid RAT POST. Raid failed	
			owing to wire not being cut. Bombardment with Lewis on flank was during the day	
			Enemy continued desultory shelling.	

Army Form C. 2118.

WAR DIARY
or
INTELLIGENCE SUMMARY

(Erase heading not required.)

16th LAN. FUS.

July 1917

Place	Date	Hour	Summary of Events and Information	Remarks and references to Appendices
ST GEORGE'S Sub Sectr.	July 11		Casualties. O.R. Died of Wounds 1. Wounded 1. T&T	
	12.	1-30 A.M.	Heavy Bombardment of enemy on Sector on our left. At 2 A.M. Bombardment slackened.	
		3-20 A.M.	Heavy Bombardment commenced on NIEUPORT. At 3-45 A.M. bombardment became intense.	
		4 A.M.	Enemy fire slackened. 4-30 A.M. enemy fire ceased. Heavier continued on beach and at	
			Enemy front line during day, mostly on NIEUPORT & Left Sub Sectr.	
		8-30 A.M. to 8-30 A.M.	was heavily shelled with 5.9 & 8". Bomb & S.A.A store blown up	
			Capt Powell killed.	
		11-45 P.M.	Enemy raid on one of our posts near POLDER FARM. Sergeant with 1 post killed &	
			2 men wounded by bomb. Enemy driven off by patrols under 2/Lt McClymont. 1 O.R. wounded &	
			missing.	
			Casualties. Killed J. Capt Powell 2 O.R. Wounded 7 O.R.	
	13.		Intermittent shelling during the day. At 9 p.m. heavy hostile Bombardment commenced on Left Sub	
			Sectr & NIEUPORT & continued with great intensity - until 11 p.m. when fire slackened.	
			Casualties. O.R. Killed 1. Wounded 6. Missing 1. Gassed 1. Gassed 1. T&T	
			Capt Knox. Wounded. O.R. Wounded 2. Gassed 1. T&T	
	14.	1-45 A.M.	14th Bde commenced attack on Left Sub Sectr. Enemy replied vigorously to our Bombardment T&T	
	15.		O.R. 3 Wounded.	
	16.	1-20 A.M.	2/Lt McClymont & 3 Section 'B' Co. carried out bombing attack on enemy sap at Nieuport R.D.	
			Enemy were both encountered & bombed. Two of enemy known to have been killed.	
			Intermittent shelling during day. Casualties: O.R. Wounded 4. T&T	
	17.	1-30 A.M.	Lt Watts & 3 Sections C & D Coys. attempted Bombing raid on RAT POST. Hostile	
			Raid Post about 30 strong was encountered in No Man's Land. After sharp fight enemy party	
			was driven in & bombed in their trenches. Casualties 5 & 6 Heavy.	

Original

WAR DIARY
or
INTELLIGENCE SUMMARY
(Erase heading not required.)

Army Form C. 2118.

16th LAN. FUS.
July 1917.

Place	Date	Hour	Summary of Events and Information	Remarks and references to Appendices
ST. GEORGES Sub Sector	July 17		Casualties. Wounded 2/Lt Billcock. O.R. Killed 2 Wounded 4 Wounded (at duty) 3	T/F
	18.	4 p.m.	Heavy bombardment of our front line & support for 15 minutes. Retaliation for our gun fire.	
			Same day. Casualties. Died of Wounds 2/Lt Oxford. O.R. Killed 2 Wounded 7 Wounded (at duty) 4	T/F
	19	2.30 A.M.	S.O.S. fired from Left Sub Sector. B.H.Q. shelled with light guns.	T/F
		3.00	Handed over Sector to 1/5 West Yorks. Bn (Douglas). & moved to KUHN	T/F
KUHN CAMP	21		CAMP. R. & Q.M. Munir wounded to hospital. Large working parties at night carrying up ammn. & stores. Handed over command to Lt Col Abercrombie	was Thomas F. Major
	22		Our Bat. 1 O. & 120 men came under gun shelling & a number (6 men slightly affected). Symptoms continued troublesome after return to camp. Discharging the presence of a new gas; generally described as smelling (like mustard) but not unpleasant. Men's eyes mostly affected later. Throats hoarse; handkerchiefs quite saturated for 10 days & more with common. Result 1 Off. 1 Off (Lt C.S. Marriott) + 12 men sent to hospital.	
	23		1 Off + 26 men kept in camp under regimental treatment. Sufferers from effected for inwards 5. 2 off & 30 men	
	24		Camp shelled intermittently through night – one shell hit above (Queen Cossack) Allée C Company. Killed 4. Wounded 12 Emma	

Original

WAR DIARY
INTELLIGENCE SUMMARY

16 KAN Fd S
July 1917

Army Form C. 2118.

Place	Date 1917	Hour	Summary of Events and Information	Remarks and references to Appendices
KOYEN CAMP.	July 25		D Coys work party shelled whilst burying cable at night. Casualties Killed 2, hand[ed] 15 Lt Foss to Hospital, effects of gas	
	26		Marched to Camp at BRAY DUNES. Capt R B Knott rejoined from	
	31		Marched to billets in OOST DUNKIRKE.	
			Total Casualties	
			Officers — Killed 3, Wounded 6, Gassed 2.	
			Other ranks — Killed 23, Wounded 109, Missing 1, Gassed 15	
			[signature] Lt Col	

Vol 22

War Diary
of
16 Kauverhi Division
for
August 1917.
China.

Original

Army Form C. 2218.

WAR DIARY
or
INTELLIGENCE SUMMARY

16 LAN FUS.
August 1917.

(Erase heading not required.)

Instructions regarding War Diaries and Intelligence Summaries are contained in F.S. Regs., Part II. and the Staff Manual respectively. Title Pages will be prepared in manuscript.

Place	Date 1917	Hour	Summary of Events and Information	Remarks and references to Appendices
Oost Dunkirk	Aug 1st		Took over left subsector ST GEORGES sector from 1/7 W. Yorks (49th Div.)	Casualties K.W.M. Gas(s) Other
	2			2
	3		Heavy bombardment Nieuport. Handed over to 16 north? Fusiliers & marched to RIBAILLET Camp. He expected attack about 4th but on the 9th was postponed because not of the weather to have come.	2.18. 1. 9.
	9		Took over left subsector ST GEORGES sector from 16 N.F. having 15/L/F. on our right and 4 W. Yorks on our left flank.	
	10		Special patrols have been sent out to find if enemy's front line was occupied. Patrol officers 2 Lt Lewis, 2 Lt Gould. Bombing march not (pro) on patrols have found up, delay caused by detailing fresh patrols, made it too late to get much information.	3. 12 11
	11		Reconnaissance in force to take possession of enemy front line (Lewis RAT French & ROSE Trench). B.Co. did the operation with 2 Capt Cr Smith officer in charge (Patrol 2 Lts SHAFFER McCLYMONT and BOOTH - Enemy's line two strong held & failed to take in.	2 12 2 1
			2 Lt BOOTH wounded	
	12		2 Lt TONGUEMAN wounded	5 6
	13		Enemy bombarded whole sector	
	14		ditto	7 3
	15		Back areas gassed, casualties in support Co. (C Co.)	3 10
				12. 62 3 32

Army Form C. 2118.

WAR DIARY
or
INTELLIGENCE SUMMARY

(Erase heading not required.)

16 A.V. F.U.S.
August 1917.

Place	Date 1917	Hour	Summary of Events and Information	Remarks and references to Appendices
	August		Casualties from last sheet K.W.M.G. 12 62 3 32	
	16		Enemy much quieter.	
	17		Relieved by 1 Middlesex, 98 Bde, 33 Div. marched to OOST DUNKERK Train.	
	18		Marched to camp at BRAY DUNES	
	25		Major V.F. Fneed left the Batt; to take command 1/11 Border Regt. Train	
	29		Moved to Forward Area. Billets in Cox 40 E. B'lk in Divisional Reserve	

Ewalwaterli Lt Col
Comdg 16 Lanton.

31.8.17.

Original
Confidential

War Diary
of
1/6 Lancashire Fusiliers
for
September 1917

Original

WAR DIARY or INTELLIGENCE SUMMARY.
(Erase heading not required.)

Army Form C. 2118.

16 Lanc. Fus.
September 1917.

Place	Date 1917	Hour	Summary of Events and Information	Casualties		Remarks and references to Appendices
				K.	W.	
COXYDE	Sept 6		Training. Finding working parties. Zuis	1.		
	12		Billets shelled. Zuis	1	9	
			Relieved 15H L.I. a support in LOMBARTZYDE sub sector. Casualties		2	
			caused by shell on march in			
	14		Zuis			
	16		Took over LOMBARTZYDE LEFT Subsector from 15.L.F. (Lt. Col. Hunter Grey) having 16.M.F. main right – Capt. M. 30 x. 16 + L.I. joined from redoubt as 2 W in Command	1.	9	
	17		Enemy bombard front line at 9 a.m. – he attack made in but raid attempted on 16 M.F. Zuis	1	3	
	18				1	
	19		Draft of 100 reinforcements arrived. Well trained men, including a number of specialists + 1 m.o. v.c. o gun		2	
	20		Started raid 15 L.F. In sub sector Zuis		2	
	21		I went sick handing over command to of Major Fox. Zuis			
	22		2 x 2 cells wounded h f		5	
	23		Casualties mining h f	2	1	
	24		Relieved 15 L.F. in front line. h f		2	
	26				4	
	27		Enemy bombarded front and to support lines 6·15 – 6·30 a.m. h f	1	3	
				7	43	

Original

WAR DIARY
or
INTELLIGENCE SUMMARY.
(Erase heading not required.)

Army Form C. 2118.

16/Lan: F.U.S: 2/
September 1917.

Place	Date 1917	Hour	Summary of Events and Information	Remarks and references to Appendices
	Sept 28		Relieved by 17th H.L.I. moved back to LA PANNE h.q.	Casualties K. W. 7 43 2 — 7 45
	29		I reported & took over command. Ennis.	

Ennis Lieut Col.
Cmdg 16 L.F.
30.9.17.

Confidential

War Diary
of
16 Lancashire Fusiliers
from 1st October 1917 to 31st October 1917

Volume I

W Ong Lapham
Lieut & Q

WAR DIARY or INTELLIGENCE SUMMARY.

(Erase heading not required.)

Army Form C. 2118.

16 Lan. Fus.
October 1917.

Place	Date 1917	Hour	Summary of Events and Information	Remarks and references to Appendices
LA PANNE	Oct 2		marched to AUSTRALIA CAMP, COXYDE, working parties	W?
	5		marched to BRAY DUNES. Took over Reserve for Coast Defences Training	9.
	19		2Lt J.W. Lunn accidentally wounded at Practice bombing ground	
	21		Saulieu 1.9 C.M. on 2Lt G.F Grant and 2Lt J. McClymont Immediate	
			Cha-U. Drunken on Sentries - km Veninck & Secre Reprimand	
	25		marched to WHG in Teteghem area, handing on Coast Defence duties	
			20 O.Lynts	
	26		marched to WHG in ERINGHEM area	
Owing in	2		Draft of 178 untrained men taken on the strength sent to GAMACHES for training	
			under one officer & N.C.Os.	
	29		Handed on command to Lt Col. A. Gillon	
			Zwica	

Congratulations
War Diary
GA 63 Division
16 Van Dr
November 1917

A Gillon Lt Col
Cmdg 16 Van Dr

W 95
Box 2397

WAR DIARY or INTELLIGENCE SUMMARY

Army Form C. 2118.

Place	Date	Hour	Summary of Events and Information	Remarks and references to Appendices
	29		In the line. Fighting patrols went out from A & D Coys. (casualties K.W.) They did not succeed in getting a prisoner but reported that there was no wire on the enemy front.	13 21 amn. 2(a/duty)
	30"		In the line. At 7am the enemy started a heavy barrage just behind our front line. The SOS was sent up on our right by the 8"D. This was repeated on our immediate right by the 2nd R Innis Fus & Reg by the Artillery Liaison Officer at Pill Box 83 (Bn Hd Q). Our Art. replied & a heavy bombardment by both sides continued for about 1 hour. No infantry action followed on our front. During the bombardment our T.M. was reported as firing short. Our casualties were eg. hr. Relieved by 15 Lan. Fus & proceeded in relay at 12.35am to IRISH FARM.	ofr
				16.44

A. Gillon Lieut Colonel
Comdg 16th Lancashire Fusiliers

Box/1939y
No 95

Confidential

War Diary
of
16th Lancashire Fusiliers
for
1st to 31st Dec. 1917.

Vol 26

16th Lancashire Fusiliers

December

WAR DIARY
or
INTELLIGENCE SUMMARY.

Army Form C. 2118.

Place	Date	Hour	Summary of Events and Information	Remarks and references to Appendices
Birch Farm	1st		At IRISH FARM.	K W
ditto	2nd		At IRISH FARM.	
WURST FARM	3rd		Bn. moved to WURST FARM & took over from 1st Dorsets. 6...1 Camp was shelled about midnight with 4.2 cm.	
ditto	4th		At WURST FARM. Improving & Cleaning Camp.	1
ditto	5th		At WURST FARM. Area round KANSAS Dump heavily shelled on the 2...1 afternoon. One of "D" Coys Bivouacs was hit by a 5.9 cm.	
ditto	6th		At WURST FARM. Batteries West of the Camp were shelled. Several shells 3 fell between Bn. H.Q & the Caledonia Road.	
ditto	7th		Between 1pm & 2pm the camp was heavily shelled with 5.9cm. 13 1 /4 Bivouacs received direct hits. Bn. H.Q. Dump also hit.	
ditto	8th			
TRENCHES	9th		Bn. relieved 5/6 Royal Scots in the Right Sector.	
ditto	10th		"C" Coy were in difficulties owing to the mud	
ditto	11th		in the line.	
ditto	12th		Enemy Coy raided. Gas shells were fired round KRON PRINZ & the 6...1 two ¾ back down our own trenches. Gas helmets were worn for about 2 hour.	
ditto	13th		In the line. Things were fairly quiet. 2...1	
ditto	14th		Bn. relieved by 15th R. Scots Fus. & proceeded to IRISH 4...1 FARM on relief. Relief was difficult owing to the Darkness	
IRISH FARM	15th		& was not completed until 4. V. Shells fell near the Camp.	
			At IRISH FARM. Several H.V. Shells fell near the Railway	

Army Form C. 2118.

WAR DIARY
or
INTELLIGENCE SUMMARY.
(Erase heading not required.)

Instructions regarding War Diaries and Intelligence Summaries are contained in F. S. Regs., Part II. and the Staff Manual respectively. Title pages will be prepared in manuscript.

Place	Date	Hour	Summary of Events and Information	Remarks and references to Appendices
	15th		At IRISH FARM.	K. W
	16		At IRISH FARM. St Jean Railhead shelled - 4 shells fell near Hd. Qrs. Batman's Tent - no casualties	
	17.		Bn. moved to SIEGE Camp & took over from 5/6th Royal Scots.	h.8
	18.			
	19		At SIEGE CAMP.	
	20			
	21			
	22		Bn. moved to IRISH FARM Camp & took over from 5/6th Royal Scots	
	23		At IRISH FARM. Working Parties on Corps Line etc.	
	24			
	25		Several H. Velocity Shells fell in the Camp between 12 Noon & 6 pm. -1	2
	26		At IRISH FARM.	
	27			
	28		Camp Eig Alley shelled with Shrapnel	1
	29		Bn. moved by train to LICQUES Area, - detrained at AUDRUIQ & marched to LICQUES. arriving about 11.30 p.m.	C
	30		At LICQUE	22 24
	31		ditto. Coy Inspections etc.	

YK 27

M.I.   27/25
         3 sheets

Confidential

War Diary

of

16th Lan: Fus

for

January 1918

16th Lancashire Fusiliers
WAR DIARY
or
INTELLIGENCE SUMMARY. January 1918

Army Form C. 2118.

Place	Date	Hour	Summary of Events and Information	Remarks and references to Appendices
LIQUES	1st		Bn in Billets carrying out training	
"	2nd			
"	3rd		Bn. Route March - Snow fell heavily most of the time	
"	4th		Training	
"	5th		Bn Holiday. Officers Dinner at night	
"	6th		Sgts Mess Dinner	
"	7th		Training	
"	8th		Corps Commanders Inspection was cancelled just before we reached the ground. Snow fell extremely heavily during the march	
"	9th			
"	10th			
"	11th			
"	12th		Bn. in billets carrying out Bn & Coy Training.	
"	13th			
"	14th			
"	15th			
"	16th			
"	17th			
ZOUAFQUES	18th		Bn marched to ZOUAFQUES & took over billets personnel returned	
"	19th		Bn marched to AUDRUICQ & entrained for ELVERDINGE from here Key Officers from 2 K.O.Y.L.I.	
DIRTY BUCKET CAMP	20th		marched to DIRTY BUCKET CAMP & took over from the 2nd K.O.Y.L.I. Sgt. GOODWIN was presented with the D.C.M. by the Brigadier	
CAMP	21st			
CANAL BANK	22nd		Bn marched to the YSER Canal & took over Dug Outs from the 23rd Manchesters.	

Army Form C. 2118.

WAR DIARY
or
INTELLIGENCE SUMMARY.
(Erase heading not required.)

Instructions regarding War Diaries and Intelligence Summaries are contained in F. S. Regs., Part II. and the Staff Manual respectively. Title pages will be prepared in manuscript.

Place	Date	Hour	Summary of Events and Information	Remarks and references to Appendices
Canal Bank	23rd 24th 25th		Coys on Working Parties ditto.	
BOESINGHE Camp	26th 27th		Bn marched to BOESINGHE Camp & relieved 8th NORFOLKS	
	28.		2n Comp Col. Gillou left & proceed on leave. Major M.S. Fox assuming temporary command. Relieved the 1th BEDFORDS in the left subsector of the right sector (HOUTHUARST FOREST) of the 32nd Divn Front - quiet relief.	
	29 30		In the line. Quiet Day (B + D Coys Front line D Support A Reserve)	
	31		In the line. Relief.	
			On the line. Day was very misty.	

Lt Col. Maj. Finlay
C/1.6 Hams

16 L F

Army Form C. 2118.

WAR DIARY
or
INTELLIGENCE SUMMARY.
(Erase heading not required.)

Instructions regarding War Diaries and Intelligence summaries are contained in F. S. Regs., Part II. and the Staff Manual respectively. Title pages will be prepared in manuscript.

Place	Date 1918	Hour	Summary of Events and Information	Remarks and references to Appendices
BIXSCHOOTE AREA. HOUTHULST FOREST SECTOR.	Feb 1st		Bn relieved by 15th Lancs Fusiliers. On relief 2 Coys proceeded to Erpe Line and 2 Coys Relieved Bn HQrs to ABRI CAMP	K — W.
	Feb 2nd		At ABRI CAMP.	
	Feb 3rd		At ABRI CAMP. (Working Parties)	
	Feb 4th		Bn relieved the 16th Bn Northumberland Fusiliers. Bn HQrs. EGYPT HOUSE. Pulls H.E. shell wounded at Duty. Raid took place on our Right by the 38th Division. 2nd/L. Tudor wounded	2.
	Feb 5th		Bn relieved by 15th H.L.I. and moved to BABOON Camp	
	Feb 6th		Bn at BABOON CAMP. Drafts of 5 Officers and 150 O.Rs from 9th Bn Lancs Fus joined Bn	1. — 11.
	Feb 7th		Relieved party the 15. A.L.I. and 96th Bn Royal Scots in Corps Line. B & C Coys in Corps Line "D" at COLONEL'S FARM. "A" at WOOD 16. Bn. HQrs. at LA CHAUDIERE.	
	Feb 8th		Bn on working parties	
	Feb 9th		— do —	
	Feb 10th		"A" Coy moved to LA CHAUDIERE	
	Feb 11th		Bn relieved 2nd Bn Manchesters in the line. A & D Coys in front line B & C Coys in Support.	1.
	Feb 12th		In the Line	1.
	Feb 13th		In the Line	
	Feb 14th		C.O. returned from leave.	
	Feb 15th		Relieved by 15th Bn Lancashire Fus. Bn moved to ABRI CAMP.	
	Feb 16th		Bn working parties for Army Line	
	Feb 17th		do do do do	

WAR DIARY or INTELLIGENCE SUMMARY

Army Form C. 2118.

Place	Date	Hour	Summary of Events and Information	Remarks and references to Appendices
BARSCHOETE AREA.	Feb 18.		The Bn. took part in a raid on the Divisional front. 15th Lancs Fus on the right and 97th Inf. Brigade on the left. The raiders consisted of two parties. The right party under 2nd Lieut. Lines and 2nd Lt. McClymont with 32 O.Rs. The left party under Lt. Wright and 2nd Lt. Riley with 32 O.Rs. The right party started from the assembly position (just in front of the ford), advanced and moved forward in a northerly direction along the road. Nothing was encountered up to the Cross Roads where the party turned to the left and worked their way down the road at the top of the road meeting a party of the Border Regt. The party then went through the enemy wire at U.5.a.30.65 encountered an enemy post where there were four or five dead or badly wounded Germans. One wounded was taken prisoner. Moving forward the party next entered the wood at about U.5.a.20.70 and attacked a post at about U.5.a.20.27 which was garrisoned by 8 or 10 of the enemy. 2nd Lieut. shot three and took one prisoner. 2nd Lt. McClymont shot an officer and one man and also took a prisoner. This party reported numerous dead and wounded of the enemy lying about, caused by our barrage. The left party under Lt. Wright and Lt. Riley in front of our post moved forward at 300x. They advanced a distance of about 100 yds but owing to heavy shell fire became disorganised and were unable to get to the Cross roads. Capt. Johnson Repr. O.C. were informed of progress of operations and frequent intervals. Prisoners Taken – 3. Identifications taken – 2.	K – 11 W – 32 1. Missing
		3.0 a.m.	Zero hour. 11.0 p.m.	
	Feb 19.		Bn. left A.B.21. Camp. for the Corps Line relieving 2nd Manchester Bn. "B" & "C" Coys in Corps Line "A" Coy + Bn. H.Qrs at LA CHAUDIÈRE. "D" at COLONELS FARM.	
NEUTHULST FOREST SECTOR	Feb 20.		Bn on Working Parties.	

WAR DIARY
or
INTELLIGENCE SUMMARY.

(Erase heading not required.)

Army Form C. 2118.

Place	Date	Hour	Summary of Events and Information	Remarks and references to Appendices
AREA - BIXSCHOOTS	21/Feb.		Bn on Working Parties	
	22 "		do do do	
	23 "		Bn relieved 2nd Bn Manchester Regt on front line. "A" & "D" Coys front line. "C" "B" Coys Support. In the line.	K. - W. 1. - 1.
	24 "		do do	
	25 "		Coys relieved. "B" & "C" in Front Line. "A" & "D" Coys in Support.	- 9.
	26 "		In the Line.	
	27 "		Bn in the Line. The 2 Support Coys were relieved by 2 Coys of 15/75th Bn Lancs. Fus: at 7. P.m. On relief the Right Support Coy, i.e. "A" Coy moved up to the Eastern edge of Owrs Wood to take part in operation. Zero being 7-52.p.m. whilst two raids were being carried out; by the 14th & 16th Bde on its left and the 2nd Bn Manchester Regt on its right, "A" Coy under Capt Waugh searched the wood - thoroughly by sending out 4 Patrols each consisting of one officer and a Platoon. These patrols reconnoitered the whole area and located many evacuated enemy posts. Two machine enemy Machine Guns were located on the right. An attempt was made to storm them without success. On patrol returning, the 2 Coys in the front line were relieved by 2 Coys of the 15 Bn. Lancashire. Total Casualties during the operations were	2 - 0. 10. 19.
	Feb. 28		Bn moved to ABRI-CAMP. Bn on Working Parties.	

J. Gillow Lt Col
Comdg 16th Lanc. Fus.

32nd Division.
96th Infantry Brigade.

16th BATTALION

THE LANCASHIRE FUSILIERS

MARCH 1 9 1 8

War Diary

1/6th Bn Lancashire Fusiliers

From 1st to 31st of the Month of March 1916.

A Gillon Lt Col.
Commanding 1/6th Bn Lancashire Fusiliers

Army Form C. 2118.

WAR DIARY
or
INTELLIGENCE SUMMARY.
(Erase heading not required.)

Instructions regarding War Diaries and Intelligence Summaries are contained in F. S. Regs., Part II. and the Staff Manual respectively. Title pages will be prepared in manuscript.

Place	Date	Hour	Summary of Events and Information	Remarks and references to Appendices
Asbri Camp	1st March		Working Parties	K. W.
"	2nd		Raiding party complimented by Divnl. and Commander	
"	3rd		i/c ordered to Reimingher relieved 2nd K.O.Y.L.I.	
Reiminghet	4th/5		Training in progress	
"	6th		" "	?.
"	6th		" "	1.
"	7th		" "	
"	8th		" "	
"	9th		" "	?.
Baton Camp	10th		Bn moved to Baton Camp	
Inth. Line	11th		Working Parties	
(Hen Hutte Sector)	12th		do	
"	13th		Bn relieved 15th Bn. H.L.I. "D" Coy Front line. "A" Coy. Support. "B" & "C" in Reserve	
"	14th		Sector quiet. Mining quiet.	
"	15th		do S.O.S. sent up on right sector	
"	16th		do	
"	17th		Intr Company relief. "C" Coy front line "B" Support "A" & "D" in Reserve	
"	18th		Quiet day. Sector shelled with Mustard Gas	
"	19th		" "	Various '5. to 3.
"	20th		15th Bn. Lancashire Fus. carried out a raid in front of our sector.	
"	21st		Intr company relief. "B" Coy front line. "C" Coy in support. "A" & "D" in reserve.	1.
"	22nd		15th Bn Lancashire Fus. carried out a raid on the left of the sector	2.
"	23rd		Hostile T.M. strafe on Sector	
"	24th		Quiet Day.	
"	25th		Intr Company relief "B" Coy in Front line. "C" Coy in Support. "A" & "D" in reserve. Intended raid cancelled.	1.
"	26th		Sector shelled heavily.	2.
"	27th		Bn relieved by 1st & 3rd Battalions of 10th Belgian Regt (Companies of)	1.
Bister Camp	28th		Bn moved by rail to Savy	
Latre Gueret	29th		Bn marched to Latre Guerrel	3.
Adinfer Wood	30th		Bn marched to Adinfer Wood and relieved 11th Border Regt	
In the line	31st		Bn relieved Grenadier Guards in Sector S. W. of Atlas.	

96th Inf.Bde.
32nd Div.

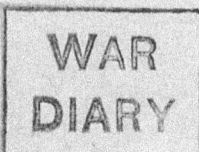

16th BATTN. THE LANCASHIRE FUSILIERS.

A P R I L

1 9 1 8

WAR DIARY
or
INTELLIGENCE SUMMARY.
(Erase heading not required.)

Army Form C. 2118.

8/16th Bn/Lancashire Fusiliers

From Hyplie - 30/4/18.

VM 30

Place	Date	Hour	Summary of Events and Information	Remarks and references to Appendices
AYETTE South of ARRAS.	April 1st		Battalion relieved 4th Bn Grenadier Guards in front line, patrols were very active but were driven off by heavy M. Gun fire.	K – W – 2. 1 m missing
	" 2nd	2 a.m.	"C" Coy 1/5th Battn attacked posts south of AYETTE but had to withdraw owing to left flank being in the air. 2/Lt Jamieson Killed and 2nd Lt Lowis wounded	–
	" 3rd	9 a.m.	"D" Coy again attacked posts and recaptured two these were consolidated. Remainder of "D" Coy attacking force dug themselves in in front of posts which were still held by the enemy on the right. Three attempts were made to storm the remaining posts under cover of Stokes mortar Barrage. M. Gun fire was heavy and no progress was made.	23 – 64 9 missing
		9 p.m.	"B" Coy attacked posts at F.11.c.90.60 will two strong sections under 2nd/Lt. W. Clayment and 2nd.Lt. Vasey. & platoon under 2nd Lt Riley acted as mopping-up party along Bugeole & Road from F.11.c.70.80 to F.11.c.90.60. The attacking party gained all objectives and captured 3. Enemy M. Guns. As soon as this operation was completed "A" Coy under Capt. F Waugh constructed a line of 8 posts from F.11.c.10.30 to F.11.c.90.60. These were completed and occupied. Casualties during this day and the previous day's fighting were heavy. Capt Summer, 2nd Lt. Buckley and Le Gregory, 2nd Lt Cooke were wounded. 3 Prisoners were taken.	
	April 4th		Bn was relieved by 2nd Bn Manchester Regt and moved to purple line at Greenway Farm.	
	April 5th		Sect was shelled very heavily from farm to N.a.m. Shelling appeared to be the fringe of a heavy bombardment on the Corps on the right (about) shells 59 and 4.2" with large proportion of gas shells. "D" Coy was affected by the gas to a great extent suffering rather heavy casualties. Capt Johnson, Lt. Rankin, 2nd Lt Howarth were gassed and evacuated to U.K.	13 – 32 gassed 46
	April 6th		Bn still in purple Line. Gas still hung about the area.	–
	April 7th		Bn relieved the 15th & 13th Lancashire Fusiliers in Right front sects.	gassed 10. 1 30 C

Commanding 16th Bn/Lancashire Fus.

Army Form C. 2118.

WAR DIARY
or
INTELLIGENCE SUMMARY.
(Erase heading not required.)

Instructions regarding War Diaries and Intelligence Summaries are contained in F. S. Regs., Part II. and the Staff Manual respectively. Title pages will be prepared in manuscript.

Place	Date	Hour	Summary of Events and Information	Remarks and references to Appendices
AYETTE SECTOR South of ARRAS	April 8th		Bn in the line. very quiet day.	K — W 3 — 1
	April 9th		do do do do Short heavy bombardment on front line posts.	6 — Gassed 4
	April 10th		do do do do Support Coys lines were lightly shelled	2 — Gassed 8
	April 11th		do do do do Short heavy bombardment on front line posts	1 — Gassed 6
	April 12th		do do do do very quiet day. Capt Brooks and 2nd Wright wounded	5 Gassed 1
	April 13th		Bn relieved by 2nd Bn Manchester Regt and moved to Purple line very quiet day	—
	April 14th		Bn in Purple line Reserve	—
	April 15th		Bn do do do Light Shelling at intervals	4 Gassed 3
	April 16th		do do do do do	3
	April 17th		Bn relieved 15th Lancashire Fusiliers in Left Sector front line	1 Gassed 3
	April 18th		Bn in the line, the enemy heavy shelling at 12 noon falling in rear of posts	2 Gassed 2
	April 19th		do do do Light shelling in rear of front line during the day. Inter Coy reliefs Coys front to Supports	6 Gassed 1
	April 20th		Bn in the line. Heavy Shelling on the Right Sector held by 15th B Lancashire Fus. S	1
	April 21st		Bn do do Very quiet day.	1

A Stones Lt Col.
Commanding 16th Bn Lancashire Fus c

Army Form C. 2118.

WAR DIARY
or
INTELLIGENCE SUMMARY. of 16th B/Lancashire Fus.
(Erase heading not required.)

Place	Date	Hour	Summary of Events and Information	Remarks and references to Appendices
Aveluy Sect. Souly Area	April 22nd		Bn in the line relieved by 2nd Manchester Regt. and moved to Purple Line quiet Relief	K/1. W/1.
	April 23rd		Bn in Purple Line Reserve. Bn "Stood to" 4.30 a.m. to 5.30 a.m. on Purple Line	1
	April 24th		do do do do. Purple Line improved by 3 Coys working during the night	1
	April 25th		do do do do. Relieved by 1st Bn Grenadier Guards, very quick relief. Bn moved	—
	April 26th		to Billets in BIENVILLERS au BOIS.	
	April 27th		Bn moved to Billets in BARLY.	
	April 28th		Bn at Rest. Billets arranged and cleaned.	
	April 29th		do do do. Day spent in cleaning Equipments	
	April 30th		Bn commenced Training programme issued. Training to be done in the mornings. Sports during afternoon. Bn Training	

A. Shute Lt Col
Commanding 16th Lancashire Fus?

WAR DIARY
or
INTELLIGENCE SUMMARY.
(Erase heading not required.)

Army Form C. 2118.

16 Lancs Fus

Vol 31

Place	Date 1918	Hour	Summary of Events and Information	Remarks and references to Appendices
Burley	May 1		Training in Progress — Sports in the afternoon.	
"	2			
"	3			
"	4			
"	5			
"	6		2nd Lt Ivory awarded M.C. — No 11701 Pte Strapp awarded M.M.	
"	7		STRAPP	
"	8			
"	9			
"	10			
(In the line) BOISLEUX AU MONT	11		Battalion relieved the 17th R.F. and proceeded into the line at BOISLEUX AU MONT (one wounded).	
"	12		In the Trenches. One wounded	
"	13		" One S.I.W.	
"	14		" One killed Eight wounded	
"	15		" Inter Coy Relief C Co Patrol captured Two prisoners of Reserve Ers Reg 15 Comp 11 Batt.	
"	16		" 15th L.F. Raided by the Enemy	
"	17		"	
"	18		"	
"	19		Battalion relieved by the 2nd Manchesters and went into reserve at BLAIRVILLE. One wounded.	
BLAIRVILLE	20		Battalion in Reserve. One wounded	
"	21		" One killed Five wounded	
"	22		" One wounded.	
"	23			
"	24			
(In the line) BOISLEUX AU MONT	25		In the Trenches. Battalion relieved the 15th Bn L.F. Three killed Nine wounded.	
"	26		" Two wounded	
"	27		" No 12594 Cpl Hilton awarded the M.M.	
"	28		" Two killed Ten wounded	
"	29		" Six wounded	
"	30		" One wounded	
"	31		Battalion relieved by the 2nd Bn Manchester Regt. One killed one wounded	

A Stone
Lt Col
Cmdg 16 Lan. Fus.

31.2

WAR DIARY or INTELLIGENCE SUMMARY.

Army Form C. 2118.

16 LF
32

Place	Date 1916	Hour	Summary of Events and Information	CASUALTIES		Remarks and references to Appendices
				KILLED	WOUNDED	
NEUVILLE	JUNE 1st		In reserve	0	0	
"	2nd		"	0	0	
"	3rd		"	0	0	
"	4th		"	0	0	
In the trenches	5th		Battalion relieves 15th LAN FUS. C & D Coys in line	0	0	
"	6th		Quiet day	4	7	
"	7th		Heavy bombardment for 1 hour of the B posts to right of railway embankment	8 or 10	12	2/Lt P. Hubbard
"	8th		Quiet day	0	4	
"	9th		Quiet day. Inter Coy relief A & B Coys in line	0	4	
"	10th		"	0	0	
"	11th		"	0	1	
"	12th		"	0	0	
BARLEUVILLE	13th		In reserve. 6 officers relieved by 2nd MANCHESTER REGT.	0	0	
"	14th		"	0	0	
"	15th		"	0	0	
"	16th		"	0	0	
In the trenches	17th		Battalion relieves 15th LAN FUS. C & D Coys in line	0	0	
"	18th		Quiet day	0	0	
"	19th		"	0	4 + 1 S.TM.	
"	20th		9pm raid by A Coy. No prisoners nor material taken. Enemy his own and 2 batteries	1	9	
"	21st		Quiet day. Inter Coy relief A & B in line	2	11	
"	22nd		Quiet day	2	1 injured	
"	23rd		"	0	1	
"	24th		" Battalion relieved by 2nd MANCHESTER REGT:	0	2 + injured	
NEUVILLE	25th		In reserve	0	0	
"	26th		"	0	0	
"	27th		"	0	0	
"	28th		"	0	0	
"	29th		"	0	0	
"	30th		"	0	0	

WAR DIARY
INTELLIGENCE SUMMARY

(Erase heading not required.)

Army Form C. 2118.

16 L F
95 33

July, 1918

Place	Date 1918	Hour	Summary of Events and Information	Casualties Killed Wdd. Missing	Remarks and references to Appendices
Blaireville	July 1st		On reserve. Training for raid on 3rd July.	0 0 0	
"	2nd		" " " " " " "	0 0 0	
"	3rd		Raid by "B" "C" "D" Coys on "BOYGIES" at "1 AM. through 15th LAN: FUS: 1 Prisoner, 1 light Machine gun, & orders captured. Enemy retired before our advance, Enemy heavy owing to camouflaged dugouts in BOYSELLES. Capt. Waugh (O.C. Raid) wounded a missing. Lt. Ellis " 2nd Lt. Ellis "	0 46 18	
"	4th		Awards for raid. 111384 Sgt. Hughes W.H., 36226 Sgt. Faulkner G. 2336/8, Pte Mohan F.W. (all from "C" Coy) Military Medal 16/272, Pte Rogerson J.H. ("D" Coy) Military Medal.	0 0 0	
"	5th		On reserve. Col. Stone D.S.O. returned from leave, but remained at Transport Lines.	0 0 0	
"	6th		" " " " "	0 0 0	
"	7th		2nd Bn. Scots Guards relieved this Battn. at 18.30 Hrs. 100.		
A A BAZEQUE	8th		Left BLAIREVILLE at 12.30 A.M. After relief. Travelled via Currie to LA BAZEQUE. Bn. taken over from Major Uniacke D.S.O. Col. Stone D.S.O. took over command.		
"	9th		Bn. Resting and re-organizing.		
"	10th		Started training and recreational training		
"	11th		Training and recreational training		
"	12th		" " " "		
"	13th		" " " "		
"	14th		" " " " . Major Uniacke D.S.O. went on course.		
"	15th		" " " " . Col. Stone D.S.O. to the Wolepithre		
"	16th		" " " " went to hospital		
"	17th		" " " " Entrained at DOULLENS. Major Uniacke D.S.O.		
"	18th		Battn Left LA BAZEQUE for PROVEN, BELGIUM. took had and took command 7 Batt. now in G.H.Q. Reserve.		
PROVEN	19th		Battn. Billeted in PENTON CAMP. now in G.H.Q. Reserve.		
"	20th		Training and recreational training		
"	21st		Church parade		
"	22nd		Training and recreational training		
"	23rd		" " " "		
"	24th		" " " "		
"	25th		" " " "		
"	26th		" " " "		
"	27th		Church parade. Battn. sports.		
"	28th		Bn. moved to McDonnell, Moncrieff & Mieghem Camps.		
"	29th		Training and recreational training.		
"	30th		" " " "		
"	31st		First move to Battle Position. Aeroplane attack.		

J.B. Uniacke Major
16th Bn. L.A.H. Fus:

Official Commanding 16/ Bn L A R. Fus:

16 Lanc Fus
9/31
34/31

Army Form C. 2118.

WAR DIARY
INTELLIGENCE SUMMARY.
(Erase heading not required.)

Instructions regarding War Diaries and Intelligence Summaries are contained in F. S. Regs., Part II. and the Staff Manual respectively. Title pages will be prepared in manuscript.

Place	Date 1918 August	Hour	Summary of Events and Information	Remarks and references to Appendices
PROVEN	1st		MINDEN DAY. Bn in B.H.Q. reserve. Inspection of 15th & 16th Lan. Fus. by Brig. Gen. Girdwood D.S.O. (96th Bde.) Dining at MIESGHEM Camp for Lan. Fus. officers & Sgts guest. Brig. Gen. Girdwood D.S.O. 96th Bde present.	
"	2nd		Training. Heavy rain.	
"	3rd			
"	4th		Sunday. Anniversary Service. 4th Anniv. of War.	
"	5th		Training.	
"	6th		Representative party from the Bn. went to be inspected by H.M. the King at SCHOOL CAMP.	
"	7th		Entrained at HEIDEBEEK and detrained at HANGEST-SUR-SOMME. 12 hrs on journey.	
SAISEVAL	8th		March of 9 miles to SAISEVAL. Travelled in lorries to BOVES and we re-rejoined to Cana during the attack started 8/8/18. Marched to DOMART arrived midday 8th and bivouacked.	
DOMART BEAUCOURT	9th 10th		Marched to BEAUCOURT through captured territory. Received orders at 2.30 p.m. to march at 5 a.m. of 10th. Marched off at 4 a.m. through BOUCHOIR, the starting point of the attack. Objective:- DAMERY WOOD. Bn. went over 600 yds. behind 1st Lan. Fus. with 22nd Manchester Regt. 2nd Lieut. of front 2200yds. Artillery formation taken up under fire from QUESNOY WOOD & "M". Witnessed information. REYOLECOOL taken by Canadians & 1st Lan Fus. Wood on left was M.G. swamp and looks to by 18th Lan. Fus. Commanding Officer. Of 16th Lan Fus wounded by the first form before its capture by us (Severe fighting at Wood (M) left of heavy Sylvan sky road. Three were taken & BOIS DE LA FUTOSE reached by us and taken after the 2nd Lt. Knott 4 days alone with Rifle & 4.9 H.K. guns captured, complete with 4 of Sunday party at 3.5 Mm. 4/16th 1/15th 5th take the Combed Seconded Major Mr. Knott M.C. (16th Lan. Fus.) Bur' at BROCKMAN (15th Lan. Fus.) 3 m. Gs. established. Officer casualties :- KILLED. 2/Lt VASE, M.C. Wounded : Lt. Col. Knott 4 days alone Bar; 2/Lt's G. ROBINSON & 2/Lt MORGAN. Missing:- Major KNOTT, M.C., C.S.M. HANRLEY, 2/Lt TONGEMAN, TOBIN & GARDINER.	34/192 2

SHEET II

WAR DIARY
INTELLIGENCE SUMMARY.
(Erase heading not required.)

Army Form C. 2118.

Place	Date 1918 August	Hour	Summary of Events and Information	Remarks and References to Appendices
DAMERY	11th		14th & 97th Bgde took BOIS D'EQUERRE. 16th Lan. Fus. followed and established line E. & west with posts on DAMERY ROAD. Office casualties:- wounded. Capt. LORD M.C. 2/Lts. OWEN & BURNS. Lt. RIGDEN R.A.M.C. att. (North. [remain and Bn.)	0 1 0
"	12th		Enemy troops massing for counter attack dispersed by Artillery. M.G. + rifle fire. Bn. relieved at 6 p.m. by the Canadians and came out to QUESNEL. 2/Lt. ATN. W. Bgde in Barnard and commanded to 9th Canadians and came out to QUESNEL. 2/Lt. ATN. W. Bgde in Barnard and commanded to 9th work by Brig. Gen. GIRDWOOD & Go. Thon Bgde. moved to IGNAUCOURT.	0 1 0
IGNAUCOURT FOUENCAMPS	13th 14th		Rested till afternoon. Marched back to FOUENCAMPS & bivouacked in field 2 kilos. west of village. Resting. Bgde. paraded and thanked by the Divisional Commander. (Gen. Lambert)	
"	15th 16th		"	
"	17th		Travelled to Amiens evening to HARBONNIÈRES. Relieved 27th Bn. Australian Infantry in a wood.	
HARBONNIÈRES	18th		Major MACDONALD D.S.O. sent to take command of Bn. Major ROBOTTOM M.C. 2nd in Command. Frm. 12/5/18 of 8/18 Capt. GILL O.C. A Coy. in command of Bn. Received news of Capt. WAUGH temp. officer Reported MISSING after raid by his Bn. on BAYELLES on 3/7/18. Moved off in evening to occupy support trench in front of VAUVILLERS.	
VAUVILLERS	19th 20th 21st		Moved up and support position and consolidated. Quiet day. "	1 0 2 0 1 0
"	22nd 23rd		Relieved 2nd MANCHESTER REGT. in front line between HERLETVILLE and MADAME WOOD. Attacked enemy trench line at 4.45 A.M. Objective:- Enemy trench in 300 yds. in front. Taken early 18 95 2 3 Prisoners. 72 M.Gs. 2L.T.M.S. Officer casualties:- Wounded. 2/Lts. JD WEST + GLADWYN. Kt. HEARD. R.A.M.C.	5
"	24th 25th		Held line and consolidated. Much trouble from Snipers. Much of pm. shelling from 12.12 p.m. - 3.1/3 p.m. Men moved in morning. Returned line + left 4.30 p.m. after 5. Took 1 survived. Wounded officers casualties:- 2/Lt. Capt. SMITH. 2/Lts. GOODE + PIRCE. 2/Lts. ELLIS, SHAW, TURMAN. OLLIER, ALCOTT, COKAINS, MILES, BROWN, SIDDALL, MURPHY, DEAN, SPENCER, HELLIS. Killed 2/Lt. Relieved in evening by 5th Border Regt. Moved to reserve at VAUVILLERS. Capt. WATTS L. Lieut. LEE 2nd MANCHESTER REGT. wounded. Scale. Scale attd. Bn. suffered miss. air attacks by air craft.	0
VAUVILLERS	26th 27th		" " " "	
ROSIERES MERIES	28th 29th 30th 31st		MANCHESTERS relieved 2nd Bn. Somme. Bgde. relieved by 97th Bgde. Bn. moved to MISERY. MISERY. Bn. Relieved to BERNY.	479/9

Bgde. H.Q. MISERY. Relieved. Bgde. moved to BERNY.

WAR DIARY
or
INTELLIGENCE SUMMARY

(Erase heading not required.)

Army Form C. 2118.

16. Lanc. Fus.

96/32

WD 35

Place	Date	Hour	Summary of Events and Information	Remarks and references to Appendices
BEAUNY	SEPTEMBER 1918			
	1st	In reserve		
	2	do.	New draft of 97 men and 10 officers arrived.	
	3	do.		
	4	do.		
	5	do.	Orders received rd. ready to move out at 2 hr. notice. No move.	
	6	do.	Moved in the morning to ENNEMAIN.	
ENNEMAIN	7	do.	Moved in the morning to MONCHY LAGACHE.	
MONCHY LAGACHE	8	do.	Lt PALMER, 2nd Lt BOSWORTHICK, BOONHAM, & HULTON rejoined from course.	
	9	do.	Orders for attack on ST QUENTIN & VERNON WOODS. Cancelled in afternoon.	
Bn line	10	do.	Orders to be ready to move in afternoon to take over line from the French at 11pm via VILLEVEQUE.	
	11		Advanced to West edge of HORNON WOOD. TOOK ATTILLOY + HILL 135. C Coy lost FRENCH at night. Remained in same position. Edge of HORNON WOOD heavy shell 2/Lt ARCHIBALD gassed. 2/Lt MOFFAT WHALE	
	12		Transport moved up 3m. from TERTRY to CORBIE. 2/Lt GILLMORE wounded. A Coy. 3 men killed, 3 wounded, 12 men prisoners. During the night A Coy. Relieved	
CORBIE	13			
	14		moved 3m. from TERTRY to CORBIE. Bath available at MONCHY LAGACHE at 2p.m. Reached CORBIE from town.	
	15		do. do.	
	16		do. do.	
	17		Training.	
	18		do. do. Training — 2/Lt LEWIS rejoined Bath from wounded. Beaux R.T.O.	
	19		do. do. Training — recreational tournament. Lt. Col. STONE D.S.O. returned & took on command of Batt.	
	20		do. do. Training. Major MACDONALD D.S.O. relinquished command of Batt. and returned to Co. Pool Base	
	21		do. do. Training.	
	22		Church Parade.	
	23		Training. CAPT W.N. WATT'S rejoined Batt. from Hospital.	
	24		Training. CAPT. A.E. HALL (a/adj) went to ENGLAND to RAF.	
TERTRY	25		Training. Left in morning by bus for TERTRY & Bivouac.	
	26		Training.	
	27		Training.	
	28		Received orders for the attack. 96th 2/Fl Brigade direct attack 3rd day 2/Fl 46th Division from early HINDENBURG-	
VENDELLE'S	29		Resting. Bath meantime.	
MAGNY LA FOSSE	30		BELLENGLISE and moved into bivouac at MAGNY LA FOSSE. R.S.M. EANDERSON M.M. wounded slightly.	

BRPatham
Capt & Col a.m. 16

357 others

Confidential

War Diary
of
16th Lan. Fus.
for
October 1918.

Army Form C. 2118.

WAR DIARY
or
INTELLIGENCE SUMMARY.
(Erase heading not required.)

OCTOBER 1918

Place	1918 Date	Hour	Summary of Events and Information	Total Casualties Killed Wounded Missing	Remarks and references to Appendices
IN TRENCHES Sth. NE of LA BRIQUE FOSSE WOOD	Oct 1		Battn. moved up to FOSSE WOOD to withdraw 2nd bn Brown Watch		
	2		Battn. attacked RAMICOURT. Heavy casualties owing to enfilade machine gun fire from both flanks. Lt. Col. Stow DSO & Kitter, Major Robotham comdg. 4 from transport and 2nd in Command of Battn. Casualties Kitter Lt. Col. Stow DSO and his Adjutant Captain Shelton Robert Shuttleworth wounded. Lt. Parker 2nd Lt. Nolan Killed. Lt. King W 2nd 1341 18 Cauder Bootman		
	3		At 3 am the battn. was withdrawn to comply with standing orders. The owing to the night and fog, the brigade had been able to relieve us on the right and outs during the night. It was believed in		
LEHAUCOURT	4		Battn. moved to LEHAUCOURT where it was billeted.		
VENDELLES HANCOURT	5		At ST QUENTIN CANAL Battn. moved to VENDEULES and examined in billets under Canvas it		
	6		Canvas for the night		
	7		Battn. arrived at HANCOURT 12.30 PM the next Brigade of Division		
	8		Brigadier Bayley Brig. General A.E. Govenon DSO made a short speech which he congratulated the Brigade on its Performance and		
	9		Informed us its ability service. Colonel Stow DSO lately bringing M.G.B. Gun Battalion & Lt. Col. CB. Ottley Div. Com. AMG. Brig. Gen. No. Govenon DSC DSO were present. Those killed Map ref 9 7 81 75 sht 62 C G 8 C 75 75		
	10		Battn. in Billets day of Battle at ESTREES Right of 108 & 2nd Battn Rabs		
	11		Wai 0 129 to as Sniper Infected Canada Carried Out		
	12		Major Marsham M.C. ARTH and Patr. and Bowman & A Bathn. Major. Robotham 2nd in Command.		

284 25 147 18

WAR DIARY
or
INTELLIGENCE SUMMARY.
(Erase heading not required.)

Army Form C. 2118.

Place	Date 1918	Hour	Summary of Events and Information	Remarks and references to Appendices
HANCOURT	OCT 13		Church Parade. Wash & Officers	
	14		Battn Drill. Sniper Lewis Gunner Scouts and Specialist training in afternoon	
	15		Coy. reorganisation. Officers and O.R.s Casualo report for duty. Specialist training in afternoon	
	16		Battn Training. Afternoon allotted to Specialist and recreational training	
	17		—do—	
	18		Battn moves to LEHAUCOURT area. Billets along CANAL BANK. Draft of three officers and new arms scout Coy Commanders. Major Robertson goes to hospital Capt Pentecost from 2nd Battn reports for duty with us. Capt Pentecost will	
LEHAUCOURT	19		Battn leave for BOHAIN area then at 10pm. Arrive at 2.30am	
BOHAIN	20		Battn Parade after which new bad day at HQ for cleaning up in afternoon	
	21		Bam was at pres on at usey alters by Major Gamon 7.S Lauked C.B.C.M.G. The following reinor the following 2/RSM Aldridge M.C. and M.S. and McFarlane 2627. 26 Cpl R. Gill M.M. Cpl L.S. Dunning Sgt Gastene Battn wages by way Cpl R. Ryan M.M. L/Sgt Turner Sgt L.S. Neal L/Cpl M.M. Cpl R. Dean L/Cpl R. Hall M.M. Pte Mobbings J Roan, L/Cpl B. Grue M.M. Pte Thomas L/Cpl M.M.	
	22		Battn remains at BUSIGNY. Afternoon devoted to cleaning up. Circuit tactical report for duty.	
BUSIGNY	23		Battn parade in morning afternoon cleaning up. Battn proceeds by rail for lunch.	
	24		New Draw Training and Capt Potts G.A. reports for duty.	
	25		Battn parade in casualo report for duty.	
	26		"	
	27		Battn moves to BECQUIGNY. In afternoon Battn carried out simple tactical exercise (attack)	
BECQUIGNY	28		Battn parade. 2nd Lt Steele returns to duty.	
	29		Bn moved to ST SOUPLET	
	30		Bn moved to BAZUEL	
	31		Bn Bathing	

Bruce [signed] Capt.
Commdg 16th Lan. Fus.

WAR DIARY
or
INTELLIGENCE SUMMARY.

Army Form C. 2118.

16 Lond? R Vol 37

Place	Date 1916	Hour	Summary of Events and Information	Remarks and references to Appendices
BAZEL (Nr Le Sars).	Nov.1.		Officers & Bn. reconnoitred line held by 1st Lancashire Fusiliers in neighbourhood of Ply Sun N.E. of Ors. A. Coy. sent up to relieve 1st Lancashire Fusiliers.	9/17
BAZEL & LINE	Nov 2.		B. & C. Coys. sent to relieve 1st Lancashire Fusiliers and withdrew tired of Senart in Supersession for big attack on Gurd. Capt. P.B. Dunn M.C. (1st H.L.I.) joins Bn on 1st Oct 16 to Hdqs 1st Lancs Fus Furbey.	9/17 9/18
BAZEL & LINE	Nov 3.		Operations entered and jumping off place cleared. The following casualties reported to officers. Lt. H. Whitehead (A Coy) wounded. Lt. F. Bowmer, B Coy (wounded). 2 Lt. H.E. Jones (B Coy). Wounded. 2 Lt. Rhys C.W. (B Coy) killed. B. Coy lost its prisoners in this operation. While this prisoners were are Jumpers where returned for the Guards Can'l which was to take the Stone Zero 05.45 Nov 4. B.H.Q Off Bazon at 6 P.M. Nov 3 for Bake Hays due to Rolean Entertained. Capt F. B. Dunn M.C. (1st H.L.I.) relieved the Cooper and conveyed him in a Road by S.H.Q. nearly to the jumping off place.	9/12
SUNKEN ROAD & ground East of CANAL	Nov 4.		Battalion moved to assembly place one ordered there is Battle at 5.30 AM on close silence of boys lying down following Corps Brigade Troops at 05.15 having fire handle on small tank there the onwopy by them o 12 lucks speed forward N.E. of Ors. Bogdan of attack at 05.50 The troops were exceled about 1500 yds sleeping small track N.E. of Ors. Bogdan of attack. No more cared and advance with sleep hands on cannon & right up of this Barge. In fact Attacks on the hour Landbarn Rd. He Buttln met wiles of ht Barge in while of heavy Enfeld strengthy to cover. Many Enemy turbine gave them into action against this Barge which before. All really cared cars broken of still free. Lt Cr. Morsdale M.C. with B.H. came forward when his Bn was beat up and decedent as we after fuel to capture the Badger. Filly update to the Enemy Care he wasn't this Stuff through the track.	

3725
Wolse

WAR DIARY or INTELLIGENCE SUMMARY

Army Form C. 2118.

Place	Date	Hour	Summary of Events and Information	Remarks and references to Appendices
Suez Canal & Ground East of Canal.			Capt. J. B. Dunn. M.C. (K.H.L.I.) came up from Bn. Hqs. and took over Command. The surrendered Companies and effected a mustering of his Comd. over the Bde Ridge. Advancing in a wide extended formation the Battalion met and overcame stiff resistance from enemy M.G. posts and Snipers. At dusk the Bn. consolidated in depth for the night with its left on the Canal bank and its right in touch with the 2nd Manchesters on the road Meunieres-Vendeville Village. The Battalion suffered severe casualties during the day. Officers casualties were:- Lt. Col. Marshall M.C. into Bn. Commanding Officer (Killed). Lt. C.H.G. Hulton M.C. Offr. C. Coy. Killed. 2/Lt. S. A.H. Law. Bn. Intelligence Officer. Killed. 2/Lt. F.N. Livingstone. A.Coy. Died of Wounds. 2/Lt. J. Moore. C.Coy. Killed. 2/Lt. J. Hollis. C.Coy. Killed. Wounded. 2/Lt. Schofield. Offr. D.Coy. Wounded. 2/Lt. R.H. Potts. D Coy. wounded. Capt. G.A. Potts. M.O. Attd. Wounded. 2/Lt. Selwyn. Bn. Signals Officer. Wounded. 2/Lt. E. Lyons. D Coy. Missing.	gws.
La Folie.	5 Nov.		The advance continued in the morning, the Battalion tactically up the ground east of the Canal and the advancing as far as the village of La Folie. Two tanks were in efficient but wounded both in the mopping up operations. The Bn. captured two Field guns, i.e. 8 guns except the stores of ammunition, Kochers guns; and a certain amount of transport. Attacked at La Folie. The Bn. billeted in La Folie. The 27 Sept parties through the 96 Aug. Sept.	gws.
La Folie.	6 Nov.		Refit during and and reorganization.	gws.
"	7 Nov.		"	gws.
"	8 Nov.		Funeral of Lt. Col. Marshall. M.C. who has been late Commanding Officer of Battalion at the attended by Major General J.S. Lambert. C.B. C.M.G. Commanding 32. Div. and Brigadier General F.C. Yatman. D.S.O. Commanding 96. Inf. Bde. attended. Capt. J.B. Dunn. M.C. (K.H.L.I.) Commanding 16. Lanes Fusiliers. Capt. M.E. Buchanan & Lt. Kerr representing the R.S. Glam. Major Cardiff. R.E. Chaplain to his troops performed the Burial service.	

WAR DIARY
or
INTELLIGENCE SUMMARY.
(Erase heading not required.)

Army Form C. 2118.

Instructions regarding War Diaries and Intelligence Summaries are contained in F. S. Regs., Part II. and the Staff Manual respectively. Title pages will be prepared in manuscript.

Place	Date	Hour	Summary of Events and Information	Remarks and references to Appendices
La Folie	Nov. 8	—	The Bn sent a fatigue party to the Overwal & Remades, Quinal all other units on the Bougek were dispersed	appx.
La Folie	Nov. 9	—	Baths. Billeting. Lt. Col. F.E. Ashton. D.S.O. joined Battalion and took over command of Battalion vici Capt. J.B. Dunn M.C.	appx.
La Folie	Nov. 10	—	Resumed C.O.'s Salute.	appx.
Harbre See Petit Fayt (Suring)	Nov 11	—	Battalion move to Petit Fayt Quin. News received on march that armistice was will action of 11 A.M. News quickly with cheers.	appx.
"	Nov 12	—	Orders received that Rumels move as far forward as possible up to have Divisional Billeter hot be force, in order to these good starting point for march to Rhine in Abity.	appx.
Avesnes	Nov 13	—	Battalion move to Avesnes billets.	appx.
Rumories	Nov 14	—	Battalion move to Rumories. Draft arrived approx 250. O.R.	appx.
"	Nov 15	—	Battalion carries out training	appx.
"	Nov 16	—	Battalion bathed, trained and refitted with clothing	appx.
Felleries	Nov 17	—	Battalion moved to Felleries. Good Billets.	appx.
"	Nov 18	—	Baths built by Battalion. Training under Company arrangements. Men unfit for march sent to rear to follow Battalion by train.	appx.
Rousies	Nov 19	—	The following officers joined the Battalion from Reinforcement camp. Captain Shoel. 2 Lt. Cutts. F. 2 Lt. Maynard. F.E. 2 Lt. Stafford. F. 2 Lt. Thursby B.E. 2 Lt. Wittrick S.J. 2 Lt. Tomlinson H.W. 2 Lt. Wilks A.B. 2 Lt. Pickering M.E.	appx.
Rouvie.	Nov 20	—	Battalion marched to Rouvie (Belgium).	appx.
" "	Nov 21	—	Battalion cleaning up.	appx.

Army Form C. 2118.

WAR DIARY
or
INTELLIGENCE SUMMARY.
(Erase heading not required.)

Instructions regarding War Diaries and Intelligence Summaries are contained in F. S. Regs., Part II. and the Staff Manual respectively. Title pages will be prepared in manuscript.

Place	Date	Hour	Summary of Events and Information	Remarks and references to Appendices
Ronse (Belgium)	Nov 21		Battalion Rested. Rued during foliage. Sergeants Mess suppers.	
"	Nov 22		Training by Companies.	
Forêt Chapelle	Nov 23		Moved to Forêt Chapelle by March Route. Buyee trouble in appearance.	
" "	Nov 24		Lt Building Reynard Barker from 15 Lancashire Fusiliers. Battalion Ruin in Jown Hall Frondschaffelle.	
" "	Nov 26		Company training.	
" "	Nov 27		Lt. Col. G. L. Compton-Smith. D.S.O. R.W.F. joined the Bn and took over duties of Commanding Officer.	
" "	Nov 28		Funeral given by Battalion in Jown Hall.	
" "	Nov 29		The following officers joined the Battalion. 2 Lt. R.F. Smith. 2/Lt Williams A.W. 2/Lt E.H.P. Edmondson & Lt Haworth G. 2Lt. Harvey A. & Lt Cox A.C.	
" "	Nov 30		Battalion Sports held on Football Ground.	

Humphris Miller Lt Col.
16th Lancs Fusiliers

WAR DIARY
or
INTELLIGENCE SUMMARY.
(Erase heading not required.)

Army Form C. 2118.

16 Kans 4/38

Place	Date	Hour	Summary of Events and Information	Remarks and references to Appendices
Festubert	Dec. 1.		Church Parade. Concert in evening attended by Brig. General Gibwood, G.O.C. 96. Inf. Bde.	
"	Dec. 2.		Dance in Town Hall attended by some civilians in village.	
"	Dec. 3.		Battalion Route March. A & B. Coys. bathing in Bethune.	
"	Dec. 4.		Coys. drill A & B. Coy. very successful. Battalion Drill & Route march.	
"	Dec. 5.		Paper chase C, D Coys.	
"	Dec. 6.		Brigade Concert Party at E. Coy. Billet attended. By Brig-General Gibwood, G.O.C. 96 Inf. Bde.	
"	Dec. 7.		Batt. Relieving equipment to take coys uniform extra clothing on Parade	
"	Dec. 8.		Church Parade. Civilian Sports in Town Hall 16 Lanc. Battn. invited. Football match Officers 16 Lan Fus.	
"	Dec. 9.		Result 116 Lan Fus. 3. 15 Lan Fus. 1.	
"	Dec. 10.		Bn. Route March. Football Match afternoon. Result. 16. Lan. Fus. 3. 15. Lan Fus. Nil.	
Philippville	Dec. 11		Commanding Officer inspected Bn. in full marching order.	
"	Dec. 12.		Left Festubert and marched to Philippville. About 10 miles. Rain.	
Aubin Ko	Dec. 13		Marched to Aubichillies. approx 12 miles. Rain.	
Methel-	Dec. 14		Marched to Methel. approx 13 miles. Rain.	
Gezures.	Dec. 15		Marched to Gatonthin Gezures. Rain.	
"	Dec. 16		Bn. drying up.	
"	Dec. 17		Bn. still drawing up.	
"	Dec. 18		Inspection of transport by C.O. Work on Roads in village.	
"	Dec. 19		Lecture by Commanding Officer on The Grenade.	
"	Dec. 20		Bn. Parade & Short Route March.	

Army Form C. 2118.

WAR DIARY
or
INTELLIGENCE SUMMARY.
(Erase heading not required.)

Instructions regarding War Diaries and Intelligence Summaries are contained in F. S. Regs., Part II. and the Staff Manual respectively. Title pages will be prepared in manuscript.

Place	Date	Hour	Summary of Events and Information	Remarks and references to Appendices
Eyeuls	Dec 21		Following decorations awarded Officers of 1st Bn Sussex Buad attack. Major E.B. Dunn M.C. H.L.I. attached 16 Lancashire Fusiliers. Awarded D.S.O. Capt. H.E. Pendleton. Awarded D.S.O. Lt. ? W. Lewis. M.C. award Bar to M.C. a/Capt. Lt. G.H. Potts. award M.C. 2 Lt. C.P. Stapley award M.C. a/Capt P.G. Horsfall award M.C. a/Capt. R.G. Boden award M.C. Demolition of ruined Square.	gpus
	Dec 22			gpus
	Dec 23		Preparations for Xmas Day.	gpus
	Dec 25		Xmas Day Dinner for the men. Prize for best decorated room won by D. Coy. Dance at A Coy Hostel. A very successful day.	gpus
	Dec 26		Holiday. Football Matches. B. Coy beat A. 6-0. D v C. Drew. No score.	gpus
	Dec 27		Coy Pounds.	gpus
	Dec 28		Coy Pounds.	gpus
	Dec 29		Dance D. Coy. Rileli. Heavy Rodgrier on Band attended.	gpus
	Dec 30		Br. Parade & Drill. Afternoon Paper Curse ; Bn. Bathing.	gpus
	Dec 31		Br. Route March & recreational Training.	gpus

Y Humphrey Smith
Lt. Col. Cdg
16 Lancs Fusrs

LANCASHIRE DIVISION
(LATE 32ND DIVN)

96TH INFY BDE (2ND LANCS INFY BDE)

16TH BN LANCS FUS.
JAN - OCT 1919

WAR DIARY or INTELLIGENCE SUMMARY

Army Form C. 2118.

16 Lanc[ashire] Fus[iliers]

Place	Date	Hour	Summary of Events and Information	Remarks and references to Appendices
Bertrancourt	Jan 1.		Holiday for Battalion. Dinner A + D. Coy. Billets.	
"	Jan 2.		Battn. Parade. Lecture by Capt. H.C. Poulsson. D.S.O. on Production of Newspapers.	
"	Jan 3.		Bn. Parade & Route March. Recreational Training. Dance at Bn. Recreation Room.	
"	Jan 4.		Lewis gun classes started. Bn. Paper Chase in afternoon.	
"	Jan 5.		Church Parade. Dance in evening.	
"	Jan 6.		Brigade Football Competition. 16 Lanc. Fus. 1 Goal, 2 Manchesters 3 goals. Brigade	
"	Jan 7.		Inspection of Brigade by Brig. Gen. Lambert. Brigade Surgeon Inspection by Divisional Staff. ARTS. Play "Better 'ome than the first Brig." (at 106 horses) attended by 95% wants. Bn. also by Rifle Stevens. Chaps Communication with expected Lieus. Sub's return with audition of Bn. & recruiting.	
"	Jan 8.		Bn. Parade. Rugby Football Match in afternoon. Lecture by Padre in evening. Bn. Went Drive very successful.	
"	Jan 9.		Bn. Parade. Hoech. Recreational Training.	
"	Jan 10.		Rugby Football Match. 11 Lancashire Fusiliers. 3 Pts. 2 Manchesters. 9 Pts. The Bn was handicapped by lack of practice run. Losing the 3rd game played by the Batn.	
"	Jan 11.		Bn. Paper Chase. Concert by Bn. Concert Party of Ye Chateau.	
"	Jan 12.		Church Parade. Dance in the evening.	
"	Jan 13.		Presentation of Ribbons by Major General Lambert. Divisional Commander at Wagny who presentation of Lt. to 16 Lancashire Fusiliers for Gallantry & past services, and a farewell in the Division for the month. Lt. Col. Cuxton-Smith, D.S.O. succeeded to 9'c Eg. Brigade to take Command. Major Dunn, D.S.O. M.C. assumed command.	
"	Jan 14.		Bn. Batn. Cross Country run & Rugby Football Match in the afternoon. Capt H.C. Poulsson D.S.O. assumed the duties of acting Second Command from D.S.O.	

WAR DIARY
or
INTELLIGENCE SUMMARY.
(Erase heading not required.)

Army Form C. 2118.

Instructions regarding War Diaries and Intelligence Summaries are contained in F. S. Regs., Part II. and the Staff Manual respectively. Title pages will be prepared in manuscript.

Place	Date	Hour	Summary of Events and Information	Remarks and references to Appendices
Gezves.	Jan 15	—	Bn Parade. 1st Meeting of Bn. Debating Society.	
	Jan 16	—	Bn. Route March. Lecture by 2nd Lt. Withers on Kruppe Brecci.	
	Jan 17		Bn. Parade.	
	Jan 18		Kit Inspection. Concert by R.A.M.C. Concert Party.	
	Jan 19		Church Parade. Dance in evening.	
	Jan 20		Bn Parade. Inter Company Sports held in afternoon. New billets in GEZVES. Dance at A Coy billets.	
	Jan 21		Bn Parade. Very football match for Division played.	
	Jan 22		Bn. Parade. Cross country run. Cinematograph show for children in afternoon.	16 Jan Jan on by officers & Sgt. Cinema at 6.0pm	
	Jan 23		17th Parade. School Dance by B Coy billets. Cinematograph show at GEZVES Chateau.	
	Jan 24		18th Parade. Inspection by D.A.A.G. The Dance of Wales. Officers introduced to H.R.H. Cinematograph show.	
	Jan 25		Kit Inspection. Cinematograph.	
	Jan 26		Church Parade. Dance at A.D.S. Mess Room.	
	Jan 27		Batt / Parade. Recreational training. Cinema in evening. To Batt Cinema Coathan Lecture by Brig / General Sir Francis Lloyd Commanding 1st London Divn. To all assembling from all	
	Jan 28		Batt / Orange. Recreational training.	and all the evening. Cinematograph Exhibition.	
	Jan 29		Place AS Cinema & Dance at Q Coy. Bn Batten Cadre march 12 forth.	
	Jan 30		Route March. Cinema Performance.	
	Jan 31		BATT. PARADE. Recreational training.	

Bruce Dunn Major
Col 16 January
2/19

WAR DIARY or INTELLIGENCE SUMMARY

Army Form C. 2118.

16th Lancs. Fusiliers.

FEBRUARY, 1919.

Place	Date	Hour	Summary of Events and Information	Remarks and references to Appendices
GESVES BELGIUM	1.2.19		Battn. kit inspection. Paper chase in afternoon. Whist drive at B Coy School. H.15 odon 1st Prize.	
"	2.2.19		Divine service at Chateaux, Gesves. Dance at B Coys School.	
"	3.2.19		Battn. parade + parades under company arrangements. Dance at A Coys School.	
"	4.2.19		General cleaning up of billets prior to vacation.	
"	5.2.19		Battn. move. Left Gesves 08.30 hrs., arrived NAMUR 16.00 hrs. – 26 kilos march. Billeted at Scaill School, NAMUR.	
"	6.2.19		Entrained NAMUR 18.50 hrs. Night of 6-7.2.19 in train. Comfortable journey.	
BONN 6/Rt.	7.2.19		Detrained at BEUEL 11.30 hrs. and marched to BONN – billets in INFANTERIE KASERNE.	
"	8.2.19		All day devoted to cleaning up new billets.	
"	9.2.19		Divine service at UNIVERSITY CHURCH, BONN. Dress – Drill Order with rifle.	
"	10.2.19		Completion of cleaning up billets – clean fatigues provided. Parade under company arrangements. Recreational training.	
"	11.2.19		Rearrangement of billets in consequence of reallotment of accommodation at INFANTERIE KASERNE. Recreational training.	
"	12.2.19		Lt Col Boyd-Moss Swift DSO assumes command of Bn. (then Colonel 94th 2nd Bn Surrey (A.B. Batcheroes & Cmn)) Short route march to VENUSBERG. Battalion drill on EXERZIER-PLATZ, BONN. Recreational training.	
"	13.2.19			
"	14.2.19		Battn. parade + parades under company arrangements. Battery parade. Transport inspection.	
"	15.2.19		Battn. kit inspection. Football match between winning half Coy 2 A 13 and 13 runners up. Staff Captain Smith DSO referee. Stop for extra time. Result 1-1.	
"	16.2.19		Divine service at EVANGELICAL KIRCHE. Drums play rebeats in KAISER PLATZ, BONN.	
"	17.2.19		Company parades. NCO's under RSM. Drum lecture nights 2.90. Batt-n-lieut Army Commander at 12 noon 1/4 hr	

Army Form C. 2118.

WAR DIARY
or
INTELLIGENCE SUMMARY.
(Erase heading not required.)

16th LANCS FUSILIERS

FEBRUARY, 1919.

Instructions regarding War Diaries and Intelligence Summaries are contained in F.S. Regs., Part II. and the Staff Manual respectively. Title pages will be prepared in manuscript.

Place	Date	Hour	Summary of Events and Information	Remarks and references to Appendices
BONN	18.2.19		Short route march + Batt. drill on EXERZIER PLATZ, BONN. Recreational training.	
"	19.2.19		Adjutant's parade; company parades. Education + Lewis Gun classes. Batt. football league. C + D. Routt - 1 each.	
"	20.2.19		Short route march + Batt. drill. Practice drill for 'Presentation of Colours'. Batt. football league. H.Q. + T. Routt - H.Q. 3, T. 2.	
"	21.2.19		Adjutant's parade; company parades. Education + Lewis Gun classes. Recreational training.	
"	22.2.19		Batt. kit inspection.	
"	23.2.19		Divine service at EVANGELICAL KIRCHE. Bonn play-match on KAISERPLATZ. Whole BRIDGE GD, BONN.	
"	24.2.19		Adjutant's parade; company parades. Education + Lewis Gun classes. Brigade Cross Country Run: Routt 1. 15th L.F. 2. 2nd MR's 3. 16th L.F.	
"	25.2.19		Practice for Guard Mounting on KAISERPLATZ 26.2.19. Cleaning up equipment etc.	
"	26.2.19		Mounting Guards on KAISERPLATZ at 11.00 hr. A + B Coys Piquets under A.P.M., B Coy Guards. Brig. Gen. Cunliffe inspected Guards.	
"	27.2.19		Batt. less C Coy on Cinemas. C Coy clean up barracks. Brigade Boxing tournament.	
"	28.2.19			

Bruce Drum

WAR DIARY or INTELLIGENCE SUMMARY
(Erase heading not required.)

16th Lancs Fusiliers

MARCH 1919

Army Form C. 2118.

Place	Date	Hour	Summary of Events and Information	Remarks and references to Appendices
BONN	1.3.19		Batt. less C Coy on guards in Bonn.	
"	2.3.19		Batt. less C Coy on guards in Bonn. Non-commissioned officers' parade only.	
"	3.3.19		Batt. less C Coy on guards in Bonn.	
"	4.3.19		Batt. less C Coy on guards in Bonn. Bonn-Beuel Bridge Guard relieved at 11.30 hrs by 2nd M.R.	
"	5.3.19		Relief of guards in Bonn by 2nd Manchester Regt at 11.45.	
"	6.3.19		Batt. practice of the enemy of formation of colours. Football match. 'OR staff v Runners & Drivers. Result 2-2.	
"	7.3.19		" " " " " " The X Coys commander (Lt Gen Stephens) inspects barracks.	
"	8.3.19		Presentation of Colours to the Battn on Hofgarten, Bonn at 10.30 by 2nd Army Commander General Sir Herbert Plumer G.C.B, G.C.M.G, G.C.V.O, A.D.C. 3/Lt Williams M.M, Colour Subaltern. Colours taken to H.Q Mess by Colour party. 'C' Coy + band.	Bruno Play wheat on Kaiserplatz.
"	9.3.19		Divine Service in University Church Bonn. Brown - Drill Order + rifle. Battn. League football match. 'A' v 'B'. Result A. 4, B. 1.	
"	10.3.19		Adjutant's parade; company parades. Lewis Gun - Subcalibre drill. Recreational training in afternoon.	
"	11.3.19		Draft of 24 Officers + 226 O.Ranks arrive from 6th King's Own Lancaster Regiment. Batt. route march - battalion drill. Recreational training in afternoon.	
"	12.3.19		Draft of 10 Officers + 240 O.Ranks arrive from 2nd Batt. Lancashire Fusiliers. Officers 7/16 L.F. v Officers 2/15 L.F. Rule 16-1 15-0. Adjutant's parade; company parades. Lewis Gun - Subcalibre drill. Batt. League football match. H.Q. v D Coy. Result H.Q. 3 - D. 0	

WAR DIARY or INTELLIGENCE SUMMARY

16th Lancs Fusiliers   March 1919.

Place	Date	Hour	Summary of Events and Information	Remarks and references to Appendices
BONN	13.3.19		Adjutant's parade; company parades; Lewis Gun & Education classes. Recreational training.	
"	14.3.19		Adjutant's parade; company parades; Lewis Gun & Education classes. Battn. League football match: Transport v 'B' Coy. Result T.1 – B.3	
"	15.3.19		Battn. kit inspection by Commanding Officer. Battn. League football match 'C' v 'A'. Result 'C' 5 – 'A' 3.	
"	16.3.19		Divine Service in University Church, Bonn. Dress: Drill Order – rifle.	
"	17.3.19		Adjutant's parade; company parades. L.G. & Education classes: N.C.O's under R.S.M. Class of instruction for soldiers. These commenced under Capt. H.C. Cox. Battn. League football match H.Q. v 'C' Coy. Result 'H.Q.' 2 – 'C' 0.	
"	18.3.19		Adjutant's parade; company parades. L.G. classes. Officers' class under Capt. Cox. Practice for General Salute.	
"	19.3.19		Battn. ceremonial parade in Bonn at 12.00 hrs. Inspected by the Brigade Commander (Lt. Gen. Stephens) & Brigadier General Commander (Major Gen. Glubbens) on Kaiserplatz.	
"	20.3.19		Adjutant's parade; company parades. L.G. classes; Officers' class. Education classes (Rev. B.S.W. Boulton). Still detained from leave. Class on guards.	
"	21.3.19		Adjutant's parade; company parades. L.G. classes. Officers' class. Education classes (Lesson on prisoners). Draft of 1 Officer + 12 ORanks arrived from 2nd Bn Lancs Fus	

Army Form C. 2118.

WAR DIARY
or
INTELLIGENCE SUMMARY.
(Erase heading not required.)

16th Lancs Fusiliers.

MARCH, 1919.

Instructions regarding War Diaries and Intelligence Summaries are contained in F.S. Regs., Part II. and the Staff Manual respectively. Title pages will be prepared in manuscript.

Place	Date	Hour	Summary of Events and Information	Remarks and references to Appendices
BONN	22.3.19		Battalion kit inspection by Commanding Officer. Officers classes. Notification of award of "Star of Roumania" to Capt. W.N. Watts.	
"	23.3.19		Divine service in Evangelical Church, Rathi Platz.	
"	24.3.19		Adjutant's parade; company parades; Lewis Gun, education classes. Officers classes. Inspection of Lampposts, O.C. Lancs Divn. Train.	
"	25.3.19		Adjutant's parade, company parades; Lewis Gun + education classes. Officers classes. Football match, Officers 16th L.F. v Officers 15th L.F. Result 16th L.F 1 – 15th L.F. 0.	
"	26.3.19		Adjutant's parade, company parades. Lewis Gun + education classes. Officers classes. Patrol of Town Guards in Bonn. Divn. Guard furnished by batt – inspected on Wapplatz by Brigade Commander. Football match 16th L.F v 13th L.N.L Result L.N.L 2 – L.F. 1½.	
"	27.3.19		Adjutant's parade company parades. Lewis Gun, Musketry + Signalling classes. Officers classes.	
"	28.3.19		" " "	
"	29.3.19		Kit inspection by Coy Commanders. Lecture (4 - 200 O.R.) by Professor Adkins at Beethoven Hall on "The Growth of Germany".	
"	30.3.19		Divine service in Evangelical Church, Rathi Platz.	
"	31.3.19		Adjutant's parade; company parades. Lewis Gun, education + signalling classes. Officers classes.	

G/Fourpton Smith
Bonn 16th Lancs Fusiliers

WAR DIARY or INTELLIGENCE SUMMARY

Army Form C. 2118.

16 Lancs Fusiliers

APRIL 1919

Place	Date	Hour	Summary of Events and Information	Remarks and references to Appendices
Bonn	1-4-19		Lieut Colonel W J Woodcock DSO assumed command 16th Battalion	
	2-4-19		Battalion Route March (less Officers & NCOs detailed for Town Guards. BONN) Town Guards furnished for Inniskillen	
			Adjutants Parade. Coy. Parade. Subalton Officers Class. Lewis Gun, Signaller & Education Classes.	
	3-4-19		Battalion (less Town Guards) Route March	
	4-4-19		Adjutants Parade. Coy Parade: Officers Class. Lewis Gun Signallers & Education Classes	
	5-4-19		Inspection by C.O. Football 16 Lane F v 1st Royal N.W.F. Rangers. Result L.F 1 – R.W. 2	
	6-4-19		Divine Service in Evangelical Chapel. BONN. Gun-Drill, Bren & Rifle	
	7-4-19		Adjutants Parade. Coy Parade. Lewis Gun, Signallers & Education Classes	
	8-4-19		Adjutants Parade. Coy Parade. Classes for Lewis Gunners, Signallers & Signallers	
	9-4-19		Adjutants Parade. Company Parades. Lewis Gun, Musketry, Signallers & Education Classes	
	10-4-19		Bn Route March. Specialists Classes.	
	11-4-19		Adjutants Parade. Company Parade. L.G., M.G. & Education Classes.	
	12-4-19		Commanding Officers Inspection of Kits & Barracks. Football 16 Lanc Fus v 168 Bde RFA Result LF 1, 168 Bde RFA 1.	
	13-4-19		Divine Service in University Chapel. Gun-Drill Bren Rifles	
	14-4-19		Adjutants Parade. Coy. Parade. "A" Coy to go to Range. Specialist Classes	
	15-4-19		Adjutants Parade. Coy Parade. "B" Coy to go to Range. L.Gun, Musketry, Signallers & Education Classes.	
	16-4-19		Adjutants Parade. Coy Parade Physical Training. "C" Coy to go Range. Lecture illustrated by Lt. Col. Hoare on "Citizenship". Specialist Classes in Lewis gun, Signaller, Musketry.	
	17-4-19		Battalion (less "D" Coy) Route March. "D" Coy to go Range. Specialists Classes.	

WAR DIARY
or
INTELLIGENCE SUMMARY.

Army Form C. 2118.

1st LANCS FUSILIERS

APRIL 1919

Place	Date	Hour	Summary of Events and Information	Remarks and references to Appendices
Bonn	18.4.19		Divine Service (Good Friday) in Evangelical Church. Bonn. Bren Gun Rifles.	
	19.4.19		Commanding Officer Inspection of Kits & Barracks.	
	20.4.19		Divine Service in Evangelical Church. Bonn Bren Gun Rifles	
	21.4.19		Adjutants Parade. Coy parades. A Coy 20 yds Range. Specimen Clames in Lewis Gun Signallers & Musketry. Education Clames. Football. B Coy Y & C Coy Route Moore. Lecture by Doctor to 'A' Tgroon on "The British Empire from a Doctors point of view"	
	22.4.19		Adjutants Parade & Coy Parades. B Coy 20 yds Range. Specialist Clames. Education Clames.	
	23.4.19		Adjutants Parade & Coy parades. C Coy 20 yds Range. Clames in Lewis Gun Musketry Signalling. Education Clames. Transport on Route March. Lectures by Medical Officer. Football. B Coy Y HQ Coy Runner. B Coy 3. HQ 1.	
	24.4.19		Ceremonial Parade in Kaiser Platz. Bonn. Presentation of Flags by Municipal Authorities of AVESNES SUR HELPE to Brig General T.S. LAMBERT CB CMG + LIEUT COL SIR I.A. ARMITAGE BART CMG. DSO. in commemoration of relief of town by 32 Division (3 April 1918 BR'S)	
			Remainder Battalion, Route March. Specimen Clames.	
	25.4.19		Adjutants Parade Coy Parades (D Coy Range Practise) Lewis Gun Musketry Signalling & camp Education Clames.	
	26.4.19		Inspection by CO of Kit & Barracks. Lecture by Canon T.J PARCITT on "BAGDAD"	

WAR DIARY
or
INTELLIGENCE SUMMARY.
(Erase heading not required.)

Army Form C. 2118.

16th Lanc. Fusiliers

April 27th to April 30th 1919

Place	Date	Hour	Summary of Events and Information	Remarks and references to Appendices
Bonn	27.4.19			
	28.4.19		Divine Service in University Church (BONN) A + B Coys - 30 yds range - (drill order & rifles) Special stand on ministry, Cy Ds Coys PT, BF, Squad drill, Musketry, Guard mounting, L.G., & Signalling - Education classes.	
	29.4.19		Battalion practice guard mounting in B arrack square	
	30.4.19		B attalion take over guard & piquet duties in BONN from 15th Lanc Fus	

Bruce Drum Major
Commanding 16th Lanc. Fus.

WAR DIARY OR INTELLIGENCE SUMMARY.   16th LANCASHIRE FUSILIERS.

MAY 1919.

PLACE.	DATE.	HOUR.	SUMMARY OF EVENTS & INFORMATION.
BONN.	1-5-19.		Battn. engaged on Guard & Picquet duties in BONN. Remainder under Coy arrangements, minature range practice -B.F.&.P.T. Close Order & Arms drill-specialist & Education Classes.
	2-5-19.		Battn engaged on Guard & Picquet duties in Bonn - remainder C.Os. Kit Inspection.
	3-5-19.		Battn engaged on Guard & Picquet duties in Bonn - remainder under Coy arrangements Musketry, B.F.&.P.T. Close Order and Arms Drill, Specialist & Education Classes.
	4-5-19.		Battn engaged on Guard & Picquet duties in Bonn - remainder Divine Service. Football - 16th Lancs. Fusrs. Sgts. 3 gls v 53rd Mcr.Regt.Sgts. 3 gls.
	5-5-19.		Battn engaged on Guard & Picquet duties in Bonn - Remainder "A" & "B" Coys on 30 Yards Range "Venusberg". - "C" & "D" Coys P.T. Close Order - Gas Drill. Specialist Classes L.G. Sigs & Musky.
	6-5-19.		Battn engaged on Guard & Picquet duties in Bonn. "C" & "D" Coys (Remainder) 30Yds Range (Education Classes). "A" & "B" Coys P.T. Close Order - Gas Drill Specialist Classes L.G. Siglg. and Musky.
	7-5-19.		Battn engaged on Guard & Picquet Duties in Bonn - Remainder Musky - 30 Yards Range, Education Classes.
	8-5-19.		Battn engaged on Guard & Picquet Duties in Bonn - Remainder Route March.
	9-5-19.		Battn engaged on Guard & Picquet Duties in Bonn - Remainder Musky & P.T. at 30 Yards Range. Education Classes. Duke of Connaught witnessesrelief of Bonn Brigade Guard.
	10-5-19.		Battn engaged on Guard & Picquet Duties in Bonn - Remainder Kit Inspection s under Coy arrangements. Barrack Inspection by C.O.
	11-5-19.		Battn engaged on Guard & Picquet Duties in Bonn - Divine Service in the Museum Coblenzer Strasse - Dress:- Drill Order.
	12-5-19.		Battn engaged on Guard & Picquet Duties in Bonn - Sir William Robertson C.in.C. Rhine Army Inspects 2nd Lancs. Infantry Brigade on the "Venusberg" Dress:- Fighting Order.
	13-5-19.		Battn engaged on Guard & Picquet Duties in Bonn - Remainder Musky & P.T. on Range at "Venusberg" Inspection of Barracks by Sir William Robertson,C.in.C. Battalion relieved of Guard duties by 1/5th Border Regt. Football. "HQ" Coy and Transport 4 gls v rest of Battalion. 1gl.
	14-5-19.		Battn parade on Banks of Rhine & Cheer Marshall Foch. Remainder of morning under Coy arrangements. Specialist and Education Classes.
	15-5-19.		Parades under Coy arrangements. Interior Economy.
	16-5-19.		0900 hours on Barrack Square. P.T. Close Order Drill Musketry & Gas Training. Education Classes. 1030 Lecture in Stadt Theatre on "WONDERFUL SCENERY & HOW IT WAS FORMED" by Mr. J. Mc.Cabe. Battn Officers Mess opened in Bonner Talweg.

WAR DIARY OR INTELLIGENCE SUMMARY.   16th LANCASHIRE FUSILIERS.

MAY 1919.

PLACE.	DATE.	HOUR.	SUMMARY OF EVENTS & INFORMATION.
BONN.	17-5-19.		Battn Kit Inspection.
	18-5-19.		Divine Service in University Church, Bonn at 1100 hours. Dress:- Drill Order.
	19-5-19.	0815 hours	"A" Coy. 30 Yards Range "Venusberg" "B" Coy Tactical Training "Venusberg" "C" Coy. 30 Yards Range Sports Platz. "D" Coy Barrack Square. P.T. Musketry, Gas Training & Drill. Education and Specialist Classes
	20-5-19.	0820 - 1230 hours.	"A" Coy Barrack Square. P.T. Drill, Musketry, Gas. Tng. "B" Coy 30 Yards Range Venusberg. "C" Coy Tactical Training Venusberg. "D" Coy 30 Yards Range Sportsplatz. Colnstrasse. Specialist Classes in L.G. and Signalling. Education Classes.
	21-5-19.		Rhine Steamer Trip. 8 Officers and 400 Other Ranks. 1430 Lecture by Lt.Col. Tysham in Beethoven Halle on the "FALLACIES OF BOLSHEVISM".
	22-5-19.	0820 to 1230	"A" Coy 30 Yards Range Sportsplatz. "B" Coy Barrack Square. P.T. Musketry, Drill, and Gas Training. "C" Coy 30 Yards Range Venusberg. "D" Coy Tactical Training Venusberg. Specialist & Education Classes.
	23-5-19.	0820 - 1230	"A" Coy Tactical Training Venusberg. "B" Coy 30 Yards Range Sportsplatz. "C" Coy Barrack Square. P.T. Musketry, Gas Training & Drill. Specialist and Education Classes. Cricket. 16th Lancs. Fusrs. 73 91st F.A. 38 runs.
	24-5-19.	0930 hours.	Battalion Kit Inspection and Medical Inspection.
	25-5-19.	1100 hours	Divine Service in Evangelical Church Reuter Strasse. Nonconformists. Y.M.C.A. 1000 hours.
	26-5-19.	0820 - 1230	"A" & "C" Coys. 30 Yards Range practice at Venusberg & Colnstrasse. "B" Tactical Training "D" Coy Barrack Square (General Training) Specialist & Education Classes. Riding School for Officers under 2nd Lieut. Witherick.
	27-5-19.	0820 - 1230	"B" & "D" Coys 30 Yards Range practice at Venusberg & Colnstrasse. "C" Coy Tactical Training Venusberg. "A" Coy Barrack Square Training, Specialist Classes and Education.
	28-5-19.	0900 - 1200	0945 Disposal O.C. Coys. 1000. uster Parade in full Marching Order. 1100 hours Lecture in Stadt Theatre on War Savings.
	29-5-19.	0820 - 1230	"A" & "C" Coys 30 Yards Range Colnstrasse & Venusberg. "B" Coy Barrack Square Training "D" Coy Tactical Training Venusberg. Specialist Classes and Education.
	30-5-19.	0830 - 1015.	All Coys P & R.T. on Barrack Square. At 1100 hours Lecture by Rev. G. H. HEASTLETT B.A. in Stadt Theatre on "VENEREAL DISEASE"
	31-5-19.	0930	Kit Inspection by Commanding Officer, followed by Medical Inspection.

Army Form C. 2118.

WAR DIARY
or
INTELLIGENCE SUMMARY.
(Erase heading not required.)

16 Bn LANCS FUSILIERS

Ref. No. 272
6 - JUL 1919
16th SERVICE BATTALION LANCASHIRE FUSILIERS

44 V
3 shut

Place	Date	Hour	Summary of Events and Information	Remarks and references to Appendices
BONN	1-6-19	10.20	Batt Parade for Divine Service in University Church. Nonconformists 09.30. R.C. 09.50	
"	2-6-19	08.30	A & B Coys Tactical Exercise in Venusberg. & 30 yds Range Practice. "C" Coy 30ˣ Range Practice & Lobbing Volunteers. "D" Coy Barrack Square Training. Specialist & Education Classes.	
"	3-6-19	08.00	Batt Parade for Brigade Ceremonial Parade in HOFGARTEN at 09.30 hours to celebrate the Birthday of "HIS MAJESTY KING GEORGE V."	
"	4-6-19	08.00	Rhine Steamer Trip. 130 Officers & men. A. B. C Coys. Remainder Barrack Square Training.	
"	"	08.30	"D" Coy Tactical Exercise in Venusberg. Divisional Commander Inspected.	
"	5-6-19	08.30	A & B Coys Tactical Exercise on Venusberg	
"	"	08.30	C Coy Barrack Square Training. D Coy 30ˣ Range Practice at Colmaheim Musketry Instructional Classes	
"	6-6-19	08.20	C & D Coy Tactical Exercise on Venusberg	
"	"	08.30	A Coy Barrack Square Training. B Coy 30ˣ Range Practice at Colmaheim Musketry Instl Classes	
"	7-6-19	05.30	Something at Barracks. Battalion War Savings Committee Meets	
"	"	02.30	Cricket matches Officers versch. west	
"	8-6-19	10.20	Whitsun day. Batt. Paraded for Divine Service in University. Nonconformists 09.30 R.C. 09.50	
"	9-6-19		Whitsun day. General Holiday. Sergeants won by 7 runs.	
"	"	14.30	Cricket Match. Officers v Sergeants	

Army Form C. 2118.

WAR DIARY
or
INTELLIGENCE SUMMARY.
(Erase heading not required.)

16 Bn LANCS FUSILIERS

Instructions regarding War Diaries and Intelligence Summaries are contained in F. S. Regs., Part II. and the Staff Manual respectively. Title pages will be prepared in manuscript.

Place	Date	Hour	Summary of Events and Information	Remarks and references to Appendices
Bonn	10.6.19	08.30	Battalion Parade under R.S.M. for preliminary instruction in Regtal Duties	
		11.30	do under the Adjutant	
		14.30	Cricket Match. Battalion v. 1st Welch	
			Score: 7/Lt Mitchell 29. Pte Bray 64. T.M.B. Battalion won by 107 runs	
	11.6.19	10.00	Battalion took over Iron Piquet and Guards from 15 Bn. Lancashire Fusiliers	
	12.6.19	08.00	Battalion in Iron Piquet & Guards	
			9 Officers & 1 Serjeant proceeded to WAHN to see Stokes Mortar Artillery Demonstration	
	13.6.19		Battalion engaged on Iron Piquet & Guards	
			Remands of Batt on Chevron of Barrack Church Parade	
	14.6.19		do	
	15.6.19		do	do
	16.6.19		do	
		08.15	Cricket Match. 5. of Welch Regt v. Battalion 52 All Out 203 for 7 Iron Piquet	
			Battalion 132 for 6 Match drawn. In Bn. Pte Earl 55 Not Out. Lt Watel 38.	
			Battalion engaged on Iron Piquet & Guards	
	17.6.19		General Packing up for non formal - Surplus stores to dump Ermitte Barracks.	
	18.6.19	08.15	Batt moved to Heiden - MINDEN	
Minden	19.6.19	06.30	Batt Route march to SIEGBURG	
	20.6.19	06.30	Coy Parades. General Training. Lewis Gun Classes under L.G.O. Bathing Parade & Games.
		15		
		08.30		
	21.6.19	06.30	Training under Coy arrangements. Musketry. P.T. & Close Order Drill. Lewis Gun Classes.	
		08.30	Bathing Parade. Games.	

Army Form C. 2118.

WAR DIARY
or
INTELLIGENCE SUMMARY.
(Erase heading not required.)

16 Bn. LANCS FUSILIERS

Place	Date	Hour	Summary of Events and Information	Remarks and references to Appendices
Minden	22-6-19	06.20 07.30	Training under Coy Arrangements. P.T. Close Order Drill & Lewis Gun Firing etc Classes. Bathing Parades Games. Cricket.	
	23-6-19	08.30 07.30	Training as for 22-6-19. Cricket.	
	24-6-19	06.20 07.30	Coy Training. P.T. Close Order Extended Order Drill. Platoon Schemes. Lewis Gun & Appendix Games. Bathing Parade Games.	
	25-6-19	"	Coy Training as for 24-6-19. C.B & S.B.etc Games. Bathing Games.	
	26-6-19	"	Training as for 25-6-19. Cricket. O. Coy. (100 frs S) v Rest of Batt (44)	
	27-6-19	"	Training as for 26-6-19. Cricket. Officers (112) v Sergt (76)	
	28-6-19	07.00	Medical Inspection & Interior Economy	
	29-6-19	10.00	Divine Service in Hall. Minden. R.C. Minden Church.	
	30-6-19	06.30 07.30	Training under Coy Arrangements as for the 25-6-19.	
			Strength of Batt June 30th :- Officers 52. OR's 1160	1
			Officers Demobilized during month	17
			OR's " " "	

Bruce Dunn MAJOR
Comdg. 16 LANCS FUSILIERS

Army Form C. 2118.

WAR DIARY
or
INTELLIGENCE SUMMARY.
(Erase heading not required.)

16th Bn Lancashire Fusiliers

Instructions regarding War Diaries and Intelligence Summaries are contained in F. S. Regs., Part II. and the Staff Manual respectively. Title pages will be prepared in manuscript.

Ref No. 682
4 - AUG 1919
16th SERVICE BATTALION LANCASHIRE FUSILIERS

45 U.
3 whole

Place	Date	Hour	Summary of Events and Information	Remarks and references to Appendices
BONN	1.7.19	06.30	Bn. marched into NIEDER-MENDIN arriving at Kaserne BONN at 10.30 hours.	
"	2.7.19	06.00	Bn. engaged in clearing up of Barracks.	
"	3.7.19	05.00	Declaration of Peace. Signing.	
"	4.7.19	05.00	Bn. on Bayonet Sqdn. training.	
"	5.7.19	10.15	Kit inspection. Medical Officer inspected all ranks.	
"	6.7.19	10.00	C.of E., Nonconformist & Presbyterians attended United Service at Beethoven Halle.	
"	"	09.30	Roman Catholic Mass held in Munster Church.	
"	7.7.19	08.00	Bn. commenced firing General Musketry Course at Ordnance Range.	
"	"	11.00	Cricket Match at Beethoven against 51st Sussex Regt. Result. 51st Sussex Regt. - 68 - 16th L.F. 149.	
"	8.7.19	08.00	Continuation of General Musketry Course.	
"	9.7.19	08.00	Continuation of General Musketry Course.	

Army Form C. 2118.

WAR DIARY
or
INTELLIGENCE SUMMARY.
(Erase heading not required.)

Instructions regarding War Diaries and Intelligence Summaries are contained in F.S. Regs., Part II. and the Staff Manual respectively. Title pages will be prepared in manuscript.

Place	Date	Hour	Summary of Events and Information	Remarks and references to Appendices
BONN	10.7.19	06.30	Continuation of General Musketry Course.	
	11.7.19	06.30	Continuation of General Musketry Course.	
	12.7.19	06.30	Continuation of General Musketry Course.	
	13.7.19	10.45	Battalion Church Parade at Evangelical Church. Roll on Shaw.	
		10.30	Non conformist Parade at YMCA	
		18.30	Special Roman Catholic Service in the MUNSTER KIRCHE	
	14.7.19	06.30	Battalion on Barrack Square Training.	
		14.00	Battalion engaged on Training for Divisional Sports.	
	15.7.19		Battalion Continue General Musketry Course.	
	15.7.19	06.30	Continuation of General Musketry Course.	
		14.00	Cricket Match 13th Kings Liverpool Regt. v Battalion. Won 13.K.L.R. 69. 16.L.F. 171	
			Captn. BODEN M.C. made a score of 65.	
	16.7.19	06.30	Battalion on Barrack Square Training.	
		14.00	Training for Divisional Sports held.	
	17.7.19	06.30	Continuation of General Musketry Course.	
			Cricket Match 53rd Kings Liverpool Regt. v Battalion. Won. 53 K.L.R. 72. 16.L.F. 114/5	
	18.7.19	06.30	Continuation of General Musketry Course.	
		14.00	Cricket Match 1st Suffolk Regt. v. Battalion. Score 1st Suffolks 146/6 & 16.L.F. 141.	
	19.7.19	—	General Holiday for Official Celebration of Peace	

Army Form C. 2118.

WAR DIARY
or
INTELLIGENCE SUMMARY.

(Erase heading not required.)

16 R. LANCASHIRE FUSILIERS

Instructions regarding War Diaries and Intelligence Summaries are contained in F. S. Regs., Part II. and the Staff Manual respectively. Title pages will be prepared in manuscript.

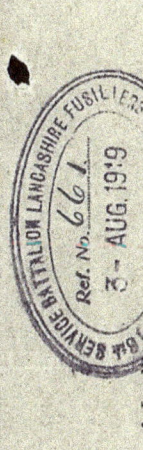

Ref. No. 661
3 – AUG. 1919

Place	Date	Hour	Summary of Events and Information	Remarks and references to Appendices
BONN.	20.7.19	10.30	Battalion Church Parade at Garrison Church R.C. 09.45 hrs. M.C. 10.00.	
	21.7.19	06.30	Battalion Parade for Trooping Trophy of the Colour	
		14.00	General or General Muster of Coys Cricket Match 92nd Field Ambulance v. Battalion (Army) Result 92 F.a. 42 16 L.F. 116.	
	22.7.19	06.30	Battalion Parade for Trooping Trophy of the Colour	
		10.00	Casual or General Muster of Coys. Trooping of Divisional Sports	
	23.7.19		Battalion engaged in Trooping the Colour & Offr. Divisional Sports	
	24.7.19		do do	
	25.7.19		do do	
		16.00	Divisional Sports commence at SPORTSPLATZ, COLNSTRASSE	
	26.7.19		Battalion engaged in Trooping Trophy of the Colour. Medical Inspection	
		16.00	Divisional Sports Concluded	
	27.7.19		Divine Service in Garrison Church at 11.00 hours	
	28.7.19	19.00	Practice Trooping the Colour Specialist Executive Classes	
		19.30	Visit by Command Paymaster to Pay & Mess Books.	
	29.7.19	09.45	Practice Trooping the Colour Commands under to Coys.	
	30.7.19	09.45	Practice Trooping the Colour " "	
	31.7.19	09.45	Practice Trooping the Colour " "	
Effective			Strength 17 Batt. Jones 31. Officers 50. O.R.s 1130	
			Officers undergoing Weekly Jay rides " 20	
			W.O.s "	

Signed
LIEUT COL
Comdg 16 LANCASHIRE FUSILIERS

WAR DIARY
or
INTELLIGENCE SUMMARY.
(Erase heading not required.)

Army Form C. 2118.

16th Bn LANCS FUSILIERS

Place	Date	Hour	Summary of Events and Information	Remarks and references to Appendices
BONN	Aug 1st	11:00	"Trooping the Colour" by the HOFGARTEN, by combined 15 + 16 Batt L.F. Brig Gen FREETH in Command. Major General Sir H.S. JEUDWINE K.C.B. took the Salute.	Appx K Training 25.20.5 12.20
"	"	4:00	CRICKET MATCH. HOFGARTEN 15th L.F. v. Rest of Division. Result DRAW.	
"	"	14:15	MINDEN DAY Dinner at BURGER-VEREIN. BONN.	
"	Aug 2nd	11:00	Batt relieve 15th L.F. from Town Guards + Piquet duties. { CRICKET 16 Lancs Fus 114 v East Div Sig 77	
"	Aug 3rd	11:00	Remainder of Bau'n: KIT + MEDICAL INSPECTIONS.	
"	"	11:00	DIVINE SERVICE for C of E members at GARRISON CHURCH. Kreuzstrasse. Y.M.C.A. Mark Platz 5 R.C. Mass Munster Church 10:00 hours.	
"	Aug 4th	8:30	Town Guards + Piquet. Remainder Batt General Training. Specialrs Classes. Education	
"	Aug 5th	12:30	Six Officers + 90 O.R. relieve various Areas of Battn Burial at Cologne Siegburg + Brmth.	
"	"	"	Training for remainder of Batt under Coy arrangements. Education.	
"	Aug 6th	"	Remainder Batt. Training under Coy arrangements.	
"	"	"	CRICKET 16 L.F. v 52 CHESHIRES Result :-	
"	Aug 7th	"	Remainder Batt Training under Coy arrangements.	
"	"	"	CRICKET 16 L.F. v 207 Squadron R.A.F. Result :-	
"	Aug 8th	"	Remainder Batt Training under Coy arrangements.	
"	"	"	CRICKET 16 Lancs Fus v 2nd Bn M.T. Coy + 1st HOFGARTEN @ 14:00 hours Result :- 16 L.F. 136. 2nd Bn M.T. Co 94.	
"	Aug 9th	"	KIT + Medical Inspection to all available men.	
"	Aug 10th	11:00	DIVINE SERVICE for C of E members at Garrison Colonel. 11:00 hrs. Non Conformists 10:00 hrs Y.M.C.A Markt Platz. R.C. Munster Church 10:00 hours.	
"	"	10:00	CRICKET 16 Lancs Fus (171) v 23 ROYAL FUSILIERS (51)	

Army Form C. 2118.

WAR DIARY
or
INTELLIGENCE SUMMARY.
(Erase heading not required.)

16 LANKASHIRE FUSILIERS

Instructions regarding War Diaries and Intelligence Summaries are contained in F. S. Regs., Part II. and the Staff Manual respectively. Title pages will be prepared in manuscript.

Place	Date	Hour	Summary of Events and Information	Remarks and references to Appendices
BONN (GERMANY)	11.8.19	08.20 to 12.30	Training under Coy arrangements for men left in barracks. Education.	
"	12.8.19	"	"	
"	13.8.19	"	"	
"	14.8.19	"	"	"CRICKET 16 L.F. (136) v 39 B.S. R.G.A. (77)"
"	15.8.19	09.00	Remainder of C & D Companies returned to WAHN (ARTILLERY BARRACKS) & took over duties from Leshin Division at LIND, TROISDORF, SIEGBURG & FOREST CAMP LOHMAR.	
"	16.8.19		Men left in Barracks to thoroughly clean out Barrack rooms, etc.	
"	17.8.19	11.00	Voluntary DIVINE SERVICE for men in Barracks at GARRISON CHURCH. R.Cs HOFGARTEN STRASSE CHURCH. Non-conformists at Y.M.C.A. BONN.	
"	18.8.19	08.30 to 12.30	Training under Coy arrangements for men left in barracks. Education.	
"	19.8.19	"	"	
"	20.8.19	"	"	Visit of Army Council to BONN.
"	21.8.19	11.00 14.30	A & B Coys relieved from Town Guards & proceeded to BONN by 5th Border Regt. CRICKET 16th Lancs Fus v Corps Signal Coy. (Result) - 16th L.F. 127 for 7 x Corps 18.	
"	22.8.19	08.30 to 12.30	Training under company arrangements for A & B Coys. Education.	
"	23.8.19	"	"	

Army Form C. 2118.

WAR DIARY
or
INTELLIGENCE SUMMARY. 16th LANCASHIRE FUSILIERS
(Erase heading not required.)

Instructions regarding War Diaries and Intelligence Summaries are contained in F. S. Regs., Part II. and the Staff Manual respectively. Title pages will be prepared in manuscript.

Place	Date	Hour	Summary of Events and Information	Remarks and references to Appendices
BONN	24.8.19	11.00	Voluntary DIVINE SERVICE in GARRISON CHURCH. C + D Coys at WAHN, TROISDORF + SIEGBURG relieved by 51st Manchester Regt.	
"	25.8.19	08.30 / 12.30	Training under Coy arrangement - all coys Education	
"	26.8.19	"	"	
"	27.8.19	"	"	
"	28.8.19	08.30 / 12.00	Battalion Route March.	
"	29.8.19		Battalion engaged in thoroughly cleaning out barracks preparatory to handing over to 17th Regt N. Lancs Regt.	
BONN – BRÜHL	30.8.19		Battalion leaves BONN for BRÜHL. Entrain 10.40. Arrive 11.15. Take over billets of 52nd Sherwood Foresters.	
BRÜHL	31.8.19		Battalion settles down in BRÜHL – Cleaning + improving new quarters. Strength of Battn. 1.8.19. 59 Officers 1 Holzr. + 1 o/ Belsa II 40 bspo 50 bpso 10.5 Ko. 12.53 Bonn others " 31.8.19. 60 " 1 " 57 " 956 " 1134 " Bonn 16. Lancs Fus.

Army Form C. 2118.

WAR DIARY
or
INTELLIGENCE SUMMARY.
(Erase heading not required.)

16 LANCS FUSILIERS

Place	Date 1919	Hour	Summary of Events and Information	Remarks and references to Appendices
BRUHL (GERMANY)	Sept 1st	08.30	Cleaning up new billets etc. Batt parade - School grounds.	
	2nd	12.30	General Training under Coy arrangements including one hours education.	
	"		A Coy stationed at Kierberg to find guard over dump at Kalem.	
	3rd	"	Coy training in School grounds. 1 hours education	
	4th	"	Batt route march. Dress - Drill order. Education nil.	
	5th	"	Coy training on Batt parade ground. Education 1 hour. 15 O.R's sent for Ammunition	
	6th	"	Inspection of billets by the Commanding Officer. Medical Inspection by M.O. Inspector of Kits by O.C. Coys.	
	7th	"	Divine Service in Garrison Church at 08.45 hour. R.C's in Parish Church 09.30. 6 O.R's despatched to dispersal Areas.	
	8th	"	Training under Coy arrangements including one hours education	
	9th	"	" " " " "	
	10th	"	" " " . No education. 49 O.R's to one hour. 40 O.R's to dispersal areas.	
	11th	"	Batt route march. Education 1 hour.	
	12th	"	Coy training. Education 1 hour.	
	13th	"	General training under O.C Coys. Education 1 hour.	
			Inspections. Billets by the Commanding Officer. Kits by O.C. Coys. Medical by Medical Officer	

Army Form C. 2118.

WAR DIARY
or
INTELLIGENCE SUMMARY.
(Erase heading not required.)

1 Lancs Fusiliers

Place	Date 1919	Hour	Summary of Events and Information	Remarks and references to Appendices
BRUHL (GERMANY)	Sept 14th	09:45	Divine Service in the Theatre at 09:45 hours. New Commandants in Recreation room 09:45 Res in Parish Church at 09:30 hour.	
	15th	08:30 & 12:30	Training under Coy Arrangements. Educations lecture. B Coy relieve A Coy at Kierberg	
	""		Inspection of Transport by G.O.C. 2nd Lancs Brigade at 10.00 hours. 10 ORs to dispersal areas.	
	16th	"	Training under Coy Arrangements including 1 hours education. 5 Officers + 116 ORs to dispersal areas.	
	17th	"	Training under Coy Arrangements. Conference by Commanding Officer. 1 Officer + 129 ORs to dispersal areas.	
	18th	"	All available men employed on guard duties at Vochem. 34 ORs to dispersal areas.	
	19th	"	" " " " " " " " 2 Officers + 92 ORs to dispersal areas.	
	20th	"	Inspection of animals by D.A.D.V.S. Coy Officer to dispersal areas.	
	21st	"	B Coy + remainder of dark men engaged on guard duties at Vochem. 11 ORs to dispersal areas. A Coy, 53 Northumberland Fusiliers take over guard duties at Vochem at 11:00 hours.	
	22nd		Bart move to EUSKIRCHEN by train. Transport by road.	
EUSKIRCHEN	23rd		to drawing up new quarters &c.	
"	24th		Training under Coy Arrangements. D/ABarns etc.	

Army Form C. 2118.

WAR DIARY
or
INTELLIGENCE SUMMARY.

(Erase heading not required.)

1 Lancs Fusiliers

Instructions regarding War Diaries and Intelligence Summaries are contained in F. S. Regs., Part II. and the Staff Manual respectively. Title pages will be prepared in manuscript.

Place	Date 1919	Hour	Summary of Events and Information	Remarks and references to Appendices
EUSCHIRCHEN (GERMANY)	Sept 25th	08:30 & 12:30	Training for available men under Coy arrangements. 37 O.R's to Hospital Centre.	
	26th	"	" " " " " " " Education (one hour)	
	27th	"	Medicine Inspection for all available other ranks. Til inspection by Company Commander	
	28th	—	No C of E parade or Service. R.C's Point Church 09:30 hour.	
	29th	"	Training for all available men under Coy Arrangements. Education (one hour)	
	30th	"	" " " " " " " " Education " "	

Effective Strength of Batt. Sept 30.
    Officers — — — 36
    Other ranks — — — 480

Demobilized during September
    Officers — — — 10
    Other ranks — — — 548

A. Morris Lt Col
Comdg 16th Bn Lancs Fusiliers

WAR DIARY or INTELLIGENCE SUMMARY

Army Form C. 2118.

OCTOBER 1919

Place	Date	Hour	Summary of Events and Information	Remarks and references to Appendices
EUSKIRCHEN GERMANY	1-10-19	08.30	Coy Parades as per programme of work. (General Training) Education Classes.	
"	2/10	12.30	" " " " " " Bath	
"	3/10	"	" " " " " "	
"	4/10	"	Medical Inspection for all O.R. Ranks. Kit Inspection &c. Football Match A Coy. 2 v B Coy. 1.	
"	5/10	10.00	Divine Service in COLNERSTRASSE CHURCH. Drill Bugle.	
"	6/10	10.30 to 12.30	Parades under O.C. Coys. Training as per Programme (General Training) Field Kitchen Competition. Fit for duty rest 10.30 by D Coy.	C Coy-2 v D Coy-3. Equal to B Coy.
"	7/10	"	General Training under " " " " But Tin rest 10.30 by D Coy.	
"	8/10	"	All Railway Billets Red back one hour at 0.400 hours. Reveille 06.00 hour Retire 17.30 " "	Football B Coy-1 v C Coy-1
"	9/10	"	Training under O.C. Coys. Education Classes.	" Education Classes.
"	10/10	"	General Training as per programme of work under O.C. Coys.	" Education Classes Bath.
"	11/10	"	" " " " " " " "	
"	12/10	"	Medical Inspection of all O.R. Ranks F.U. Inspection Barrack Inspection by CO.	
"	13/10	09.30	Divine Service in Lutheran Church Colnerstrasse. Draw Dividentes. 1 Officer + 24 O.R. Ranks.	Football A Coy-0 v D Coy-3. 3/A.Rs ?
"	14/10	"	sent to Cowl for disposal.	A Coy-2 v C Coy-3 - 15 O.R. " "
"	15/10	08.30 to 12.30	General Training under O.C. Coys. Education Classes.	
"	16/10	"	Training as per programme. Education Classes.	
"	17/10	"	Route March for all available men.	
"	18/10	"	General Training under O.C. Coys. Education Classes. 24 O.R. Ranks send for Air force	Standigder ?
"	19/10	"		" " "
"	20/10	"	Education Classes. Inspection of Small Arms Refreshments by Company Commander. 1 Officer + 35 O.R. Ranks send for Air force 2.	

WAR DIARY

Army Form C. 2118.

INTELLIGENCE SUMMARY. 11o Batt LANCASHIRE FUSILIERS

(Erase heading not required.)

OCTOBER 1919

Instructions regarding War Diaries and Intelligence Summaries are contained in F.S. Regs., Part II. and the Staff Manual respectively. Title pages will be prepared in manuscript.

Place	Date	Hour	Summary of Events and Information	Remarks and references to Appendices
EUSKIRCHEN GERMANY	18/10/19	9:30 to 12.30	Medical Inspection for all other ranks. Barrack & Kit Inspection.	
"	19/10		Church Service in Wilhelm Eduard & Luise Strasse at 12.30 hours.	
"	20/10		Coys at Disposal of OC Coy for training. Billets &c. Football Match A Coy 2 v Transport 1.	
"	21/10		Batt races Billets & mens kits attacks. Inter-gull Matches Drawn. 6 Other Ranks to Hospital.	
"	22/10		2 Officers & 22 Other Ranks sent for Air patrol.	
"	23/10		Support of O/C Coys in Disposal Education Scheme. Football Sergts 2 v Officers 1	
"	24/10		All ranks of 15 Batt have been transferred to 16th Bar. Stationed in Wilma Grunwald.	
"	24/10		& Officers sent for Air patrol.	
"	"		All available men attended in Instruction.	
"	25/10		Medical Inspection of all other ranks. Barrack inspection.	
"	26/10		Coys at disposal of Company Commanders. 5 Officers + 10 Other Ranks for Air patrol.	
"	27/10		Training under OC Coys. 6 Officers sent for Air patrol.	
"	28/10		" " 3 Officers sent for Air patrol.	
"	29/10		Re organisation of Batt. Garrison in Base (Active to be taken in Cars of Riots) 200 Division Ground.	
"	"		" Other Ranks sent for Air patrol.	
"	30/10		General Training under OC Coys. 3 Officers + 1 Other Ranks sent for Air patrol.	
"	31/10		Effective Strength of Batt. Sanctioned Armament	

Officers 34 Other Ranks 509. Officers 25 Other Ranks 184

Signed ??? Major
Comdg. 11 Batt Lancs F??